SCIENTISTS: Their Lives and Works

ISSN: 1552-8630

SCIENTISTS: Their Lives and Works

Tanya Lee Stone

VOLUME 7

Helen Plum Library
Lombard, IL

Detroit • New York • San Diego • San Francisco • Cleveland • New Haven, Conn. • Waterville, Maine • London • Munich

THOMSON
GALE

Scientists: Their Lives and Works, Volume 7

Tanya Lee Stone

Project Editor
Sarah Hermsen

Editorial
Carol DeKane Nagel

Permissions
Margaret Chamberlain

Imaging and Multimedia
Dean Dauphinais, Robert Duncan

Product Design
Tracey Rowens

Composition
Evi Seoud

Manufacturing
Rita Wimberley

ISBN 0-7876-6383-2
ISSN 1522-8630

Printed in the United States of America
10 9 8 7 6 5 4 3 2 1

Contents

*William Ramsay.
Reproduced courtesy of
the Library of Congress.*

VOLUME 7

Scientists by Field of Specialization

Includes *Scientists*, volumes 1–7.
Italic type indicates volume numbers.

Ruth Fulton Benedict. Reproduced courtesy of Library of Congress.

Anatomy

Animal Ecology

Anthropology

Archaeology

Astronomy and Space

Climatology

Computer Science

Philosophy of Science

Physical Chemistry

Physics

Physiology

Primatology

Psychiatry

Reader's Guide

Budding scientists and those entering the fascinating world of science for fun or study will find inspiration in this seventh volume of *Scientists*. The series presents detailed biographies of the women and men whose theories, discoveries, and inventions have revolutionized science and society. From Sally Ride to George Westinghouse and Jacques Cousteau to Ada Byron, *Scientists* explores the pioneers and their innovations that students most want to learn about.

Scientists from around the world and from all times are featured, in fields such as astronomy, oceanography, physics, and more.

In *Scientists,* Volume 7, students will find:

- Twenty-nine scientist biographies, each focusing on the scientist's early life, formative experiences, and inspirations—details that keep students reading

- "Impact" boxes that draw out important information and sum up why each scientist's work is indeed revolutionary

- Nine sidebar boxes that highlight individuals who influenced the work of the featured scientist or who conducted similar research, as well as related information of special interest to students
- Sources for further reading so students know where to delve even deeper
- More than sixty-five black-and-white portraits and additional photographs that give students a better understanding of the people and inventions discussed

Scientists, Volume 7, begins with a list of the scientists in all seven volumes, categorized by fields ranging from aeronautical engineering to zoology; a timeline of major scientific breakthroughs; and a glossary of scientific terms used in the text. The volume concludes with a cumulative subject index for the series so students can easily find the people, inventions, and theories discussed throughout *Scientists.*

Comments and suggestions

We welcome your comments on *Scientists,* Volume 7, and suggestions for other scientists to be featured in future editions. Please write: Editors, *Scientists,* U•X•L, 27500 Drake Road, Farmington Hills, Michigan, 48331-3535; call toll-free: 800-877-4253; fax to: 248-699-8097; or send e-mail via http://www.gale.com.

Timeline of Scientific Breakthroughs

1672 Astronomer **Gian Domenico Cassini** calculates the distance between Earth and the Sun, leading to the creation of the astronomical unit (AU).

1791 **Benjamin Banneker** becomes the first African American man to publish an almanac.

1843 **Ada Byron, Countess of Lovelace,** writes her Notes—later credited as the first computer program—on Charles Babbage's Analytical Engine.

1849 **Elizabeth Blackwell** graduates from Geneva Medical School in New York and becomes the first female doctor in the United States.

1690
John Locke's essays
introduce the
Enlightenment in Europe

c. 1750
Industrial
Revolution begins
in England

1848
Karl Marx and Friedrich
Engels write the
Communist Manifesto

| 1650 | 1700 | 1750 | 1800 | 1850 |

1865–1914 **George Westinghouse** secures hundreds of patents for his inventions, including a rotary engine, signal and braking systems for trains, and safe ways to supply communities with natural gas and electricity.

1881 Cuban doctor **Carlos Finlay** proposes a theory that the mosquito is responsible for the transmission of yellow fever.

1886 **Charles Martin Hall** develops a process to produce aluminum in a cost-effective way.

1904 Scottish chemist **William Ramsay** receives the Nobel Prize in chemistry for his work discovering the inert gases argon, xenon, neon, krypton, helium, and radon.

1921 **Frederick Banting** discovers that the hormone insulin can be extracted from pancreatic tissue and used to treat patients with diabetes.

1925 German physicist **Werner Heisenberg** publishes a groundbreaking physics paper about matrix mechanics and develops a fundamental principle of physics called the uncertainty principle.

1930–31 Physicist **Ernest Lawrence** builds the first cyclotron—a high-speed particle accelerator.

1934 Anthropologist **Ruth Fulton Benedict** publishes the groundbreaking book *Patterns of Culture,* describing the idea of cultural relativism.

1935 Astrophysicist and mathematician **Subrahmanyan Chandrasekhar** publishes his theory on stellar evolution that stars evolve into neutron stars.

1938 Nylon, invented by chemist **Wallace Carothers,** begins to be mass-produced by the DuPont chemical company.

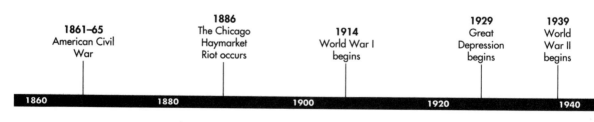

1861–65
American Civil War

1886
The Chicago Haymarket Riot occurs

1914
World War I begins

1929
Great Depression begins

1939
World War II begins

1860   1880   1900   1920   1940

1940s–60s **Robert Woodward** synthesizes many substances in the laboratory, including quinine, used to treat malaria; tetracycline antibiotics, used to fight infection; the antibiotic cephalosporin C; and penicillin.

1950 **Thor Heyerdahl** publishes *Kon-Tiki: Across the Pacific by Raft* about his exploration across the Pacific.

1951 **George H. Hitchings and Gertrude Belle Elion** develop 6-mercaptopurine (6MP), a drug to treat childhood leukemia.

1953 Shark expert and ichthyologist **Eugenie Clark** publishes her autobiography *Lady with a Spear,* which becomes a best-seller.

1953 **Jacques Cousteau** publishes *The Silent World,* an account of his underwater discoveries.

1959 **Mary Leakey** discovers human remains over 1.75 million years old at the Olduvai Gorge in Africa.

1960–62 **Leon Lederman,** Melvin Schwartz, and Jack Steinberger discover a previously unknown neutrino, or a type of subatomic particle, called a muon.

1967 South African heart surgeon **Christiaan Barnard** performs the world's first heart transplant in a human being.

1967 Argentinean heart surgeon **René Geronimo Favaloro** pioneers the use of heart bypass surgery as a standard surgical procedure.

1970–71 American geneticist **Leland Hartwell** discovers a class of genes that control the cell division cycle.

1971 **Judah Folkman** discovers that tumors depend on a blood supply in order to grow and terms this process "angiogenesis dependency."

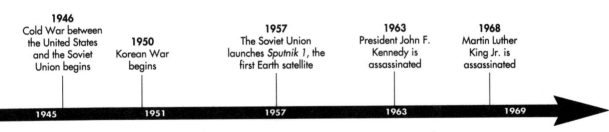

1946
Cold War between the United States and the Soviet Union begins

1950
Korean War begins

1957
The Soviet Union launches *Sputnik 1,* the first Earth satellite

1963
President John F. Kennedy is assassinated

1968
Martin Luther King Jr. is assassinated

1945   1951   1957   1963   1969

1971 Meteorologist **Tetsuya Theodore Fujita** develops the F Scale, used to measure the strength of tornadoes.

1975 **Richard Leakey** discovers a 1.5 million year old human skull at Turkana, proving that several different types of humans coexisted there.

1982 American neurologist **Stanley Prusiner** discovers proteinaceous infectious particles, or prions, a previously unknown cause of infectious disease.

1983 Astronaut **Sally Ride** becomes the first American woman to fly in space.

2000 The Human Genome Project, led by **Francis Collins,** releases the first draft of a map of the complete DNA sequence of humans.

| 1973 U.S. troops pull out of Vietnam | 1979–80 52 Americans are held hostage in Iran | 1900 Persian Gulf War begins | 2001 Terrorists attack the World Trade Center and the Pentagon |

1970   1980   1990   2000   2010

Words to Know

A

Absolute zero: the theoretical point at which a substance has no heat and motion ceases; equivalent to -276°C or -459.67°F.

Algae: a diverse group of plant or plantlike organisms that grow mainly in water.

Alpha particle: a positively charged nuclear particle that consists of two protons and two electrons; it is ejected at a high speed from disintegrating radioactive materials.

Alternating current: the flow of electrons first in one direction and then in the other at regular intervals.

Amino acids: organic acids that are the chief components of proteins.

Anatomy: the study of the structure and form of biological organisms.

Anomaly: deviation from the normal or common order or rule; not easily classified.

Anthropology: the science that deals with the study of human beings, especially their origin, development, divisions, and customs.

Aorta: the main artery of the human body that starts out at the left ventricle of the heart and carries blood to all organs except the heart.

Archaeology: the scientific study of material remains, such as fossils and relics, of past societies.

Artificial intelligence: the branch of science concerned with the development of machines having the ability to perform tasks normally thought to require human intelligence, such as problem solving, discriminating among single objects, and response to spoken commands.

Asteroid: one of thousands of small planets located in a belt between the orbits of Mars and Jupiter.

Astronomical unit (AU): standard measure of distance to celestial objects, equal to the average distance from Earth to the Sun: 93 million miles (150 million kilometers).

Astronomy: the study of the physical and chemical properties of objects and matter outside Earth's atmosphere.

Astrophysics: the branch of physics involving the study of the physical and chemical nature of celestial objects and events.

Atom: the smallest component of an element having the chemical properties of the element.

Atomic bomb: a weapon of mass destruction that derives its explosive energy from nuclear fission.

Atomic weight: the mass of one atom of an element.

B

Bacteria: a large, diverse group of mostly single-celled organisms that play a key role in the decay of organic matter and the cycling of nutrients.

Bacteriology: the scientific study of bacteria, their characteristics, and their activities as related to medicine, industry, and agriculture.

Bacteriophage: a virus that infects bacteria.

Ballistic missile: a self-propelled object (like a rocket) that is guided as it ascends into the air and usually falls freely.

Behaviorism: the school of psychology that holds that human and animal behavior is based not on independent will or motivation but rather on response to reward and punishment.

Beta decay: process by which a neutron in an atomic nucleus breaks apart into a proton and an electron.

Big bang: in astronomy, the theory that the universe resulted from a cosmic explosion that occurred billions of years ago and then expanded over time.

Binary stars: a system of two stars revolving around each other under a mutual gravitation system.

Binary system: a system that uses the numbers 1 and 0 to correspond to the on or off states of electric current.

Biochemistry: the study of chemical compounds and processes occurring in living organisms.

Biodiversity: the number of different species of plants and animals in a specified region.

Biofeedback: a method of learning to gain some voluntary control over involuntary bodily functions like heartbeat or blood pressure.

Biology: the scientific study of living organisms.

Biophysics: the branch of biology in which the methods and principles of physics are applied to the study of living things.

Biosynthesis: the creation of a chemical compound in the body.

Biotechnology: use of biological organisms, systems, or processes to make or modify products.

Black holes: regions in space that exert an extremely intense gravitational force from which nothing, including light, can escape.

Botany: the branch of biology involving the study of plant life.

Byte: a group of binary digits (0 and 1) that a computer processes as a unit.

C

Carbon filament: a threadlike object in a lamp that glows when electricity passes through it.

Carburetor: the device that supplies an internal-combustion engine with a mixture of vaporized fuel and air that, when ignited, produces the engine's energy.

Carcinogen: a cancer-causing agent, such as a chemical or a virus.

Catalyst: a substance that enables a chemical reaction to take place either more quickly or under otherwise difficult conditions.

Cathode: a negatively charged electrode.

Cathode rays: electrons emitted by a cathode when heated.

Cerebrum: the uppermost part of the brain that, in higher mammals, covers the rest of the brain and is considered to be the seat of conscious mental processes.

Chemical synthesis: the process of building up a desired compound from simpler and readily available components.

Chemistry: the science of the nature, composition, and properties of material substances and their transformations.

Chromosome: threadlike structure in the nucleus of a cell that carries thousands of genes.

Circuit: the complete path of an electric current including the source of electric energy; an assemblage of electronic elements.

Classification: a system of naming and categorizing plants and animals in which they are grouped by the number of physical traits they have in common. The ranking system goes from general to specific: kingdom, phylum, class, order, family, genus, and species.

Climatology: the scientific study of climates and their phenomena.

Combustion: a rapid chemical process that produces heat and light.

Conductor: a substance able to carry an electrical current.

Conservation biology: the branch of biology that involves conserving rapidly vanishing wild animals, plants, and places.

Conservation laws: laws of physics that state that a particular property, mass, energy, momentum, or electrical charge is not lost during any change.

Cosmic rays: charged particles, mainly the nuclei of hydrogen and other atoms, that bombard Earth's upper atmosphere at velocities close to that of light.

Cosmology: the study of the structure and evolution of the universe.

Cross-fertilization: a method of fertilization in which the gametes (mature male or female cells) are produced by separate individuals or sometimes by individuals of different kinds.

Cryogenics: the branch of physics that involves the production and effects of very low temperatures.

Crystallography: the science that deals with the forms and structures of crystals.

Cytology: the branch of biology concerned with the study of cells.

D

Deforestation: the process of cutting down all the trees in a forest.

Desertification: the changing of productive land to desert, often by clearing the land of trees and other plant life.

Diffraction: the spreading and bending of light waves as they pass through a hole or slit.

Direct current: a regular flow of electrons, always in the same direction.

DNA (deoxyribonucleic acid): a long molecule composed of two chains of nucleotides (organic chemicals) that contain the genetic information carried from one generation to another.

E

Earthquake: an unpredictable event in which masses of rock shift below Earth's surface, releasing enormous amounts of energy and sending out shockwaves that sometimes cause the ground to shake dramatically.

Ecology: the branch of science dealing with the interrelationship of organisms and their environments.

Ecosystem: community of plants and animals and the physical environment with which they interact.

Electrocardiograph: an instrument that makes a graphic record of the heart's movements.

Electrochemistry: the branch of physical chemistry involving the relation of electricity to chemical changes.

Electrodes: conductors used to establish electrical contact with a nonmetallic part of a circuit.

Electrolysis: transforming chemical substances by the passage of electric current.

Electromagnetism: the study of electric and magnetic fields and their interaction with electric charges and currents.

Electron: a negatively charged particle that orbits the nucleus of an atom.

Embryo: an animal in the early stages of development before birth.

Embryology: the study of embryos and their development.

Entomology: the branch of zoology dealing with the study of insects.

Environmentalism: the movement to preserve and improve the natural environment, and particularly to control pollution.

Enzyme: any of numerous complex proteins that are produced by living cells and spark specific biochemical reactions.

Epidemiology: the study of the causes, distribution, and control of disease in populations.

Equinox: the two times each year when the Sun crosses the plane of Earth's equator; at these times, day and night are of equal length everywhere on Earth.

Ethnobotany: the plant lore of a race of people.

Ethnology: science that deals with the division of human beings into races and their origin, distribution, relations, and characteristics.

Ethology: the scientific and objective study of the behavior of animals in the wild rather than in captivity.

Evolution: in the struggle for survival, the process by which successive generations of a species pass on to their offspring the characteristics that enable the species to survive.

Extinction: the total disappearance of a species or the disappearance of a species from a given area.

F

Flora: the plants of a particular region or environment.

Foramen magnum: the opening at the base of the skull through which the spinal cord enters the cranial cavity.

Fossils: the remains, traces, or impressions of living organisms that inhabited Earth more than ten thousand years ago.

Frontal systems: a weather term denoting the boundaries between air masses of different temperatures and humidities.

G

Gamma rays: short electromagnetic wavelengths that come from the nuclei of atoms during radioactive decay.

Game theory: the mathematics involved in determining the effect of a particular strategy in a competition, as in a game of chess, a military battle, or in selling products.

Gene: in classical genetics, a unit of hereditary information that is carried on chromosomes and determines observable characteristics; in molecular genetics, a special sequence of DNA or RNA located on the chromosome.

Genetic code: the means by which genetic information is translated into the chromosomes that make up living organisms.

Genetics: the study of inheritance in living organisms.

Genome: genetic material of a human being; the complete genetic structure of a species.

Geochemistry: the study of the chemistry of Earth (and other planets).

Geology: the study of the origin, history, and structure of Earth.

Geophysics: the physics of Earth, including studies of the atmosphere, earthquakes, volcanism, and oceans.

Global warming: the rise in Earth's temperature that is attributed to the buildup of carbon dioxide and other pollutants in the atmosphere.

Gravity: the force of attraction (causing free objects to accelerate toward each other) that exists between the surface of Earth (as well as other planets) and bodies at or near its surface.

Greenhouse effect: warming of Earth's atmosphere due to the absorption of heat by molecules of water vapor, carbon dioxide, methane, ozone, nitrous oxide, and chlorofluorocarbons.

H

Heliocentric: having the Sun as the center.

Herpetology: the branch of zoology that deals with reptiles and amphibians.

Histology: the study of microscopic plant and animal tissues.

Hominids: humanlike creatures.

Hormones: chemical messengers produced in living organisms that play significant roles in the body, such as affecting growth, metabolism, and digestion.

Horticulture: the science of growing fruits, vegetables, and ornamental plants.

Hybridization: cross-pollination of plants of different varieties to produce seed.

Hydraulics: the study of the forces of fluids as they apply to accomplishing mechanical or practical tasks.

Hydrodynamics: the study of the forces exerted by fluids in motion.

Hydrostatics: a branch of physics that studies fluids at rest and the forces they exert, particularly on submerged objects.

Hypothesis: an assumption made on the basis of scientific data that is an attempt to explain a principle in nature but remains tentative because of lack of solid evidence.

I

Ichthyologist: a scientist who specializes in the study of fish.

Immunology: the branch of medicine concerned with the body's ability to protect itself from disease.

Imprinting: the rapid learning process that takes place early in the life of a social animal and establishes a behavioral pattern, such as a recognition of and attraction to its own kind or a substitute.

In vitro fertilization: fertilization of eggs outside of the body.

Infrared radiation: electromagnetic rays released by hot objects; also known as a heat radiation.

Infertility: the inability to produce offspring for any reason.

Internal-combustion engine: an engine in which the combustion (burning) that generates the heat that powers it goes on inside the engine itself, rather than in a furnace.

Invertebrates: animals lacking a spinal column.

Ion: an atom or groups of atoms that carries an electrical charge—either positive or negative—as a result of losing or gaining one or more electrons.

Isomers: compound that have the same number of atoms of the same elements, but different properties because their atoms are arranged differently.

Isotope: one of two or more atoms of a chemical element that have the same structure but different physical properties.

L

Laser: acronym for light amplification by stimulated emission of radiation; a device that produces intense light with a precisely defined wavelength.

Light-year: in astronomy, the distance light travels in one year, about six trillion miles.

Limnology: the branch of biology concerning freshwater plants.

Logic: the science of the formal principles of reasoning.

Lunar eclipse: the passing of the Moon either wholly or partially into the shadow created by Earth's position in front of the Sun; that is, when the three bodies align thus: Moon—Earth—Sun.

M

Magnetic field: the space around an electric current or a magnet in which a magnetic force can be observed.

Maser: acronym for microwave amplification of stimulated emission of radiation; a device that produces radiation in short wavelengths.

Metabolism: the process by which living cells break down organic compounds to produce energy.

Metallurgy: the science and technology of metals.

Meteorology: the science that deals with the atmosphere and its phenomena and with weather and weather forecasting.

Microbiology: branch of biology dealing with microscopic forms of life.

Microwaves: electromagnetic radiation waves between one millimeter and one centimeter in length.

Molecular biology: the study of the structure and function of molecules that make up living organisms.

Molecule: the smallest particle of a substance that retains all the properties of the substance and is composed of one or more atoms.

Moving assembly line: a system in a plant or factory in which an item that is being made is carried past a series of workers who remain in their places. Each worker assembles a particular portion of the finished product and then repeats the same process with the next item.

Mutation: any permanent change in hereditary material, involving either a physical change in chromosome relations or a biochemical change in genes.

N

Natural selection: the natural process by which groups best adjusted to their environment survive and reproduce, thereby passing on to their offspring genetic qualities best suited to that environment.

Nebulae: large, cloudy bodies of dust in space.

Nerve Growth Factor (NGF): the nutrients that determine how nerve cells take on their specific roles in the nervous system.

Nervous system: the bodily system that in vertebrates is made up of the brain and spinal cord, nerves, ganglia, and other organs and that receives and interprets stimuli and transmits impulses to targeted organs.

Neurology: the scientific study of the nervous system, especially its structure, functions, and abnormalities.

Neurosecretion: the process of producing a secretion by nerve cells.

Neurosurgery: surgery on the nerves, brain, or spinal cord.

Neurosis: any emotional or mental disorder that affects only part of the personality, such as anxiety or mild depression, as a result of stress.

Neutrino: a subatomic particle with no electric charge and, generally, no detectable mass that interact very weakly with matter.

Neutron: an uncharged particle found in atomic nuclei.

Neutron star: a hypothetical dense celestial object that consists primarily of closely packed neutrons that results from the collapse of a much larger celestial body.

Nova: a star that suddenly increases in light output and then fades away to its former obscure state within a few months or years.

Nuclear fallout: the drifting of radioactive particles into the atmosphere as the result of nuclear explosions.

Nuclear fission: the process in which an atomic nucleus is split, resulting in the release of large amounts of energy.

Nuclear physics: physics that deals with the atomic nucleus, atomic energy, the atom bomb, or atomic power.

Nucleotides: compounds that form the basic structural units—the stairs on the spiral staircase—of DNA, and are arranged on the staircase in a pattern of heredity-carrying code "words."

Nutritionist: a person who studies the ways in which living organisms take in and make use of food.

O

Oceanography: the science that deals with the study of oceans and seas.

Optics: the study of light and vision.

Organic: of, relating to, or arising in a bodily organ.

Ornithology: the study of birds.

Ozone layer: the atmospheric layer of approximately twenty to thirty miles above Earth's surface that protects the lower atmosphere from harmful solar radiation.

P

Paleoanthropology: the branch of anthropology dealing with the study of mammal fossils.

Paleoecology: the study of prehistoric organisms and their environments.

Paleontology: the study of the life of past geological periods as known from fossil remains.

Particle accelerator: any of several machines, such as the cyclotron, that allows atomic particles such as protons and electrons to speed up to very high velocities in order to learn about the structure and composition of matter at very high velocities.

Particle physics: the branch of physics concerned with the study of the constitution, properties, and interactions of elementary particles.

Particles: the smallest building blocks of energy and matter.

Patent: a government grant giving an inventor the right to be the only person to sell an invention for a set length of time.

Pathology: the study of the essential nature of diseases, especially the structural and functional changes produced by them.

Pediatrics: a branch of medicine involving the development, care, and diseases of children.

Pendulum: an object that hangs freely from a fixed point and swings back and forth under the action of gravity; often used to regulate movement, as the pendulum in a clock.

Periodic table: a table of the elements in order of atomic number, arranged in rows and columns to show periodic similarities and trends in physical and chemical properties.

Pharmacology: the science dealing with the properties, reactions, and therapeutic values of drugs.

Phylum: the first division of the animal kingdom in the Linnaeus classification system. The ranking of the system is in order from the general to the specific—kingdom, phylum, class, order, family, genus, and species.

Physics: the science that explores the physical properties and composition of objects and the forces that affect them.

Physiology: the branch of biology that deals with the functions and actions of life or of living matter, such as organs, tissues, and cells.

Planetologist: a person who studies the physical bodies in the solar system, including planets and their satellites, comets, and meteorites.

Plankton: floating animal and plant life.

Plasma physics: the branch of physics involving the study of electrically charged, extremely hot gases.

Primate: any order of mammals composed of humans, apes, or monkeys.

Prions: a protein particle that lacks nucleic acid and is sometimes held to be the cause of various infectious diseases of the nervous system.

Projectile motion: the movement of an object thrust forward by an external force—for example, a cannonball shot out of a cannon.

Protein: large molecules found in all living organisms that are essential to the structure and functioning of all living cells.

Proton: a positively charged particle found in atomic nuclei.

Psychiatry: the branch of medicine that deals with mental, emotional, and behavioral disorders.

Psychoanalysis: the method of analyzing psychic phenomenon and treating emotional disorders that involves treatment sessions during which the patient is encouraged to talk freely about personal experiences, especially about early childhood and dreams.

Psychophysiology: a branch of psychology that focuses on combined mental and bodily processes.

Psychology: the study of human and animal behavior.

Psychotic: a person with severe emotional or mental disorders that cause a loss of contact with reality.

Q

Quantum: any of the very small increments or parcels into which many forms of energy are subdivided.

Quark: a type of elementary particle; the smallest known building block of matter.

Quasar: celestial object more distant than stars that emits excessive amounts of radiation.

R

Radar: acronym for radio detection and ranging; the process of using radio waves to detect objects.

Radiation: energy emitted in the form of waves or particles.

Radio waves: electromagnetic radiation.

Radioactive fallout: the radioactive particles resulting from a nuclear explosion.

Radioactivity: the property possessed by some elements (as uranium) or isotopes (as carbon 14) of spontaneously emitting energetic particles (as electrons or alpha particles) by disintegration of their atomic nuclei.

Radiology: the branch of medicine that uses X rays and radium (an intensely radioactive metallic element) to diagnose and treat disease.

Redshift: the increase in the wavelength of all light received from a celestial object (or wave source), usually because the object is moving away from the observer.

RNA (ribonucleic acid): any of various nucleic acids that are associated with the control of cellular chemical activities.

S

Scientific method: collecting evidence meticulously and theorizing from it.

Seismograph: a device that records vibrations of the ground and within Earth.

Seismology: the study and measurement of earthquakes.

Semiconductor: substances whose ability to carry electrical current is lower than that of a conductor (like metal) and higher than that of insulators (like rubber).

Shortwave: a radio wave having a wavelength between ten and one hundred meters.

Slide rule: a calculating device that, in its simplest form, consists of a ruler and a sliding attachment that are graduated with logarithm tables.

Social science: the study of human society and individual relationships within it, including the fields of sociology, anthropology, economics, political science, and history.

Sociobiology: the systematic study of the biological basis for all social behavior.

Soil erosion: the loss of usable topsoil, often due to clearing trees and other plant life from the land.

Solar eclipse: an event that occurs when the Moon passes between Earth and the Sun, partially or totally blocking the Sun's light.

Solid state: using semiconductor devices rather than electron tubes.

Solvent: a liquid substance capable of dissolving another substance.

Spectrum: the range of colors produced by individual elements within a light source.

Statics: a branch of physics that explores the forces of equilibrium, or balance.

Steady-state theory: a theory that proposes that the universe has neither a beginning nor an end.

Stellar spectra: the distinctive mix of radiation emitted by every star.

Stellar spectroscopy: the process that breaks a star's light into component colors so that the various elements of the star can be observed.

Sterilization: boiling or heating of instruments and food to prevent proliferation of microorganisms.

Supernova: a catastrophic explosion in which a large portion of a star's mass is blown out into space, or the star is entirely destroyed.

T

Theorem: in mathematics, a formula, proposition, or statement.

Theory: an assumption drawn from scientific evidence that provides a plausible explanation for the principle or principles behind a natural phenomenon. (A *theory* generally has more evidence behind it and finds more acceptance in the scientific community than a *hypothesis*.)

Thermodynamics: the branch of physics that deals with the mechanical action or relations of heat.

Trace element: a chemical element present in minute quantities.

Transistor: a solid-state electronic device that is used to control the flow of electricity in electronic equipment and consists of a small block of semiconductor with at least three electrodes.

V

Vaccine: a preparation administered to increase immunity to polio.

Vacuum tube: an electric tube from which all matter has been removed.

Variable stars: stars whose light output varies because of internal fluctuations or because they are eclipsed by another star.

Variation: in genetics, differences in traits of a particular species.

Vertebrate: an animal that has a spinal column.

Virology: the study of viruses.

Virtual reality: an artificial computer-created environment that seeks to mimic reality.

Virus: a microscopic agent of infection.

Voltaic pile: a basic form of battery that was the first source of continuous and controllable electric current.

W

Wavelength: the distance between one peak of a wave of light, heat, or energy and the next corresponding peak.

X

X ray: a form of electromagnetic radiation with an extremely short wavelength that is produced by bombarding a metallic target with electrons in a vacuum.

Z

Zoology: the branch of biology concerned with the study of animal life.

Zooplankton: small drifting animal life in the ocean.

SCIENTISTS: Their Lives and Works

Benjamin Banneker

November 9, 1731
Baltimore County,
in present-day Maryland

October 9, 1806
Baltimore County, Maryland

Benjamin Banneker was an African American astronomer and mathematician who was born free at a time when slavery was legal in America. He was extremely intelligent and, when he was not working on his family's farm, spent most of his free time reading books and solving math problems. When Banneker was older, his friend and neighbor George Ellicott lent him a high-quality telescope and some astronomy books, which Banneker used to teach himself astronomy. He had such a natural talent for it that he quickly learned how to chart the paths of the planets and compile information for an almanac, which was the first almanac to be published by a black man. Banneker's accomplishments were championed by abolitionists, or people who opposed slavery, as an example of what all free black men could hope to achieve.

A proud and humble beginning

Benjamin Banneker was born on November 9, 1731, before the United States was formed and before slavery was

"The colour of the skin is in no ways connected with strength of mind or intellectual powers."

Benjamin Banneker is remembered as a remarkable mathematician, astronomer, and pioneer for racial equality in America. Born a free black man during the time of slavery in America, he was given the rare opportunity to go to school where he learned to read and write. His fondness for stargazing and his talent for making astronomical calculations helped him to generate tables that predicted the paths of the Sun, Moon, and planets. This skill enabled him to successfully predict a solar eclipse in 1789 and have an almanac published in 1791. Abolitionists held Banneker up as an example of what free black men could achieve when given fair opportunities at a time in American history when credit and respect were rarely given to African Americans.

abolished. His grandmother, Molly Welsh, was a white woman from England who had been sent to work on a tobacco farm in Maryland after being accused of stealing from her English employer. Molly had to complete seven years as an indentured servant; that is, the plantation owner paid for her passage to America and Molly worked for him to pay off the debt. After her debt was paid off, she bought a small farm and two slaves and began to work for herself growing and selling tobacco. She was successful and, in 1696, Molly freed her slaves and married one of them named Bannaky.

Molly and Bannaky had four daughters. Mary, the oldest daughter, grew up and bought a slave named Robert. She later married him and the couple took the last name Banneky, in honor of Mary's father, who died shortly before their wedding. They bought a small farm near Molly and had four children; Benjamin was the oldest and the only boy. Over time, the spelling of Banneky became Banneker.

Over the next several years, Benjamin learned how to plow the land, grow tobacco and vegetables, pick fruit from the orchards, hunt and fish, and take care of the farm animals. His grandmother, Molly, meanwhile, taught him to read and write using the Bible as a lesson book. When Benjamin was twelve, a Quaker named Peter Heinrich set up a one-room schoolhouse and taught both black and white boys. (At this time in American history, blacks were rarely educated, and more rarely socialized with whites. Quakers belong to a religious group that does not believe in slavery or keeping people separated because of race.) Benjamin loved school, especially reading, writing, and mathematics. For the

Slavery in America

The practice of slavery was adopted in the United States in the 1680s. Slavers forcibly took people from their homes in Africa and shipped them under horrible conditions to America. There, the slavers sold the slaves throughout the American colonies, but they were used most in the South, where agricultural production of crops such as tobacco, rice, and cotton was the heaviest. After 1808, slaves were no longer brought from Africa, but children born to slaves were still considered slaves and were put to work. By 1860, there were nearly four million slaves in America.

When the American colonies secured their own freedom from England in 1776, many people, including Benjamin Banneker, began to speak out against slavery. The words of the Declaration of Independence, in which "all men are created equal," were in sharp contrast to the idea of slavery, in which slaves were considered possessions. Beginning in the North, states began to abolish slavery, and most of the North was free territory by the 1830s. Many slave owners living in areas where slavery was still legal also began to free their slaves. Thousands of slaves escaped and fled to the North. Still, slavery in rural parts of the South flourished, causing a large split within the United States: the South was pro-slavery while the North favored abolition. Slavery was not officially abolished until December 1865, when the Thirteenth Amendment to the Constitution was passed, freeing more than three million slaves.

next several years, he worked on the farm and spent his free time continuing his studies. He even learned how to play the violin and flute.

Benjamin was fascinated with figuring out how things are made. When he was twenty-two years old, he borrowed an English pocket watch from a friend and took it apart. He studied it, drew its parts, and figured out mathematically how to enlarge its parts. He then built a larger version of the clock out of wood and a few bits of metal. Remarkably, this large clock kept perfect time for the next forty years and brought fame to young Banneker. He began his own clock and watch repair business, which led to a meeting that would change his life.

New neighbors

In 1771 the Ellicott family moved onto land about a mile from the Banneker farm. They began to build gristmills, or mills that grind grain, houses for the workers, and a small village. Banneker watched in amazement as machines at the mills did the work of many men. The Ellicotts were Quakers, as Banneker's old teacher had been. They believed all people were equal, and welcomed everyone into the general store they built. Banneker loved to visit the store and talk to people about ideas. This new social gathering place opened his world dramatically.

Banneker became friends with the Ellicott brothers. They lent him astronomy and mathematics books and even a first-rate telescope. Banneker devoured the books and began studying the stars. He had a natural talent for mathematics that was perfectly suited to his new stargazing hobby.

Astronomy and an almanac

Banneker quickly became an accomplished astronomer. He was especially interested in solar eclipses and set out to mathematically calculate when a solar eclipse would next occur. (A solar eclipse happens when the Moon passes between Earth and the Sun, partially or totally blocking the Sun's light.)

Banneker used the information in the books, a ruler, and a compass to map out the paths of the Sun and the Moon. He made a drawing of his prediction, called a projection, and successfully calculated that the next solar eclipse in the Baltimore area would occur in 1789. Banneker extended his studies and began learning how to make an ephemeris, a chart that plots the positions of the Sun, Moon, and all the planets for every day of the coming year. It is a large part of an almanac, a reference book containing astronomical projections and weather predictions that was often consulted to figure out the best time to plant and harvest crops. Almost every household owned an almanac during the 1700s.

Banneker painstakingly completed all of the necessary calculations for an ephemeris, then he prepared an almanac

In 1791, Benjamin Banneker was part of a team that surveyed the land for the building of the nation's capital.
Reproduced by permission of Fisk University Library.

and sent it off to a publisher. This first submission was rejected, and Banneker was determined to make new sets of calculations and try again. However, an important detour delayed his plans.

Surveying the nation's capital

In 1776, the United States of America declared its independence from England. The new nation needed a new capital city and it was to be built on a piece of land given by both Maryland and Virginia. In February 1791, America's first president, George Washington (1732–1799), hired Major Andrew Ellicott (cousin of the Ellicott brothers that Banneker was friends with) to survey the land. One of the people Ellicott hired to help him was Banneker.

At sixty years old, Banneker left home for the first time in his life. He worked closely with Ellicott and with the architect in charge, Pierre L'Enfant. Because of his notorious temper outbursts, L'Enfant was fired, and he left Washington, taking all of the construction plans with him. Banneker stepped in and recreated all of the plans from memory, saving the U.S. government the effort and expense of hiring a new architect.

Abolition and more almanacs

Upon his return to the farm, Banneker resumed working on his new almanac. Goddard & Angell, the same publisher that had rejected his first manuscript, published Banneker's almanac in 1791. *Benjamin Banneker's Pennsylvania, Delaware, Maryland and Virginia Almanac and Ephemeris for the Year of Our Lord, 1792,* was well publicized as the first almanac ever to be written by a black man. This acknowledgment was done both to sell almanacs and to showcase the equality of black men.

The first almanac was very successful and Banneker became well known. Within a year, he decided to sell his land to the Ellicotts so he could concentrate on astronomy and almanacs instead of farming. Banneker continued to live on the farm and published five more editions of his almanac, the last one released in 1797.

Just before the first almanac was published, Banneker wrote a letter to Thomas Jefferson (1743–1826), George Washington's secretary of state who would later become the nation's third president. The letter discussed the unfairness of slavery and questioned why slavery would exist in a nation that had so recently fought to be free from English rule. With the writing of that letter, Banneker became one of the first black men to speak out against slavery to a white man in high political standing. Jefferson replied and agreed with Banneker's sentiments. Banneker's abolitionist friends published the letters between the two men in newspapers and fliers, showing that even some powerful white men could question the practice of slavery. Nonetheless, slavery was so deep-rooted in America that it would be more than seventy years before it would be abolished.

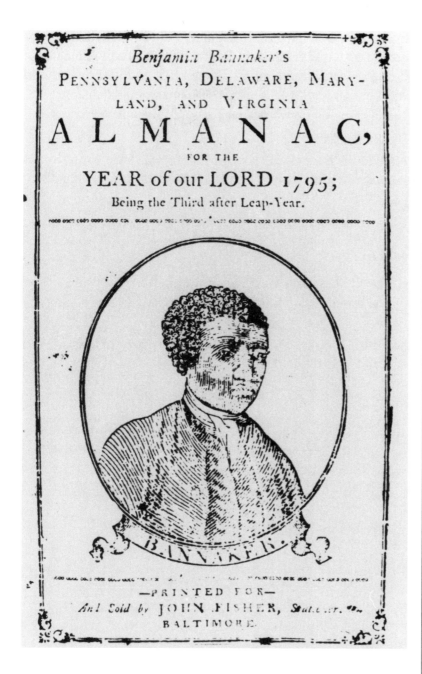

Benjamin Banneker's 1795 Almanac, was his third published almanac.

Banneker died at home on October 9, 1806, at the age of seventy-five. Modern historians have honored Banneker several times. In 1970, a traffic circle in Washington, D.C., was named after him. In 1980, the U.S. Postal Service issued a stamp with his picture on it. In 1990, his burial site was given a historical marker. And in 1998, the Benjami Banneker Historical Park and Museum was opened in Baltimore, Maryland. It sits on the original land purchased by Banneker's parents, Robert and Mary.

Further Reading

"Benjamin Banneker." *Inventors Museum.* http://www.inventorsmuseum.com/benjamin_banneker.htm (accessed on September 3, 2002).

Blue, Rose, and Corinne J. Naden. *Benjamin Banneker: Mathematician and Stargazer.* Brookfield, CT: Millbrook Press, 2001.

Litwin, Laura Baskes. *Benjamin Banneker: Astronomer and Mathematician.* Berkeley Heights, NJ: Enslow Publishers, 1999.

Maupin, Melissa. *Benjamin Banneker.* Chanhassen, MN: Child's World, 2000.

Frederick Banting

November 14, 1891
Alliston, Ontario, Canada
February 21, 1941
Newfoundland, Canada

In 1921, Frederick Banting, at the young age of 30, made a momentous discovery: the hormone insulin could be extracted from pancreatic tissue and used to treat patients with diabetes, dramatically increasing their quality of life. The Canadian doctor was awarded the Nobel Prize in physiology or medicine in 1923 for this life-saving accomplishment.

"Insulin is not a cure for diabetes; it is a treatment."

Early life

Frederick Grant Banting was born on November 14, 1891, to William and Margaret Banting. Frederick was the youngest of five children, four boys and one girl. The Banting family lived on a farm in Alliston, Ontario, where the boys helped take care of the farm animals and with other chores. Whenever an animal on the farm died, part of the boys' duties was to learn the specifics of what killed the animal so that it could be prevented from happening again. This made a big

Portrait reproduced courtesy of Library of Congress.

9

impact on Frederick and influenced his decision to pursue medical science as a career.

Frederick went to public schools in Alliston. He was a good student and an excellent athlete. In 1911, he was admitted to the University of Toronto. Influenced by his father, he studied theology (the study of the nature of God) during his first year, but quickly discovered his real desire was to become a doctor. He changed his focus to medicine the following year and received his medical degree from the university in 1916.

A doctor and a hero

After World War I broke out in 1914, doctors were urgently needed on the battlefront. Soon after graduation, Banting left for England as part of the Canadian Army Medical Corps. He spent time in army hospitals and received training to perform a variety of surgical procedures. In 1918, he was transferred to a post in France, where his arm was badly wounded. The following year, he was awarded the Military Cross for bravely treating wounded soldiers while under fire.

After the war ended in 1918, Banting returned to Canada and spent a year working as a resident surgeon at the Hospital for Sick Children in Toronto. In 1920, he opened his own surgical practice in London, Ontario. Business was slow and Banting took a part-time teaching job at the University of Western Ontario. He also had the opportunity to work in the medical research laboratory of Dr. Frederick Miller. Neither Banting nor Miller had any idea that their relationship would spark the beginning of a medical breakthrough.

A brilliant idea

When Banting was younger, one of his schoolmates had died from diabetes, establishing an interest in this disease that stayed with Banting throughout his life. In October 1920, Banting was up late one night preparing a lecture at Miller's request when he read Moses Baron's article about diabetes "The Relation of the Islets of Langerhans to Diabetes, with Special Reference to Cases of Pancreatic Lithiasis." Diabetes is a disease that occurs when a body lacks insulin. Insulin is a hormone, a chemical produced by the body that regulates specific bodily functions. Without insulin, too much sugar is allowed to build up in the blood. (Some sugar is necessary in the blood for cells to produce energy. Too much sugar can lead to diabetes, however.) Diabetes patients suffer from a range of ailments, including blindness, severe infections, and kidney failure, and it can lead to death.

It was already known that the pancreas, the gland that produces insulin, is involved with how the body metabolizes, or processes, sugar. Earlier research had shown that a dog would develop diabetes if its pancreas were taken out. Scientists had been trying to figure out a way to isolate insulin from the body so that it might be studied further. Baron's article inspired Banting to work on this problem.

The pancreas also produces an enzyme called trypsin that breaks down proteins, including insulin. In his article, Baron discussed a case in which the pancreatic cells that produce trypsin could be selectively destroyed by tying off, or surgically closing, the pancreatic duct. (A duct is a tube in the body for carrying bodily fluid, especially a fluid excreted by a gland.) Tying off the duct prevented the pancreatic gland from working properly and caused blood sugar levels to increase. Banting reasoned that even if the trypsin-producing cells of the pancreas were killed off, the insulin-producing cells, called the islets of Langerhans, would be largely left intact. He determined that by destroying the trypsin-producing cells, he could isolate the islets and then extract the insulin.

Because a dog's pancreatic system is similar to that of a human, Banting proposed experimenting with insulin on dogs

IMPACT

Frederick Banting's work had a direct impact on the lives of millions of people who suffer from diabetes, a disease that occurs when a person lacks the protein hormone called insulin. Without insulin, too much sugar builds up in the blood, causing weakness and infection and possibly blindness, kidney failure, and death. Banting isolated the cells of the pancreas that produce insulin. From those cells, called the islets of Langerhans, he was able to produce purified insulin. First tested on a human patient in 1922, insulin caused blood sugar levels to drop significantly and the patient reported feeling healthier and less fatigued. As a direct result of Banting's work, insulin rapidly developed into the standard treatment for diabetes.

before humans. He wanted to tie off the pancreatic duct in dogs and cause them to develop diabetes. After this procedure, he would wait several weeks and then remove the islet cells in order to isolate the insulin. If successful, Banting then wanted to treat the dogs with the insulin to see if it would cure their new disease.

When Banting explained his idea to Miller, Miller recommended he contact John James Richard Macleod at the University of Toronto. Macleod was well known for his research on how carbohydrates, including sugar, are metabolized. (Carbohydrates are compounds consisting of carbon, hydrogen, and oxygen found in plants and used as food by humans and other animals when they are broken down by metabolism, the bodily process by which compounds are broken down to yield energy.) Banting went to Toronto to interview for a job with Macleod, but was turned down because he lacked any real research experience. Banting persisted, however, and convinced Macleod to give him a chance. He was allowed to use Macleod's laboratory for eight weeks, given dogs with which to experiment, and also an assistant, Charles Best.

A new partner

Banting closed his practice, gave up his job at the University of Western Ontario, and moved back to Toronto in April 1921. When Banting arrived he met his new assistant, Charles Best (1899–1978). Best was a student at the University of Toronto who was studying physiology and biochemistry. He already knew how to analyze blood and urine samples and began working intensively with Banting after his graduation in May 1921.

In Macleod's laboratory, Banting and Best began experimenting on dogs. (Macleod supervised their work for the first month and then left for vacation.) Some of the dogs had their pancreases taken out and others had their pancreatic duct tied off to stop the gland from functioning properly. With the pancreas not producing insulin to control the amount of sugar in the dogs' blood, the dogs' blood sugar level rose. Then, they gave the dogs insulin. An hour after the insulin injections, they measured the blood sugar levels and they had dropped. They gave the dogs another insulin injection, which dropped the blood sugar levels again. This showed that giving a patient insulin would lower the blood sugar level and be an effective treatment for diabetes.

The two men were excited, but needed to find a way to obtain insulin more efficiently and in larger quantities. Banting had learned from his experience with breeding cattle on his family's farm that the pancreas of fetal, unborn, animals had a greater number of islet cells than adult animals to regulate sugar levels allowing for development and growth while inside the womb. He contacted a slaughterhouse, which supplied them with fetal calves. The increased number of islet cells in the fetal pigs allowed more insulin to be produced and the team was able to extract enough insulin to prepare for testing on humans. Macleod hired biochemist J.B. Collip to work on the project. Collip purified the insulin and made it ready for use in humans.

Charles Herbert Best helped Frederick Banting isolate insulin to treat patients with diabetes.
Reproduced courtesy of Library of Congress.

A human subject and the Nobel Prize

In November 1921, Banting and Best published their discovery in the *Journal of Laboratory and Clinical Medicine*. The paper, "The Internal Secretion of the Pancreas," received immediate attention from scientists all over the world. It also prompted many patients with diabetes to travel to Toronto for treatment.

The first patient to be injected with the team's insulin was a fourteen-year-old Canadian boy named Leonard Thompson. He had been diabetic for two years and his illness had deteriorated his body into a serious condition, causing him to weigh only 65 pounds (30 kilograms). On January 11, 1922, Thompson was given an injection of insulin. His blood sugar

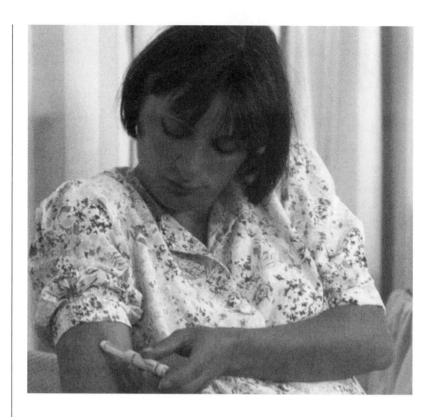

level dropped, just as it had in the dogs. But something wasn't right. Thompson's health did not improve as expected. Scientists theorized that the extract was not pure enough to be used repeatedly and researchers developed a method to produce a purer insulin extract.

About two weeks later, Banting and Best injected Thompson with the new, purer extract. This time, the patient's situation improved dramatically. The level of sugar in his blood dropped and Thompson reported feeling more alert and less fatigued than he had in a long time. The test was a huge success and insulin quickly became the standard treatment for diabetic patients.

In 1923, Banting and Macleod were awarded the Nobel Prize in physiology or medicine for the discovery of insulin. Banting felt strongly that he should have shared the prize with Best rather than Macleod. To acknowledge Best's role in the work, Banting shared the money he received from the Nobel Prize with Best.

The University of Toronto did acknowledge Best, however, honoring both men in 1923 with the creation of the Banting-Best Department of Medical Research. Banting ran the department until his death in 1941, at which point Best took his place until his own retirement in 1964. The university also acknowledged Banting in 1930, naming a new building after him.

A year after he was awarded the Nobel Prize, Banting married Marion Robertson. They had a son named William, but the marriage did not last and the couple divorced in 1932. Banting later married Henrietta Ball in 1937.

When Canada entered World War II (1939–45), Banting again served his country as an officer in the Medical Corps. He frequently flew back and forth between Canada and England. Tragically, he was killed during one of those trips when his plane crashed in Newfoundland, Canada, on February 21, 1941. Although Banting lived a short life, he left behind a gift that still benefits thousands of diabetes patients all over the world.

Further Reading

Bankston, John. *Frederick Banting and the Discovery of Insulin.* Elkton, MD: Mitchell Lane Publishers, 2001.

Banting Digital Library. http://www.newtecumseth.library. on.ca/banting/main.html (accessed on September 3, 2002).

"Frederick Grant Banting—Biography." *Nobel e-Museum.* http://www.nobel.se/medicine/laureates/1923/banting-bio. html (accessed on September 3, 2002).

Mayer, Ann Margaret. *Sir Frederick Banting, Doctor Against Diabetes.* Mankato, MN: Children's Press, 1974.

"Sir Frederick Grant Banting." *Discovery of Insulin.* http:// www.discoveryofinsulin.com/Banting.htm (accessed on June 12, 2002).

Christiaan Barnard

November 8, 1922
Beaufort West, South Africa

September 2, 2001
Paphos, Cyprus

South African heart surgeon Christiaan Barnard performed the world's first heart transplant in a human being. This historic event took place at the Groote Schuur Hospital in Cape Town, South Africa, on December 3, 1967. At the time, Barnard's decision to harvest a heart from a patient whose brain was no longer functioning but whose heart was still beating was controversial. His daring move, however, made human heart transplants an option for critically ill patients. In the decades that followed, more than 100,000 patients throughout the world received heart transplants.

Finding his path

Christiaan Neethling Barnard was born on November 8, 1922, in Beaufort West, South Africa, to Maria Elizabeth de Swart and Adam Hendrik Barnard. Christiaan's father was a minister at a mixed-race church in Beaufort West, and because

"On Saturday, I was a surgeon in South Africa, very little known. On Monday, I was world renowned."

17

South African surgeon Christiaan Barnard became known throughout the world when he performed the first heart transplant on a human patient on December 3, 1967. His decision to remove the heart from a patient who was on artificial respiration and whose heart was still beating but would never recover from her brain injuries had a major impact on the field of transplant surgery. Prior to Barnard's success, doctors were required to wait until a patient's heart had stopped beating before they could harvest donor organs. This practice made the heart unusable. Although some considered Barnard's decision controversial, most agreed that without this landmark move, heart transplant surgery would not have become a standard practice. Today, more than 2,100 heart transplants are performed yearly in the United States alone.

the town was poor, his father was not well paid. The Barnards encouraged all four of their sons to work hard and value the importance of a good education. From the time he was a very young man, Christiaan wanted to become a doctor. He went to public high school and then attended the University of Cape Town as a pre-medical student.

After graduating from college in 1946, Barnard worked at the Groote Schuur Hospital in Cape Town for one year. He then worked for two years in a medical practice in Ceres, South Africa, before going back to Cape Town. In 1950, Barnard was hired as the senior resident medical officer at City Hospital in Cape Town and continued his medical studies at the University of Cape Town Medical School. For his thesis, he did research about children suffering from tuberculosis, a disease caused by bacteria that often affects the lungs.

Gains recognition as a surgeon

After receiving his master's degree in 1953, Barnard became a research fellow in surgery at the University of Cape Town Medical School, which included working as a surgeon at the Groote Schuur Hospital. At the university, Barnard began to conduct research on gastrointestinal, or digestive, diseases. He developed a surgical procedure to fix a birth defect called congenital intestinal atresia, a gap in the small intestine, by closing the gap. The young doctor Barnard received a lot of positive attention from the medical society and the media for his new procedure.

In 1955, Barnard received a scholarship to travel to the United States to earn his doctorate degree. He enrolled at the University of Minnesota Medical School to study with the well-known cardiac, or heart, surgeon Owen H. Wangensteen. Wangensteen's work inspired Barnard to study heart surgery and he was fortunate enough to be able to observe and assist on operations being performed by several excellent heart surgeons. At Minnesota, Barnard also worked on a research project to make and test an artificial heart valve.

Barnard received his doctorate in 1958 and returned to South Africa. With him, he brought a piece of equipment called a heart-lung machine that Wangensteen had given him. This machine keeps patients alive during heart surgery by running oxygen through a patient's blood and then pumping the blood through the body. It was the first heart-lung machine in Africa and it enabled Barnard to perform heart surgery in his native country.

First steps toward transplant surgery

Back at Groote Schuur Hospital, where Barnard was now the director of surgical research, he used his heart-lung machine to perform a variety of advanced heart operations and perfect his skills. He was especially interested in taking out damaged heart valves and replacing them with artificial ones. He also experimented with transplanting a heart in a dog. Before he would be able to attempt a transplant in a human patient, however, Barnard had to better understand what would keep a patient's body from rejecting the new organ. When a body rejects an organ that is not its own, the body's immune system attacks the foreign organ much like it attacks germs.

To study organ rejection, Barnard turned his attention to the kidney. Kidney researchers around the world were already experimenting with different drugs to control the body's rejection mechanism since organ rejection was common in kidney-transplant patients at the time, resulting in many patient deaths. In 1966, Barnard traveled to the United States to take a course in kidney transplantation at the Medical College of Virginia in Richmond. There he learned the basics of anti-rejection medicines, and upon his return to South Africa, Barnard's surgical team performed the first kidney transplant in South

Africa. Barnard now felt confident that he could perform a successful heart transplant. But he had to wait for the timing to be right. The procedure not only required a patient in need of a heart transplant, it also required a compatible heart to be donated before the living patient's time ran out.

The first transplant patient

In October 1967, a fifty-four-year-old patient named Louis Washkansky was admitted to Groote Schuur. He had diabetes (a disease that occurs when the body lacks the hormone insulin, thus allowing too much sugar to build up in the blood), an enlarged liver (caused by the diabetes and other ailments), and a failing heart. By November, doctors believed he would live only a few more weeks if he did not receive a new heart. Barnard explained the procedure of a heart transplant to him, and Washkansky agreed to have the operation. The surgi-

Robert Dowling and Laman Gray

On July 2, 2001, another milestone was achieved in the field of heart transplant surgery. Robert Dowling and Laman Gray, surgeons from the University of Louisville School of Medicine in Kentucky, led a surgical team that successfully placed the first artificial heart into human patient Robert Tools. The operation took seven hours and was performed at the Jewish Hospital in Louisville. Dowling and Gray also led the investigation team that developed the artificial heart called AbioCor. It had taken more than twenty years of research and development to arrive at this day.

Two months after the procedure, Dowling and Gray reported that the patient was having a successful recovery and doing well in his physical therapy. Sadly, Tools died on November 30, 2001, after complications from a preexisting condition that he suffered from before he received the artificial heart. The artificial heart was not the cause of death, and on September 13, 2001, the team placed an artificial heart into a second patient, seventy-year-old Tom Christerson. As of August 2002, the heart was still beating.

cal team then began the wait for a donor. On December 3, 1967, one family's tragedy became another family's hope.

On December 3, twenty-five-year-old Denise Darvall had been horribly injured in a car accident. She was admitted to the emergency room at Groote Schuur and was expected to die during the night. Her condition, termed brain dead, meant that although her heart was still beating she would never recover from the injuries to her brain. At the time, American transplant surgeons followed a standard procedure, waiting for the patient's heart to stop beating before removing the organ. Although considered by many surgeons as the "proper," moral procedure, this method decreased the success rate for the transplant because the heart muscle begins to deteriorate immediately after the heart stops beating. Surgeons would try to get the heart pumping once again but often it was too late for the heart to be of any use to a second recipient. Barnard thought that if he removed the girl's heart while she was still technically alive and kept her heart beating with a heart-lung machine, their chances for a successful transplant would increase. Barnard met with Darvall's father to explain the procedure and he agreed to allow his daughter's heart to be harvested while she was on artificial respiration and still physically alive.

The surgical team flew into action. By now Groote Schuur had several heart-lung machines and Barnard and his team of thirty surgeons used one to keep Darvall's heart pumping while Washkansky's diseased heart was removed. Another heart-lung machine was hooked up to Washkansky to keep blood flowing through the rest of his body during the operation. Once Barnard removed Washkansky's diseased heart, he replaced it with Darvall's still-beating heart. The surgeons still did not know if Darvall's heart would continue beating on its own once they removed the heart-lung machine that was keeping it beating. Within fifteen minutes of being off of the machine, the heart was beating on its own. Washkansky's blood was able to circulate with Darvall's heart without the assistance of the heart-lung machine.

Taking it further

Barnard's achievement made headlines all over the world. But it was just the first step. Washkansky died of infection eighteen days after the surgery. Drugs had stopped his immune system from rejecting the heart, but they had also left him susceptible to infection. An autopsy performed after death showed that the heart itself had not stopped working but that Washkansky had died from pneumonia. More work was needed to prevent the immune system from rejecting the heart.

Barnard received another patient in need of a heart transplant the following year. On January 2, 1968, he operated on fifty-eight-year-old Philip Blaiberg. This time, Barnard reduced the amount of anti-rejection drugs and kept his patient isolated in a germ-free room. Blaiberg did not develop any post-operative infections and lived for about eighteen months after the operation.

Again, Barnard was applauded throughout the world for his achievements. He began to receive awards and was seen by many as a celebrity. Barnard's success, however, was also met with controversy over the timing of when it is acceptable to harvest a donor's heart. Fame also caused problems in his marriage. His first wife, Aletta, was a nurse who had helped support him while he developed his career as a surgeon. After twenty-one years of marriage, they divorced in 1969. Barnard married his second wife, Barbara, the following year and divorced her twelve years later. He had two children, Deirdre and Andre, with his first wife and two children, Frederick and Christiaan, Jr., with his second wife.

Heart transplants began to be performed by other surgeons in the United States and Europe. In 1974, Barnard made history again. This time, he performed a double-heart transplant, thought to be less risky. Without taking the diseased heart out, he implanted another heart into a patient to boost the original heart's function. Barnard tried this technique again the following year, but neither patient lived more than a few months. After the surgery, he returned to his original technique of transplant and successfully transplanted sixty-three hearts by the time he retired in 1983.

Speaking and writing books

When Barnard retired, he left the hospital, but continued to be active in the medical profession. He gave lectures in South Africa about malnutrition and tuberculosis. He continued to write scientific articles and also wrote several novels. He even opened a chain of Italian restaurants and bought a large sheep ranch.

In 1987, Barnard married again, this time to Karin Setzkorn. At the age of seventy-three, he had his fifth child, a son named Armin, with his new wife. Barnard died from an asthma attack while vacationing in Cyprus on September 2, 2001.

Further Reading

Altman, Lawrence K. "Christiaan Barnard, 78, Surgeon for First Heart Transplant, Dies." *New York Times,* September 3, 2001.

Barnard, Christiaan. *50 Ways to a Healthy Heart.* New York: Thorsons Publishing, 2001.

Barnard, Christiaan. *Your Healthy Heart: The Family Guide to Staying Healthy and Living Longer.* New York: McGraw-Hill, 1988.

Barnard, Christiaan, and Curtis Bill Pepper. *Christiaan Barnard: One Life.* New York: Macmillan, 1969.

Barnard, Christiaan, and Peter Evans. *Christiaan Barnard's Program for Living With Arthritis.* New York: Bantam Books, 1985.

Dougherty, Steven, and Drusilla Menaker. "Lion in Winter; Christiaan Barnard has had fame, scandal—and a few regrets." *People Weekly,* April 8, 1996, p. 117.

The Implantable Artificial Heart Project. http://www.heartpioneers.com/index.html (accessed on September 3, 2002).

Ruth Fulton Benedict

June 5, 1887
New York, New York

September 17, 1948
New York, New York

O ne of the first successful female anthropologists, Ruth Fulton Benedict introduced a new way of studying human behavior by proposing that every culture has its own accepted set of behaviors. Benedict believed that only people belonging to a culture could view behavior within that culture as appropriate or inappropriate. Therefore, she believed that judging people who were not a part of one's own culture was an inaccurate and somewhat ignorant act. Her work made great strides toward fighting racism and overcoming cultural stereotypes.

"The trouble with life isn't that there is no answer, it's that there are so many answers."

A troubled childhood

Ruth Fulton was born in New York City on June 5, 1887. Her mother, Beatrice, was a schoolteacher and librarian, and her father, Frederick, was a doctor. While still a toddler, her family moved to Beatrice's parent's farm in

Portrait reproduced courtesy of Library of Congress.

IMPACT

American anthropologist Ruth Fulton Benedict proposed the idea that every world culture is unique and should be respected as such. Her work explained that one culture should not judge a different culture for its actions, as each culture has its own ideas of what is acceptable behavior. Benedict's articles and books championed the individual culture as deserving respect. She believed that the definition of what is "normal" behavior could only be determined by the specific culture to which a person belongs. This was a groundbreaking idea that helped people consider racial and cultural differences in a new light.

Binghamton, New York. Shortly thereafter, Frederick died. In Binghamton, Beatrice found work as a teacher and began to raise Ruth and her younger sister Margery with the help of her parents. Although Ruth was young when her father died, she had been very close to him and his death affected her deeply for the rest of her life. She was a sad child and her mother's grief only contributed to Ruth's personality. Ruth often showed signs of depression and had fits of rage. She also was criticized for not listening when people spoke to her. But when she was five years old it was discovered that she suffered from partial deafness as a result of the measles.

In 1892, Beatrice moved her two daughters to Missouri, then to Minnesota. In both states, Beatrice found teaching jobs, but they did not pay well. Then in 1899, she was hired as the superintendent of circulation at the Buffalo Public Library in Buffalo, New York. Life slowly improved for the family in Buffalo, and the girls received scholarships to St. Margaret's Episcopal Academy for Girls, which they attended from 1900 to 1905. During this time, Ruth began to express her feelings by writing poetry under the name Anne Singleton.

College and beyond

In 1905, Ruth and Margery both entered Vassar College in Poughkeepsie, New York, the same college their mother had attended, on two more scholarships. Ruth studied English literature and often kept to herself. She did make some friends, mainly other shy, quiet people like herself. After graduation, Ruth and a few classmates traveled to Europe together. Following that trip, she moved back to Buffalo and lived with her mother for a year.

In Buffalo, Ruth worked for the Charity Organization Society, doing a variety of charitable and social work. In 1911, she moved to California to be near her sister. In California, Ruth found work as a high school teacher and taught at the Westlake School for Girls in Los Angeles from 1911 to 1912. She then took a job at the Orton School for Girls in Pasadena, California, until 1914. However, Ruth really didn't like teaching and was struggling to discover what she wanted to do with her life.

During the summer of 1913, Ruth returned to her grandparents' farm in New York to visit. There, she spent some time with Stanley Benedict, a brother of a former Vassar classmate and a biochemist at Cornell Medical College in New York City. They fell in love and she moved to Long Island in New York and married Stanley on June 18, 1914.

An anthropologist is born

In 1919, Benedict made a quick and unexpected decision that would change her life dramatically. She enrolled in the New School for Social Research where she went to lectures and took classes with prominent anthropologists Alexander Goldenweiser and Elsie Clews Parson. (Anthropologists are scientists who study the physical, cultural, and social development of human beings.) Benedict immersed herself in the new and varied cultures she learned about in her anthropological studies. The in-depth research and self-discovery brought about by her work helped to make Benedict's life feel fuller.

After two years of classes at the New School, Benedict enrolled in the graduate program at Columbia University so she could study with the well-known anthropologist Franz Boas (1858–1942). Benedict's life changed dramatically while at Columbia. One important change was her living situation. She rented a room in the city where she stayed during the week and returned to her home with Stanley on the weekends. She was spending less time in her role as a wife and more time as an anthropologist.

Benedict went directly from earning her master's degree to working toward her doctorate, which she completed in

1923. She had taken a job as Boas's teaching assistant and published her first paper, "The Vision in Plains Culture." It discussed her work studying the role of spiritual visions in the culture of the Plains Indians. The following year, she gave a brilliant dissertation, or long paper usually required to receive a doctorate degree, about Native American religion, "The Concept of the Guardian Spirit in North America." This paper set the tone for the rest of her groundbreaking work, which took the unique approach of examining cultures through the choices made by individuals. For this first paper, she began using her full name, Ruth Fulton Benedict. It was unusual for a woman to use both her maiden and married name during the 1920s and was a move that some considered feminist.

An anthropologist at work

Edward Sapir (1884–1939), an anthropologist in Canada who had read Benedict's dissertation, was so impressed with it that he contacted Benedict soon after reading it. Benedict and Sapir became close friends, and for a few years exchanged critiques and comments of each other's poetry and anthropological work. He also helped Benedict get her teaching job at Barnard College.

From 1922 to 1931, Benedict taught anthropology at both Columbia University and Barnard College. Boas arranged for her to be the editor of the *Journal of American Folklore,* a position she held from 1925 to 1939. In 1922, while lecturing at Barnard, Benedict met a young student named **Margaret Mead** (1901–1978; see entry in volume 2). Benedict saw great promise in Mead and encouraged her to pursue anthropology. The two women developed a friendship that lasted a lifetime and Mead went on to become a famous anthropologist whose studies of disappearing cultures around the world became extremely popular and brought a lot of attention to the field of anthropology.

Benedict also spent a great deal of her time continuing with her own fieldwork studies. She traveled to California to study the Serrano tribe in 1922. From 1925 to 1927, she traveled throughout the American Southwest, gathering cultural

A close friend and colleague of Benedict, Margaret Mead, center right, visits Bali, Indonesia, as part of her extensive field work to study different cultures around the globe.

Reproduced by permission of AP/Wide World Photos/American Museum of Natural History.

myths and tales among the Pima, Zuni, and Cochiti tribes. Because of her deafness, she had some difficulty working in the field, but she was able to overcome it through hard work.

Meanwhile, Benedict and her husband had been growing increasingly apart. Stanley had never approved of her having a career and, in 1931, the couple separated. (He died five years later.) It was not until their separation that Benedict was given a true salaried position of assistant professor at Columbia. At this time in American society, women were dependant on their husbands to make money to support the household and, up to this point, it was incorrectly thought that Benedict did not need the money since her husband financially supported her.

Patterns of culture

In 1934, Benedict published what became her most important work. The book, *Patterns of Culture,* tied together

elements of all of her different fieldwork with Native Americans. The main point of her book was that cultures have their own identities and need to be looked at as a whole unit; their individual parts should not be examined separately or compared to the same parts of other cultures. Behavior that is deemed unacceptable in one culture, such as women showing off skin above the ankle, may be perfectly acceptable in another. This is the idea of cultural relativism. Cultures are not seen as "wrong" but as "different."

Benedict's work sparked a new movement of thought in the field of anthropology. *Patterns of Culture* was translated into fourteen different languages and made her one of the first women to become a leader in the field of anthropology. She was promoted to associate professor two years after the book was published.

Benedict later applied the idea of cultural relativism to both race and democracy. In 1939, she temporarily left Columbia and went to California for a year. While she was there she wrote *Race: Science and Politics,* published in 1940, that spoke out against racism. A year later, back in New York, she became a founding member of the Institute for Intercultural Studies (IIS). As a member of the IIS, she was invited by the U.S. Office of War Information to use the information they had gathered from interviews of emigrants, or people who leave one country to move to another, and other documents to learn and write about European and Asian cultures. She spent some time in Washington, D.C., compiling her research.

Continued success

In 1945, Benedict again took some time off from her teaching duties at Columbia in order to write another book. In *The Chrysanthemum and the Sword: Patterns of Japanese Culture,* published in 1946, Benedict looked at how Japanese culture's dedication to honor and loyalty greatly influences the way Japanese people behave. It was an especially important work for the time, as Americans were feeling uneasy about Japanese people living in the United States after U.S. involvement with that nation in World War II (1939–45). (The United States entered the war after the Japanese bombed the U.S. naval base at Pearl Harbor in Hawaii; the war ended after the United States dropped two devastating atomic bombs on the Japanese cities of Hiroshima and Nagasaki.) Benedict's book became a bestseller and elevated her status as an anthropologist even further. She received the Annual Achievement Award of the American Association of University Women in 1946 for her work in helping society understand different cultures through studying a variety of civilizations.

In 1947, Benedict was elected president of the American Anthropological Association. That same year, she started the Columbia University Research in Contemporary Cultures program. This project, funded by the U.S. Office of Naval Research, lasted for four years and pulled together the work of more than 120 scientists from sixteen different nations. In

1948, she flew to Europe to work on the project. A few days after she returned, she suffered a heart attack. Benedict died on September 17, 1948, just a few months after she was promoted to full professor at Columbia University. She was sixty-nine years old.

Further Reading

Benedict, Ruth Fulton. *The Chrysanthemum and the Sword.* New York: Houghton Mifflin, 1946, 1989.

Benedict, Ruth Fulton. *Patterns of Culture.* New York: Houghton Mifflin, 1934, 1989.

Benedict, Ruth Fulton. *Race: Science and Politics.* New York: Modern Age Books, 1940.

Benedict, Ruth Fulton. *Zuni Mythology.* New York: Columbia University Press, 1935.

Caffrey, Margaret M. *Ruth Benedict: Stranger in This Land.* Austin, TX: University of Texas Press, 1989.

Mead, Margaret. *Ruth Benedict.* New York: Columbia University Press, 1974.

Elizabeth Blackwell

February 3, 1821
Bristol, England
May 31, 1910
Hastings, England

Elizabeth Blackwell was the first female doctor in the United States. After being rejected by every medical school she applied to because she was a woman, Blackwell was finally admitted to Geneva Medical School in Geneva, New York. Despite resistance from her classmates and the townspeople about a woman becoming a doctor, they eventually grew to respect her intelligence and determination. Blackwell opened her own clinic and began treating poor women and children. Within a few years she raised enough money to open the New York Infirmary for Indigent Women and Children, the first hospital run by women that was dedicated to treating women. Blackwell was a pioneer whose courage and hard work changed the way people thought about women in medicine.

Hard times for a strong family

Elizabeth Blackwell was born on February 3, 1821, in Bristol, England, the third of nine children born to Samuel and

"The full thorough education of women in medicine is a new idea and like all other truths requires time to prove its value."

Portrait reproduced by permission of Corbis Corporation.

Hannah Blackwell. Elizabeth's father, who owned a sugar refinery, and mother were very open minded for the time: they believed in equal rights for men and women and made sure their daughters received the same schooling as their sons. Elizabeth was shy, but intelligent, and grew to be independent and headstrong.

In 1832, England was experiencing hard economic times, and Samuel Blackwell's refinery was suffering. He decided to make a fresh start in America, and moved his family to the United States. After a long, seven-week journey across the Atlantic Ocean, Samuel opened a sugar refinery in New York.

But Samuel was dealt another blow when his refinery burned down in 1836. Struggling to support his family, he moved them to Cincinnati, Ohio, in 1838, and established a new business. Samuel's health, which had begun to suffer before the move, quickly deteriorated and he died on August 7, 1838, at the age of forty-eight.

It was soon clear that the family's financial situation was desperate and the Blackwells were deeply in debt. To make ends meet, Elizabeth, two of her sisters, and her mother started a boarding school for girls in their house, while two of her brothers got jobs to help support the family. Within a few years, the family paid off their debts. Elizabeth then decided to make a life for herself on her own, and took a teaching job in Henderson, Kentucky, for about a year. She was unhappy there, however, and returned to Cincinnati.

A search for meaning

Blackwell felt strongly about finding something meaningful to do with her life. She did not want to get married and, as a strong believer in the rights and independence of women, was determined to support herself. While she was visiting her family, Blackwell went to see a friend named Mary Donaldson who was dying of cancer. Mary told Blackwell that the one thing that could have lifted her spirits during her illness was if she could have been treated by a female doctor. Women, however, weren't allowed to become doctors, weren't educated, and weren't allowed into most professions except teaching. Despite the obstacles, Mary encouraged Blackwell become a doctor.

At first, Elizabeth rejected the idea. Even as a child, she had always felt faint at the sight of blood. But as weeks passed, the idea stayed in her mind and she asked a few doctors what they thought about the notion of a female doctor. Every single one of them told her that it couldn't be done because of the strong opposition from the public and because it would be nearly impossible for a woman to be accepted into a medical school. Instead of discouraging Blackwell, this rejection only made her more determined to become a doctor.

The first woman doctor

In order to attend medical school, Blackwell needed to save money for tuition and to study with a doctor, in a sort of apprenticeship that was necessary at the time to help students learn as much as possible from experienced doctors before entering school. In 1845, she took a job as a schoolteacher in Asheville, North Carolina, where she studied with John Dickson, the school principal and a former doctor who had agreed to teach her privately about medicine. She spent much of her spare time reading his medical texts. In 1846, she moved to Charleston, South Carolina, to teach and study with Dickson's brother, Samuel Dickson, who was also a physician.

By May 1847, Blackwell had saved enough money to go to medical school full time. She began to apply to medical schools in Philadelphia and New England. All of them rejected her, with the exception of one. Geneva Medical School (now

IMPACT

Elizabeth Blackwell was a pioneer in medical education for women. In 1849, she became the first female doctor in the United States at a time when women were discriminated against in science and medicine. In 1857, she opened the New York Infirmary for Indigent Women and Children, which was the first hospital run by women for women. At this hospital, she introduced the now common ideas of disease prevention and follow-up care. In 1868, Blackwell and her sister Emily opened the Women's Medical College of the New York Infirmary. Satisfied that she had sufficiently paved the way for women who wanted to become doctors in the United States, Blackwell moved to England to undertake the same cause. She opened a private medical practice and helped establish the London School of Medicine for Women. Blackwell continued to practice medicine and write articles until her death in 1910.

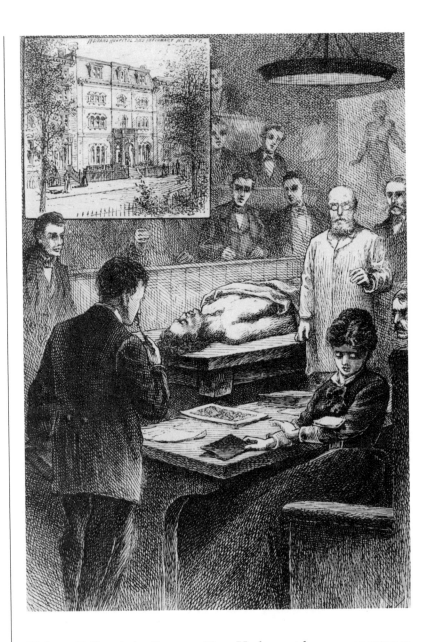

Hobart College), in Geneva, New York, sent her an acceptance letter. Years later, Blackwell found out that when she applied the faculty at the school had asked the students whether to accept a woman. The men jokingly wrote a letter stating that practicing medicine should be open to everyone. They never thought the faculty would take them seriously; they were wrong, and Blackwell was admitted to the school.

Blackwell entered Geneva Medical School on November 6, 1847, the first woman medical student in the history of the United States. At first Blackwell was treated rudely by her male classmates and by townspeople who disapproved of a woman in medical school. However, rudeness gradually became respect as Blackwell proved herself to be a dedicated student, eventually graduating in January 1849 at the top of her class. Her achievement—she was the first female doctor in the United States—was applauded in the press, both in America and abroad.

Practical experience and a new goal

After several months in Pennsylvania, during which time she became a naturalized citizen of the United States, Blackwell traveled to Paris, where she hoped to study with one of the leading French surgeons. Denied access to Parisian hospitals because of her gender, she enrolled instead at La Maternité Hospital, a highly regarded midwifery school, in the summer of 1849. Just four months after she arrived, she contracted an eye infection from a patient that left her blind in one eye and ended her dream of becoming a surgeon. Undaunted, Blackwell moved to London, England, to practice medicine at St. Bartholomew's Hospital. Strangely, the only section of the hospital where she was not welcome was Diseases of Women and Children. The head of that department disapproved of women doctors.

At St. Bartholomew's, Blackwell earned a great deal of experience taking patients' medical histories, learning how to diagnose their diseases, and caring for them. While there, she also became friendly with Florence Nightingale (1820–1910), a nurse who was famous for raising the standards of nursing while pushing for cleaner and safer hospitals. At the time, hospitals were not sanitized as they are today; most were filthy, crowded places. Without knowledge of how germs spread disease, doctors were not yet required to wash their hands before treating patients, even if they were about to operate. Many people who were middle or upper class often preferred to risk dying from their illness at home rather than go to a hospital. In

Lone Woman: The Story of Elizabeth Blackwell, the First Woman Doctor, Dorothy Wilson describes the hospitals of the time as "places of filth and evil smells and squalor. Many of the patients came from slum hovels. . . . They were crowded into bare, unaired wards in beds less than two feet apart, fifty or sixty to a room. Sheet remained unwashed from patient to patient, mattresses seldom cleaned."

Blackwell supported Nightingale's quest for cleaner hospitals and realized that she had many ideas of her own for improving health care, such as washing hands before surgery and using sanitized beds. But every time she made a suggestion to the hospital administration, her idea was ignored. Blackwell decided that she would eventually open her own hospital, and in July 1851, she left England to return to the United States.

Another challenge leads to triumph

Although some medical colleges had started admitting a few female students since Blackwell broke the gender barrier, things had not changed dramatically in America. Upon Blackwell's return, she applied for jobs at a few large hospitals but was refused. She then set out to find an office and open her own medical practice. But many landlords who had advertised rental space for doctors turned her away. They wanted only male doctors in their buildings; some disapproved of a female being a doctor, while others were afraid of the protestors a woman doctor might attract.

Blackwell finally found her own space near Washington Square Park, in New York City. Horace Greeley, the editor of the *New York Tribune,* agreed to publish an advertisement for Blackwell seeking patients for her new practice. For months, only a very few patients arrived at her door. In need of money and discouraged, Blackwell took evening walks to clear her head and to think of ways to bring in business. During these walks, she noticed the many children out at night, alone on the streets. Learning more about the poverty and slums that plagued New York City in the 1850s, Blackwell thought that some of the problems of poverty could be relieved if women and children were taught to take better care of their bodies. Though it was not seen as proper for women to discuss topics that had to do with their bodies, Blackwell began giving a series of lectures at her clinic and on the streets about cleanliness, birth, reproduction, and how the female body should be cared for. In 1852, her lectures were published as a book, *The Laws of Life in Reference to the Physical Education of Girls*. Although these topics do not seem radical in modern times, they were met with shock in 1852. Nonetheless, a few people did praise Blackwell's book. Meanwhile, her practice was still suffering.

Persistence pays off

Blackwell, although she had some doubts, was not ready to give up. She combined her desire to help the poor with her need to create a successful medical practice and devised a new plan. In 1853, Blackwell rented a small room in a very poor part of town and hung her name on the door with a sign saying that she would treat people for free, three afternoons a week, in addition to her regularly scheduled hours. Slowly, by word of mouth, free-clinic patients, as well as paying patients, began to arrive. She quickly had more work than she could handle. She treated their illnesses, delivered babies, and taught cleanliness as a preventative measure of health.

In 1856, her sister Emily lightened Blackwell's workload. Emily had followed in Elizabeth's footsteps and had graduated from medical school with high honors. The two worked together at the clinic, and soon after, were joined by Marie Zakrzewska, a German woman who had also completed medical school. Liberal and reformers' groups from as far away as France and Boston heard about Blackwell's work and contributed funds towards her practice.

This small clinic was overflowing by this time and Blackwell's two partners encouraged her to open her own hospital. On May 12, 1857, the New York Infirmary for Indigent Women and Children opened. The hospital was an immediate

Rebecca Lee Crumpler

Rebecca Lee Crumpler was the first African American woman to earn a medical degree. Born in 1833 in Richmond, Virginia, Crumpler was raised by her aunt, who had a passion for taking care of sick people in her community. From 1852 to 1860, Crumpler worked as a nurse in Massachusetts, where she was known as a talented and sympathetic caregiver, and was encouraged to go to medical school. She was accepted into the New England Female Medical College in Boston, now the Boston University School of Medicine. In 1864, fifteen years after Elizabeth Blackwell made history as the first female to graduate from medical college, Crumpler graduated.

Following medical school, Crumpler opened a practice in Boston. When the Civil War (1861–65) ended, putting an end to slavery, she moved back to Virginia to provide health care for former slaves. She spent several years practicing medicine in Virginia before moving back to Boston. In 1883, Crumpler published *A Book of Medicinal Discourses in Two Parts,* which helped teach mothers how to care for the health of their families.

success, with all of the hospital beds being filled within a month. By 1858, the doctors treated more than three thousand patients. They also introduced ideas about hygiene and the prevention of illnesses that are now common practice in medicine. The doctors at Blackwell's hospital also offered their patients follow-up care, checking on the patients after they left the hospital to make sure they were still healthy.

A college and beyond

Now that the hospital was doing well, Blackwell had yet another admirable goal. She wanted to open a medical college for women. Dramatic events in the United States, however, would delay her plans. The Civil War (1861–65) erupted and there was an urgent need for nurses. Throughout the war, Blackwell recruited and trained women to be nurses and continued to work at the hospital.

When the war ended, Blackwell and her sister turned their attention back to their dream of a medical college for women. Two other schools had already been established, but they did not have reputations of academic excellence. In 1868, the Blackwell sisters opened the Women's Medical College of the New York Infirmary.

The following year, Blackwell felt that her work helping women make progress in medicine was finished in America. There had been little progress, however, in England. She left Emily in charge of the hospital and college and went to London. While in London, she established a medical practice and helped organize the London School of Medicine for Women, where she taught until 1879. In 1871, in London, she helped start the National Health Society, an organization focused on educating people about health, hygiene, and prevention. Blackwell also continued to lecture and write medical articles. In 1895, she published her autobiography, *Pioneer Work in Opening the Medical Profession to Women*.

By 1879, at the age of fifty-eight, Blackwell's health was failing. She and her daughter Kitty, whom she had adopted in 1854, moved to Hastings, England, where Blackwell continued to write articles and conduct a small medical practice. In 1906, she suffered major injuries from a fall and her health never fully recovered. Blackwell died of a stroke three years later, on May 31, 1910, at the age of eighty-eight.

Further Reading

Blackwell, Elizabeth. *The Laws of Life with Special Reference to the Physical Education of Girls*. New York: Garland Publishing, 1986.

Blackwell, Elizabeth. *Pioneer Work in Opening the Medical Profession to Women: Autobiographical Sketches*. New York: Source Book Press, 1970.

"Elizabeth Blackwell." *National Women's Hall of Fame*. http://www.greatwomen.org/women.php?action=viewone&id=20 (accessed on September 3, 2002).

Glimm, Adele. *Elizabeth Blackwell: First Woman Doctor to Modern Times*. New York: McGraw-Hill Professional Publishing, 2000.

Wilson, Dorothy Clarke. *Lone Woman: The Story of Elizabeth Blackwell, the First Woman Doctor*. Boston, MA: Little Brown and Company, 1970.

Ada Byron, Countess of Lovelace

December 10, 1815
London, England
November 27, 1852
London, England

Ada Byron Lovelace was a mathematical pioneer. She studied scientist Charles Babbage's plans for inventing the Analytical Engine, which would have been the first computer had it been built, and published a detailed discussion of how it would work and what applications this type of machine could have. Within her "Notes," as her writings were called, she explained and illustrated the steps for writing what is now credited as the first computer program. Although her groundbreaking work was published in 1843, she did not receive any widespread recognition for her accomplishments until nearly one hundred years later when her original notes were republished in the book *Faster Than Thought: A Symposium on Digital Computing Machines*. In 1983, the U.S. Department of Defense honored her by calling their standardized computer programming language Ada.

A passion for numbers

Augusta Ada Byron was born on December 10, 1815, to Lady Anne Isabella Milbanke Byron and the famous poet Lord

"The Analytical Engine has no pretensions whatever to originate anything. It can do whatever we know how to order it to perform."

45

British mathematician Ada Byron Lovelace is credited with writing the first computer program. In 1843, she published a detailed explanation of Charles Babbage's proposed Analytical Engine, along with her Notes discussing how his machine could be programmed and how versatile it would be. Babbage never built his machine, but if he had it would have been the first model of a modern computer. Instead, the world waited more than one hundred years before the first computer was built and finally realized how important Lovelace's writings had been. To honor her achievement, the U.S. Department of Defense standardized their computer programming language in 1983 and called it Ada.

George Gordon Byron. Five weeks after Ada was born, Lord and Lady Byron separated and Lord Byron never saw his daughter again. Lady Byron was well educated and talented at mathematics. Wanting to distance her daughter from everything that reminded her of Lord Byron, Lady Byron discouraged Ada from learning about things she considered frivolous or romantic, such as poetry. Instead Ada learned mathematics, which was a very unusual subject for girls to study in traditional Victorian society. She learned to play the piano, the violin, and the harp. Ada was a quick study; she was able to spell long words and add rows of numbers by the time she was five years old.

As much as Lady Byron did not want her daughter to be anything like Lord Byron, Ada was born with his passion. While Lord Byron was passionate about poetry, Ada had a deep love for numbers and mathematics. In addition to having Ada learn languages and music, her mother arranged to have two university professors teach Ada about astronomy and complex math such as algebra and geometry.

A mentor and a husband

In November 1834, when Byron was eighteen years old, Mary Fairfax Somerville (1780–1872) invited her to a party. Somerville was a well-respected Scottish astronomer and had been one of Byron's teachers. At the party, Byron met **Charles Babbage** (1792–1871; see entry in volume 1), an experienced mathematician and inventor of several different calculating machines powered by steam. His inventions were early relatives of the computer and Byron was fascinated by the mathematical equations his machines were capable of computing. She was especially intrigued by the plans he had created for a machine called the Analytical Engine.

Although Babbage was twenty-three years older than Byron, he recognized her talent for numbers and her keen intellect. He became her mentor, supporting her work and guiding it in the right direction, and arranged for Byron to study advanced mathematical subjects, such as calculus, with the well-known mathematician Augustus De Morgan (1806–1842).

In 1835, Somerville introduced Byron to another important man in her life, William King. King and Byron married on July 8 of the same year and eventually had three children, Byron, Anne Isabella, and Ralph Gordon. In 1838, King became the Earl of Lovelace and Ada Byron King was now known as the Countess of Lovelace. (In England, both the royal family and certain members of the upper class are given titles that are passed along by birth.)

The couple's social status, combined with Lovelace's academic interests, led to an impressive circle of friends. They spent time with physicist **Michael Faraday** (1791–1867; see entry in volume 1), astronomer Sir John Herschel (1792–1871), and author Charles Dickens (1812–1870). Ada's husband was proud of her accomplishments as a mathematician and supported her intellectual pursuits.

Charles Babbage encouraged Byron to contribute her ideas about his Analytical Engine, an invention that would have been the first computer had it been built.
Reproduced courtesy of Library of Congress.

The Notes

In 1842, Lovelace was given an opportunity that resulted in the grand achievement of her career. Two years earlier, Babbage had given a lecture in Turin, Italy, about his plans for an Analytical Engine. This machine, never built by Babbage, was devised to make and analyze mathematical calculations from data that was put into it. An engineer named Luigi Federico Menabrea published the content of Babbage's lecture in a

French publication. Since Lovelace was both fluent in French and understood Babbage's work, she translated the article into English to have it published. After Babbage saw her translation, he suggested that she add her thoughts to the piece.

Lovelace worked on her "Notes" for a year. She and Babbage wrote letters back and forth, discussing the details of her ideas. By the time Lovelace was finished, her notes were three times longer than Babbage's lecture. In all, there were seven Notes, which Lovelace labeled with the letters A to G. She also included illustrations to show how the engine could be "taught," or programmed, to perform various tasks.

Note A functioned partly as an introduction, explaining the difference between Babbage's two main inventions up to that time: the Difference Engine and the Analytical Engine. His Difference Engine was a simple calculating machine that could be used to create tables of numbers based on the information put into it. The Analytical Engine, however, was a much more complex invention. Had Babbage built it, it would have been the first general-purpose computer. As history would show, the creation of such a computer would not occur for another one hundred years.

In Note B, Lovelace discussed the idea of the Engine having memory and being able to alert the user as to what was being calculated by the machine. Note C described writing a set of instructions that could be used for a variety of different tasks. Modern computer terminology calls this set of instructions a subroutine. She also detailed the idea of giving the machine "if-then" statements for it to compute, such as "if" the user answers yes to a question, "then" show a message. This is called a conditional jump. She also explained the concept of backing, called looping in modern technology, in which the machine could properly reorder instructions to be used again at a later date.

In Note D, Lovelace gave very specific directions for writing a set of instructions that the Analytical Engine could follow, today known as a computer program. Note E discussed the broad applications of such a machine and introduced the idea of what are now called function keys, or operation cards that set in motion a certain set of instructions. Note F focused on the great time- and money-saving benefits the engine could provide by solving difficult problems without the introduction of human error. Note G discussed the importance of giving the Analytical Engine quality information, touching on the concept that a computer is only as good as the data the computer programmer gives it.

Lovelace also made predictions about other uses of Analytical Engines, including composing music and making graphs and illustrations. All of her predictions came true—but not for more than one hundred years. Her translation of

Menabrea's article, along with her Notes, were published in July 1843 in the journal *Taylor's Scientific Memoirs*. "Sketch of the Analytical Engine Invented by Charles Babbage, Esq." was Lovelace's only major work. However, it was also one of the most important papers involving mathematics and computer history ever produced. For the detailed instructional information in Lovelace's Notes, she is credited with having written the first computer program. Sadly, Lovelace was told that she had cancer of the uterus in 1851 and died of this disease on November 27, 1852. She was only thirty-six years old. In honor of her achievements, in 1983, the U.S. Department of Defense named their standardized computer programming language "Ada."

Further Reading

Baum, Joan. *The Calculating Passion of Ada Byron*. Hamden, CT: Archon Books, 1986.

Computer Museum of America. http://www.computer-museum.org (accessed on September 3, 2002).

Menabrea, L.F., with Notes by Ada Augusta, Countess of Lovelace. "Sketch of the Analytical Engine Invented by Charles Babbage, Esq." *Taylor's Scientific Memoirs,* July 1843.

Toole, Betty Alexandra. *Ada: The Enchantress of Numbers*. http://www.well.com/user/adatoole/bio.htm (accessed on September 3, 2002).

Wallace Carothers

April 27, 1896
Burlington, Iowa
April 29, 1937
Philadelphia, Pennsylvania

Wallace Carothers was one of the most important chemists of the twentieth century. As head of a research team at the DuPont chemical company in the 1930s, he created the first completely synthetic, or human-made, materials that were comparable in quality to those found in nature. The synthetic rubber he developed, called neoprene, was more weather resistant than natural rubber. Nylon, Carothers's most famous invention, was a synthetic substitute for silk that had widespread applications in the commercial world, from apparel to carpeting to home furnishings. To honor his achievements in 1946, the DuPont Company named its laboratory for research of synthetic fibers the Carothers Research Laboratory.

"It took all your imagination . . . to try to reach him. And it was worth trying, because whenever anything came out it was worth hearing."

—Polly Hill, wife of a colleague of Carothers

A scientist at heart

Wallace Hume Carothers was born on April 27, 1896, in Burlington, Iowa, to Mary McMullin Carothers and Ira Hume

American chemist Wallace Carothers invented two of the most widely used synthetic materials: neoprene (synthetic rubber) and nylon. Neoprene has multiple uses in such things as wet suits, hoses, automobile parts, and medical equipment. Nylon is used in clothing, fishing line, surgical thread, toothbrushes, and hundreds of other items. Carothers's work sparked a whole new field of manufacturing synthetic materials. Sadly, he committed suicide in 1937 and did not live to see the widespread uses of his research.

Carothers, a teacher at the Capital City Commercial College in Des Moines, Iowa. Wallace, the eldest of four children, attended public school in Des Moines and was an excellent student. After graduating high school in 1914, he enrolled in Capital City to study accounting and finished his studies within a year. He was then accepted to Tarkio College in Missouri, where he studied science and excelled in chemistry and physics. During his time as a student at Tarkio, Carothers also taught accounting, English, and chemistry classes as an assistant professor.

After graduating from Tarkio in 1920, Carothers was admitted into the graduate program at the University of Illinois. He studied organic chemistry and received his master's degree in 1921. After graduation, Carothers taught chemistry at the University of South Dakota for one year where he discovered that, although he enjoyed teaching, he preferred doing research.

Carothers published his first scholarly paper in 1923 in the *Journal of the American Chemical Society*. In 1924, Carothers received his doctorate degree in chemistry from the University of Illinois and was offered a teaching position at the school. He taught there for two years, then took a position at Harvard University in 1926. In his first year at Harvard, Carothers taught structural chemistry and experimental organic chemistry. (Structural chemistry is the study of how molecules are put together in space, much like architecture. Organic chemistry is the branch of chemistry dealing with carbon compounds, which can be put together in an extremely varied number of ways. All living things contain carbon.)

Researching polymers at Harvard

Carothers had many of his own ideas that he wanted to pursue in the laboratory. During his second year at Harvard, he began researching the chemical structures of high molecular weight polymers. A polymer is a chemical compound formed of simple molecules, known as monomers, linked with themselves many times over. Carothers later proved a theory by German scientist and Nobel laureate Hermann Staudinger (1881–1965) that polymers are natural or synthetic structures made up of macromolecules, large heavy molecules made up of long chains of repeating units. Natural structures such as proteins, silk, nucleic acids, and natural rubber are made of polymers. (In the twenty-first century, in large part due to Carothers's work, human-made materials composed of polymers include synthetic rubber and plastics.)

The work Carothers did at Harvard attracted the attention of the DuPont Company, a chemical company planning a new program that would focus on developmental research. They wanted a team of scientists to pursue original ideas with the hope of coming up with new artificial materials that would serve industrial purposes. DuPont built a new laboratory, called the Experimental Station, in Wilmington, Delaware, and offered Carothers a job leading their team of chemists. Although he had not anticipated leaving Harvard, Carothers could not pass up the opportunity to be the director of DuPont's research program and develop his own areas of experimentation. He took the job at DuPont and began working there in 1928.

Inventing at DuPont

As a director, Carothers was popular among the scientists. He was hardworking, imaginative, and enthusiastic and his attitude brought out the best from his team. For the first few years at DuPont, Carothers concentrated on studying chemicals in the acetylene family. Acetylene is a colorless gas and the simplest and best-known member of the hydrocarbon series, molecules containing one or more pairs of carbon atoms linked by triple bonds, called the acetylenic series or alkynes. The first synthetic material Carothers and his team created caused initial excitement but turned out to have a low melting point. It would be ruined should any heat come in contact with it.

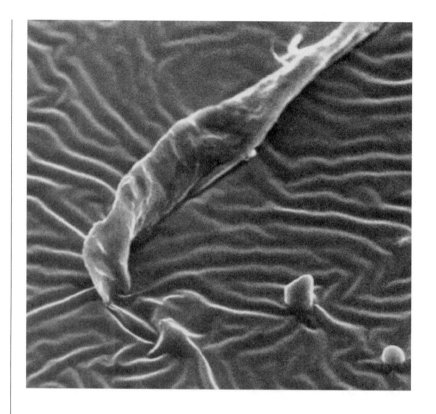

Eventually, the team combined the chemical vinylacetylene with a chlorine compound to successfully produce a polymer with rubberlike properties. They named it neoprene, and they found it to be stronger than rubber and more resistant to damaging substances such as oil, gasoline, and sunlight. Though neoprene was more expensive to produce, DuPont began manufacturing and selling the synthetic rubber neoprene in 1931. It still has many uses today, including as material in wet suits, hoses, automobile parts, and the soles of shoes.

Carothers then turned his attention to a new area of research that would prove to be even more successful than his experiments with neoprene. Natural materials such as silk and cotton are made up of polymers. Carothers wanted to try to reproduce similar structures to create synthetic fibers of equal quality, especially silk. (Due to political and trade troubles at the time with Japan, the United States's main source of silk, silk was getting harder and more expensive to find.) Between

1929 and 1937, Carothers experimented with combining different chemicals to produce the type of reaction needed to create a silk substitute. He found that by combining the chemicals amine, hexamethylene diamine, and adipic acid, and blowing the mixture through small holes, he could produce fibers of a new material. This new material, nylon, was the first completely synthetic fiber equal in quality to silk, cotton, and wool, and far more durable.

DuPont introduced nylon to the world in 1938. At the World's Fair in 1939, models showcased nylon stockings that quickly became the height of fashion. During World War II (1939–45), nylon was used in ropes, tents, shoelaces, and even paper money. Today, nylon has a huge number of uses and is found in products such as stockings, shirts, pants, sewing thread, carpet, parachutes, seat belts, and sleeping bags.

A winning reputation and a troubled soul

Carothers gained recognition throughout the scientific world for his accomplishments. He published many scientific papers in journals and gave a lecture on polymers and polymerization at Johns Hopkins University in 1935 that was extremely influential in the field of organic chemistry. He was even awarded with an invitation to join the prestigious National Academy of Sciences in 1936, the first organic chemist without a university appointment to ever be elected to this group.

That same year, on February 21, 1936, Carothers married Helen Everett Sweetman. They met at DuPont, where she worked in the patents department. In January 1937, Carothers's sister Isabelle, to whom he was very close, died. Carothers had long suffered from short periods of depression and his sister's death was an event he was not able to overcome. Although he was newly married and his wife was pregnant with their first child, Carothers took his own life on April 29, 1937. The couple's daughter, Jane, was born on November 27, 1937, just seven months after her father's death.

Further Reading

Gaines, Ann Graham. *Wallace Carothers and the Story of Dupont Nylon (Unlocking the Secrets of Science).* Elkton, MD: Mitchell Lane Publishers, Inc., 2001.

Parshall, Gerald. "Maestros of Molecules." *U.S. News & World Report,* August 17, 1998, p. 38.

Siegfried, Tom. "Chemists Whipped Up Products That Have Revolutionized Modern Life." *The Dallas Morning News,* June 21, 1999.

"Wallace Carothers." *A Science Odyssey: People and Discoveries.* http://www.pbs.org/wgbh/aso/databank/entries/btcaro.html (accessed on September 3, 2002).

Gian Domenico Cassini

June 8, 1625
Perinaldo, Republic of Genoa (now Italy)
September 14, 1712
Paris, France

Gian Domenico Cassini was one of the most important astronomers of the seventeenth century. He discovered that the planet Saturn did not have one solid ring around it, as was previously thought by such prominent scientists as **Galileo Galilei** (1564–1642; see entry in volume 4) and Christiaan Huygens (1629–1695). He also correctly theorized that instead of being solid, the rings were made up of tiny particles, and he observed a gap between the rings. This gap was later named the Cassini Division in his honor. Cassini also discovered four of Saturn's satellites, or moons, calculated the rotation of Mars and observed that planet's polar caps, tracked comets, and calculated the distance between Earth and the Sun. Remarkably, he did all of this without the use of modern astronomical technology.

"[Cassini] served science twice over, with great discoveries and the ability to advance them."

—French mathematician Jean-Baptiste Biot, 1854

An early passion

Gian, also spelled Giovanni, Domenico Cassini was born on June 8, 1625, in Perinaldo, Republic of Genoa, near what is

Gian Domenico Cassini was a talented astronomer with many interests. His work enhanced our knowledge of comets, planets, and the size of our solar system. Without the benefit of modern telescopes, he accurately calculated the rotation of Mars within minutes and observed that planet's polar caps. He discovered four moons of Saturn and detected a gap within the planet's ring system. Cassini even realized that the rings of Saturn could not be solid and correctly theorized that they are made up of tiny particles. Perhaps most dramatically, Cassini's work led to our understanding of the size of the vast solar system in which we live. His calculations were responsible for the unit of measurement used to gauge distances within the solar system, the astronomical unit (AU).

now Nice, in present-day Italy. Cassini developed an interest in astrology, the study of how the stars and planets supposedly influence events and people's actions, at a young age, while studying at a Jesuit school at Genoa. (The Jesuits are a religious order of Roman Catholics.) A wealthy amateur astronomer, the Marquis Cornelio Malvasia, was also very interested in astrology and was impressed with Cassini's knowledge of this subject. In 1648, Malvasia invited Cassini to work at Panzano Observatory, an observatory he was building near Bologna. (An observatory is a place designed and furnished with equipment for studying moons, planets, and stars.) It was common in those days for wealthy people to support artists and scientists. This was called patronage. Patrons were usually rich individuals, members of government, and members of the Church. In this way, Malvasia became Cassini's first patron and Cassini stayed at the Panzano Observatory until 1669. There, Cassini had some of the finest telescopes of the time at his disposal and was given the chance to become an accomplished astronomer. He quickly proved himself to be a hardworking scientist. He was hired as a professor in the astronomy department at the University of Bologna and, in 1650, at the young age of twenty-five, Cassini became chairman of the department.

Cassini also had a knack for engineering. In 1657, Pope Alexander VII asked him to determine ways to avoid the flooding of the Po River, which runs across most of northern Italy. Pleased with Cassini's work, the pope then hired him to inspect all of the nation's waterways. Cassini did this survey for the Italian government while still continuing with his astronomy work at Panzano.

Artist's rendition of a moment from the Cassini Mission, when an interplanetary space probe descends towards Saturn's moon Titan.
Reproduced by permission of Corbis Corporation.

Cassini was very interested in studying the planets. In 1666, he became the first person to calculate the rotation period of Venus. To calculate a planet's rotation, it is necessary to be able to see a feature on the surface in order to gauge the amount of time that elapses before you can observe that same spot again. He determined that the planet rotated on its axis once every 23 hours and 21 minutes. (The time it takes for a planet to make one turn, or rotation, around its axis—the imaginary line through the middle—is equal to that planet's day.) The following year, Cassini presented the first sketches of what he believed were Venus's surface features. Unfortunately, his drawings only showed the clouds of Venus. His rotation calculation was therefore incorrect as it was based on an inaccurate observation of the planet's surface. Cassini also mistakenly reported having observed a Venusian moon. All of Cassini's findings about Venus were eventually disproved. The primary reason for this, and for others' miscalculations about Venus at the time, was that a telescope had not yet been invented that allowed an observer to see through the thick Venusian clouds.

Cassini had also calculated the rotation period of Mars in 1666. His calculations put Mars's rotation at 24 hours and 40 minutes. He was extremely close; Mars's rotation is actually 24 hours, 37 minutes, and 22 seconds. Cassini also observed large white areas, which were polar caps, at the northern and southern poles of Mars, furthering our understanding of the red planet.

From Italy to France

In 1669, the French King Louis XIV invited Cassini to undertake research at the Paris Observatory. Because Pope Clement IX was now Cassini's employer and patron, the pope had to agree to let Cassini go. His trip to France was granted for a short time, but Cassini would never return to Italy. He became the director of the Paris Observatory in 1671 and held the position until 1710. Soon after arriving in Paris, Cassini met Genevieve de Laistre, daughter of an advisor to the king. They married in 1673 and later had two sons. Cassini also became a French citizen that same year.

One of Cassini's major achievements at the Paris Observatory was his discovery of four of Saturn's moons. In 1656, Dutch astronomer Christiaan Huygens had identified the first moon of Saturn. Astronomer John Hershel named it Titan in 1847. From the Paris Observatory, Cassini discovered four additional moons of Saturn. He named them all Louisian stars, after King Louis XIV. They were later renamed Iapeta, Rhea, Dione, and Tethys. Cassini observed Iapeta first, in 1671, and found Rhea the following year. Dione and Tethys were both discovered in 1684. Iapeta was the most interesting of these moons: Cassini correctly theorized that one hemisphere of Iapeta was a better reflector of the Sun's light than the other. This explained why the satellite looks so much brighter when it is to the west of Saturn than when it is to the east of the planet. Three centuries later, in the 1980s, the National Aeronautics and Space Administration's (NASA's) Voyager space-

Christiaan Huygens

Astronomer Christiaan Huygens.
Portrait reproduced courtesy of Library of Congress.

Dutch astronomer Christiaan Huygens (1629–1695) contributed greatly to science in the seventeenth century. He was fascinated by telescopes and worked to improve them. In 1655, he devised a new method of grinding and polishing the lens glass and was able to see with much greater definition. Through his improved lens, he discovered Titan, Saturn's first known satellite, or moon. Four years later, in 1659, he observed and described Saturn's ring. (With modern telescopes, we now know that Saturn has a complex system of rings.) When NASA's Voyager mission traveled to Saturn in 1981, the spacecraft discovered a smaller and separate gap within the Cassini Division. The gap was named Huygens in honor of the Dutch astronomer.

Huygens also contributed to our knowledge of the planet Mars. In 1659, he observed and sketched a dark area called Syrtis Major, which means "Great Wetland" in Latin. At the time, scientists thought the dark areas they saw on Mars were water, a main ingredient for the existence of life. We now know there is no liquid water on Mars. That same year, Huygens calculated Mars's rotation to be about 24 hours. In 1666, Cassini calculated it at 24 hours, 40 minutes. They were both remarkably close given the instruments they had at their disposal; Mars's actual rotation is 24 hours, 37 minutes, and 22 seconds. Huygens made many other observations of the stars, which he published in *Systema Saturnium* in 1659.

In addition to being an astronomer, Huygens was an accomplished mathematician. He developed the wave theory of light, which states that every point on the front of an advancing wave of light is itself a source of new light waves. Tying together astronomy with his love of mathematics, Huygens also developed and patented the first pendulum clock in 1656.

craft collected evidence that finally proved Cassini had been right about Iapeta. Locating any of these satellites with the telescopes of the time was an incredible achievement and a testament to Cassini's skill as an astronomer.

Cassini also improved our knowledge of Saturn's ring. In 1659, Huygens was the first scientist to correctly identify what Italian astronomer Galileo had called Saturn's "ears." What Huygens saw was a ring around the planet. In 1675, Cassini's observations told us more. From the telescopes of the Paris Observatory, he saw that Saturn did not have one single ring at all. Cassini observed two rings, as well as a gap in between them. He even proposed that the rings were composed of "a swarm of tiny satellites," as quoted by William Sheehan in *Worlds in the Sky: Planetary Discovery from Earliest Times.* This theory was in extreme contrast to those held by his colleagues, who believed Saturn's rings were solid. We know now that the rings are indeed made up of billions of particles of ice, dust, and rock that were drawn into orbit around Saturn by the planet's gravitational pull. In Cassini's honor, the gap he discovered, which is about 2,900 miles (4,666 kilometers) wide, was later named the Cassini Division.

A huge solar system

Scientists are driven by the strong desire to know as much as possible about our world. One of the things early astronomers were interested in was the size of our solar system. Before Cassini attempted to measure the distance between Earth and the Sun, two other prominent scientists had made efforts to do so. **Tycho Brahe** (1546–1601; see entry in volume 1) proposed the distance to be 5 million miles (8 million kilometers). **Johannes Kepler** (1571–1630; see entry in volume 4) then calculated 15 million miles (24 million kilometers) as the average distance from Earth to the Sun. But in 1672, Cassini and French astronomer Jean Richer (1630–1696) made observations and measurements that led to our current knowledge of distances within the solar system. The two astronomers looked at the position of Mars in the sky at the same time, Cassini observing from Paris and Richer from French Guiana in South

America. By looking at Mars simultaneously and measuring the position of the Sun in the background from two different locations on Earth, Cassini was able to accurately calculate the distance between Earth and Mars.

Cassini then calculated the distance between Earth and the Sun, leading to the creation of the astronomical unit (AU). The AU is the unit of measurement used to indicate distances within the solar system. One AU is equal to 149,597,870.691 kilometers (93 million miles), or the average distance between the Earth and the Sun. Cassini calculated the distance as 87 million miles (140 million kilometers). Although his numbers were slightly lower, Cassini gave us the first accurate way of measuring our solar system.

Cassini had varied interests and throughout his career he maintained a particularly strong fascination with comets. We learned through his work more about the history of comets crashing into planets. In his observations he discovered evidence that Jupiter sustained an impact from a comet in 1690.

The year before his death in 1712, Cassini went blind, likely the result of years of intense use of his eyes. He served the Paris Observatory and the world of astronomy well and was the king's astronomer for more than forty years. He paved the way for a succession of royal Cassini astronomers (his son and grandson) who worked at the Paris Observatory for more than a hundred years. NASA named a mission to Saturn in Cassini's honor and the Cassini spacecraft should reach Saturn in 2004.

Further Reading

Fradin, Dennis Brindell. *The Planet Hunters: The Search for Other Worlds.* New York: Simon & Schuster, 1997.

Fox, William. "Giovanni Domenico Cassini." *New Advent: The Catholic Encyclopedia.* http://www.newadvent.org/cathen/03405b.htm (accessed on June 13, 2002).

O'Conner, J.J., and E.F. Robertson. "Giovanni Domenico Cassini." School of Mathematics and Statistics, University of St. Andrews, Scotland. http://www-history.mcs.

st-andrews.ac.uk/history/Mathematicians/Cassini.html (accessed September 3, 2002).

Sheehan, William. *Worlds in the Sky: Planetary Discovery from Earliest Times.* Tucson: University of Arizona Press, 1994, p. 133.

Subrahmanyan Chandrasekhar

October 19, 1910
Lahore, India
August 21, 1995
Chicago, Illinois

update

Subrahmanyan Chandrasekhar was a brilliant Indian-born American astrophysicist and mathematician who did much to further our understanding of stellar evolution. His theory that stars with a certain mass evolved into neutron stars countered the longheld belief that all stars end their lives as stable white dwarfs, or small stars with very great densities. Chandrasekhar's theory was not widely accepted until twenty years after he first published it in 1935. Nearly fifty years after first announcing his revolutionary ideas, Chandrasekhar received the Nobel Prize in physics for his work. **(See original entry on Chandrasekhar in *Scientists*, volume 1.)**

"After the early preparatory years, my scientific work has followed a certain pattern motivated, principally, by a quest after perspectives."

An early scientific start

Subrahmanyan Chandrasekhar was born on October 19, 1910, in Lahore, India, now part of Pakistan. Known by most as Chandra, he was interested in science from an early age and, in

Portrait reproduced by permission of Mr. Subrahmanyan Chandrasekhar.

Subrahmanyan Chandrasekhar received the 1983 Nobel Prize in physics for his theory about stellar evolution that led to the realization that some stars develop into neutron stars. Prior to this theory, which took decades for scientists to accept, it was generally believed that all stars evolved into stable white dwarfs.

part, was influenced by his uncle, Sir Chandrasekhar V. Raman, a Nobel Prize-winning physicist. Chandra attended Presidency College in Madras, India, where he excelled at physics and mathematics. Chandra quickly earned his master's degree in 1930 and received a research scholarship from the Indian government to attend Trinity College in Cambridge, England. There he researched his idea about the evolution of stars and delved into the field of astrophysics, the branch of astronomy that deals with the physical processes, such as energy generation and transmission, that occur in stars and galaxies. Chandra finished the doctoral program in 1933 and began a fellowship at Cambridge, focusing his research on white dwarfs.

A radical idea

After extensive research, Chandra felt ready to announce his theory on white dwarfs at a 1935 meeting of the Royal Astronomy Society. He began by summarizing what was known about stellar evolution, explaining that as stars evolve they emit energy generated primarily by their process of converting hydrogen into helium. When a star nears the end of its life, it has progressively less hydrogen to convert into helium and therefore emits less radiation energy. Eventually, the dying star cannot generate enough pressure to sustain its size against its own gravitational pull. At this point, a star begins to contract and collapse into itself. It becomes a white dwarf, a tiny object of enormous density.

Chandra then proceeded to discuss his own radical idea. He believed that the greater a white dwarf's mass (weight), the smaller its radius (center point to perimeter). If the mass of a star increases past a certain limit, it cannot become a stable white dwarf without losing some of its mass. The alternative path the star may take is to become a supernova, releasing its excess energy in an explosion. He further reasoned that following such an explosion, any remaining mass may become a white dwarf, but will more likely form a neutron star with an even greater density than a white dwarf.

Chandra's theory disturbed several scientists who previously believed that all stars ended their lives as stable white dwarfs. It particularly upset well-known British astronomer Arthur Stanley Eddington, who spoke out against Chandra's notions during his talk. Because of this controversy, it took twenty years before Chandra's theory began to receive the attention it deserved and hurt his chances to make a name for himself in England. In search of a more permanent position, Chandra moved to the United States.

A successful career

In 1935, Chandra visited Harvard University as a guest lecturer of physics. He was offered a research position at the University of Chicago's Yerkes Observatory in Williams Bay, Wisconsin. Chandra started working at Yerkes in 1937, after a trip home to India during which he married Lalitha Doraiswamy, whom he had known since college. He taught at Yerkes, and developed a highly respected graduate program in astrophysics and astronomy that attracted top students from around the world. Although his stellar evolution theory had not been well received at first, there were many important physicists such as **Neils Bohr** (1885–1962; see entry in volume 1), Wolfgang Pauli, Paul Dirac, and Ralph H. Fowler who supported his work. Chandra continued his research and in 1939, published a book about his theory.

During World War II (1939–45), Chandra began studying the transfer of energy within stars, called radiative transfer. He became a full professor at the University of Chicago and was elected to the Royal Society of London. In 1943, to assist the American war effort, he spent part of his time working at the Aberdeen Proving Grounds in Maryland, testing the theory of shock waves as well as the motion of projectiles in flight.

In 1952, Chandra became Morton D. Hull Distinguished Service Professor of Astrophysics in Chicago's departments of astronomy and physics, as well as at the Institute for Nuclear Physics at Yerkes Observatory. That same year, he became the managing editor of the university's *Astrophysical Journal,* a position he held until 1971. He became a U.S. citizen in 1953.

Chandra was a well-respected scientist who was recognized with many honors throughout his career, most notably the Nobel Prize in physics, which he shared with William Alfred Fowler for his work with the structure and evolution of stars in 1983. In 1998, in honor of Chandra—who died of heart failure at the age of eighty-four on August 21, 1995—the National Aeronautics and Space Administration (NASA) named a new X-ray astrophysics observatory after him. The Chandra X-ray Observatory (CXO) is in orbit around Earth. CXO Director Harvey Tananbaum said, "Throughout his life Chandra worked tirelessly and with great precision to further our understanding of the universe. These same qualities characterize the many individuals who have devoted much of their careers to building this premier x-ray observatory."

Further Reading

Bethe, Hans A. "Subrahmanyan Chandrasekhar (1910–1995)." *Nature,* October 12, 1995, p. 484.

Chandrasekhar, Subrahmanyan. *An Introduction to the Study of Stellar Structure.* Chicago, IL: University of Chicago Press, 1939. Reprint, New York: Dover Publications, 1967.

Chandrasekhar, Subrahmanyan. *The Mathematical Theory of Black Holes.* New York: Oxford University Press, 1992.

Chandrasekhar, Subrahmanyan. *Truth and Beauty: Aesthetics and Motivations in Science.* Chicago, IL: University of Chicago Press, 1987.

Goldsmith, Donald. *The Astronomers.* New York: St. Martin's Press, 1991.

NASA: Chandra X-ray Observatory News. http://chandra.nasa. gov (accessed on September 3, 2002).

Parker, Eugene N. "Subrahmanyan Chandrasekhar." *Physics Today.* November 1995, pp. 107–8.

Wali, Kameshwar C. *Chandra: A Biography of S. Chandrasekhar.* Chicago, IL: University of Chicago Press, 1991.

Eugenie Clark

May 4, 1922
New York, New York

Known as the Shark Lady, Eugenie Clark is a world-renowned ichthyologist, a scientist who specializes in the study of fish. Her early fascination with fish led her to a career that she excelled at during a time when most women were offered limited work opportunities, especially in scientific fields. Clark's research has taken her all over the world to study hundreds of fish species. For twelve years, she ran a laboratory on the Gulf of Mexico in Florida. She quickly made it a respected center for marine research with an emphasis on sharks. A longtime professor at the University of Maryland, Clark continues to conduct research. In addition to her many scientific publications, she has published three books, two autobiographies and a children's book about sea life.

Mornings at the aquarium

Eugenie Clark was born on May 4, 1922, in New York City. Clark's grandmother, Yuriko, was Japanese and had

"I have always been too intrigued and awed by sharks to be scared of them, but it's important to understand their behavior and to learn how to behave when you visit their home."

Eugenie Clark has made great strides in educating the public about the intelligence and beauty of sharks. Her shark research has put to rest some common fears and misperceptions about sharks and shown that they have the ability to learn. In addition to being a scientist, Clark is a dedicated teacher and a concerned environmentalist. She has altered some of her earlier research techniques such as spearing fish and found ways to study specimens in the wild whenever possible. She has also worked toward protecting endangered reef environments. In all, Clark's body of research has added a wealth of knowledge to the field of ichthyology, and it continues to grow today.

moved from Japan to Seattle, Washington, in 1910. Yuriko emigrated, or left one place or country to live in another, with her daughter Yumiko, her son Boya, and her second husband. When Yumiko was a teenager, the family moved to New York City. Yumiko loved to swim, and took a job as a swimming teacher at a pool. There she met the manager, Charles Clark, whom she married. Eugenie Clark was born a few years later. Sadly, Eugenie's father died just two years after her birth and she was raised by her mother and grandmother.

Clark's interest in fish was sparked when she was just nine years old. Her mother worked on Saturday mornings and needed a safe place for her child to play. Luckily, the New York Aquarium was close to Yumiko's workplace, and Clark would spend many hours there, mesmerized by all the different kinds of fishes. She loved to watch how they moved and soon became as knowledgeable about the fish as the tour guides. Clark began collecting fish for a small aquarium at home. The family's small apartment quickly became crowded with aquaria filled with a wide assortment of sea life. As Clark got older, her interest only deepened and one of her favorite high school classes was biology. She went on to study zoology, the scientific study of animal life, at Hunter College in New York City. Clark's goal was to become an ichthyologist.

Important mentors

Clark had two mentors at the beginning of her career who helped guide and encourage her ideas and pursuits. After graduating from Hunter College, Clark was admitted to New York University (NYU) as a zoology and ichthyology graduate student. There she met Charles Breder, who was head of the Department of Fishes and taught an ichthyology course in the American Museum of Natural History. The museum was the perfect setting for Clark to study in because she could enter the exhibit hall and get a firsthand view of the specimens being discussed in class. For a research project, Breder asked Clark to study how blowfish are able to puff themselves up to scare off predators. Her work was so good that Breder included it in a paper he had published and credited Clark as the co-author.

In 1945, Clark met another professor who would help her enormously. Carl Hubbs was a famous ichthyologist whom Clark had met at the annual American Society of Ichthyologists and Herpetologists meeting. He was extremely impressed with her and invited her to work for him as a research assistant and to begin working toward a doctorate degree at the University of California in San Diego. Clark was thrilled. When she finished her master's degree at NYU, she moved to California. Hubbs was the first person to teach Clark how to dive with a mask and use scuba equipment so she could view fish in their natural habitat.

Living the dream

After about a year, Clark was hired by the U.S. Fish and Wildlife Service to study fish in the Philippines. During a stop in Hawaii, however, Clark was notified that one of the officials had changed his mind about hiring a woman. Clark then decided to return to New York to work at the American Museum of Natural History and finish her Ph.D. at NYU. Her work in Myron Gordon's laboratory at the museum led to discoveries about the mating habits of platies and swordtail fishes. Clark learned that although these two species will have babies together in captivity, they do not mate with each other in the wild. In the course of her laboratory work with platies and swordfishes, she produced the first test-tube, or artificially inseminated, fishes in the United States. Clark's work was beginning to get recognition within the male-dominated world of ichthyology. She had realized her dream: she was a respected ichthyologist. In fact, Clark was one of only three female ichthyologists in the United States. At a time when most women were homemakers or, if they worked outside the home, were limited to being secretaries, bookkeepers, waitresses, and nurses, or held other service jobs, her accomplishment was extraordinary.

Clark's first job as an ichthyologist was for the U.S. Office of Naval Research. After World War II (1939–45), many islands in the South Pacific had become U.S. territories. The navy was interested in learning if there were a large enough quantity of fish that were good to eat to set up commercial fishing in the waters off these islands. Clark had finished most of the work needed for her doctorate and did not want to pass up such a wonderful opportunity. She planned to present the final work for her Ph.D. when she returned from the South Pacific. Traveling from island to island, she met fascinating people and studied hundreds of different species of fish. In the fall of 1949, she finished conducting her fish survey for the navy and went back to New York.

Soon after finishing her doctorate, Clark won a Fulbright Scholarship that allowed her to travel to the Red Sea in the Middle East. There, in January 1951, she became the first woman to ever work at the Marine Biological Station in Ghardaqa, Egypt. Clark spent the next year there, swimming among the varied sea life of the Red Sea and collecting specimens. She used fish poison and learned spearing techniques to obtain some of her specimens. In all, she collected three hundred different species of fish. She even discovered three species that were previously unknown. Clark then returned to the United States to analyze the work she had done in Egypt and write scientific papers. She also decided to write an autobiography about the fascinating life she was leading at the young age of thirty, all stemming from her early passion for watching fish swim. Her book, *Lady with a Spear,* was published in 1953 and became a bestseller.

The Shark Lady

In 1954, a chance reading of *Lady with a Spear* by Anne Vanderbilt changed the course of Clark's life. The Vanderbilts were wealthy and lived on the Cape Haze peninsula in Florida.

Their young son had a deep interest in fish and the family wanted to meet the subject of *Lady with a Spear*. So the Vanderbilts invited Clark to Florida and offered her a laboratory that she would be in charge of right on the Gulf of Mexico at Cape Haze. Clark and her second husband Ilias Konstantinou, a doctor whom she had met in New York, decided it was a wonderful opportunity and moved to Florida with their two young children, Hera and Aya, the following year. (Clark had married Roy Umaki just after college, but they were divorced in 1949.) The Vanderbilt family built the Cape Haze Marine Laboratory, later called the Mote Marine Laboratory.

After receiving a call from a scientist who needed shark livers for his cancer research, Clark began collecting shark specimens so they could be dissected, or cut apart, and studied. Clark grew increasingly interested in studying sharks throughout this research process. She cut up the stomachs of more than 1,500 dead sharks to learn what they eat and found

Eugenie Clark has studied sharks for years, often interacting with them underwater, like this diver, earning her the nickname "The Shark Lady."

Reproduced by permission of Corbis Corporation.

that they consume many types of fish, including crabs, eels, octopuses, and other sharks. With the help of other scientists, Clark devised ways to study live sharks in the water. They built pens next to the dock in which to keep trapped sharks and Clark could study them from inside the tank.

Perry Gilbert, a scientist from Cornell, also helped Clark's work with live sharks. He discovered that he could spray the sharks with a chemical that would not hurt them, but would keep them unconscious for about ten minutes. This way, some of the sharks could be transported to the laboratory for further study. Partly because people are fascinated with sharks and partly because Clark was one of very few women doing extensive research with sharks, the scientific papers she published on the subject got a lot of attention. Her work began to be profiled in magazines and newspapers in addition to the scientific journals. The Cape Haze Laboratory quickly became a tourist attraction for anyone interested in sharks, and Clark became known as the Shark Lady.

Clark ran the laboratory, and later its museum, for twelve years. In that time, Cape Haze became world renowned as a marine research center with a specialty in shark studies. Clark even developed experiments to study the learning behavior of sharks, something that had never been done before. She was able to teach the sharks she had in captivity how to hit a target and receive food, thus discovering that sharks are creatures that can learn. Clark also investigated the possibility that some sharks may sleep in underwater caves.

Teaching, writing, and research

Clark and her husband had two more children, Tak and Niki, during their time in Florida. She named a new species of sandfish that she discovered in the Red Sea, *Trichonotus nikii*, after her son Niki. But in 1967 the couple divorced. Clark decided to teach at the university level, and the following year she took a position as a professor at the University of Maryland in the zoology department. In 1969, she published her second autobiography, *The Lady and the Sharks*.

In the mid-1980s, Clark began making dives in submersibles, vehicles that can be submerged and travel in deep water from which scientists can observe sea life without disturbing their environment. She was the chief scientist for the Beebe Project, a project funded by *National Geographic* that consisted of dives in many different places such as Bermuda, Japan, the Bahamas, and California. These submersible dives allowed scientists to view deep-sea creatures easier than ever before. Clark has written several articles for *National Geographic* magazine and in 1982 made a television special for them about sharks. In 1991, she wrote a children's book with author Ann McGovern called *The Desert Beneath the Sea*. Though Clark retired from the University of Maryland in 1992, she still has an office there and continues to conduct research in exotic locations around the world. Clark also married again in 1997, to Henry Yoshinobu Kon.

Clark has received numerous awards for her work. The Society of Women Geographers, the Maryland Women's Hall of Fame, the National Geographic Society, the Explorers Club, and many other organizations have honored her. She has even been awarded two medals from the government of Egypt and had four newly discovered fish species named after her.

Further Reading

Berman, Ruth. *Sharks*. Minneapolis, MN: Carolrhoda Books, 1995.

Butts, Ellen R., and Joyce R. Schwartz. *Eugenie Clark: Adventures of a Shark Scientist*. North Haven, CT: Shoe String Press, 2000.

Clark, Eugenie. *The Lady and the Sharks*. New York: Harper-Collins, 1969.

Clark, Eugenie. *Lady with a Spear*. New York: Harper & Brothers, 1953.

Dr. Eugenie Clark: Home Page. http://www.sharklady.com (accessed on September 3, 2002).

McGovern, Ann. *Adventures of the Shark Lady: Eugenie Clark around the World*. New York: Scholastic, 1998.

McGovern, Ann, and Eugenie Clark. *The Desert Beneath the Sea.* New York: Scholastic, 1991.

McLoone, Margo. *Women Explorers of the Oceans: Ann Davison, Eugenie Clark, Sylvia Earle, Naomi James, Tania Aebi.* Mankato, MN: Capstone Press, 1999.

Ross, Michael Elson. *Fish Watching with Eugenie Clark.* Minneapolis, MN: Carolrhoda Books, 2000.

Francis Collins

April 14, 1950
Staunton, Virginia

F rancis Collins is a physician and a geneticist and the director of the National Human Genome Research Institute. He leads the U.S. Human Genome Project (HGP), which is a far-reaching collaborative effort to sequence the entire human genome, or the complete genetic information of an organism, and analyze that information for medical and scientific use. One of the main goals of this project is to understand what genes in the human system are responsible for a wide range of diseases in order to more easily detect them, prevent them, or treat them.

Early knack for science

Francis Sellers Collins was born on April 14, 1950, in Staunton, Virginia, and grew up on his family's farm. His father, Fletcher Collins, taught theater at a local college and his mother, Margaret, wrote and produced plays. They also home-

"The Human Genome Project is fulfilling its promise as the single most important project in biology and the biomedical sciences—one that will permanently change biology and medicine."

Francis Collins has dedicated his career to finding genes that are responsible for causing certain diseases and for mapping and analyzing the human genome, the complete DNA sequence of humans. As director of the National Human Genome Research Institute, Collins led a team of researchers from six countries who drafted a sequence of the human genome. Scientists hope to use the knowledge gained from this analysis to vastly enhance our abilities to predict, detect, and treat a variety of diseases. Having a thorough understanding of the human genome will have a dramatic effect on the scientific world as well as raise moral questions in society.

schooled their four children. When Francis was ready for the sixth grade, his mother sent him to public school, primarily so he could interact with children his own age.

Francis was an excellent student and loved science. He graduated from high school at sixteen and went to college at the University of Virginia, where he majored in chemistry. He earned his bachelor's degree in 1970 and four years later received a doctoral degree in physical chemistry from Yale University, in New Haven, Connecticut.

An important change in plans

During graduate school, Collins began to feel that he could make more of a contribution to people's lives by working in a field that was closely related to health. Instead of pursuing a scientific career as a chemist, he decided to go to medical school and become a doctor. He was accepted at the University of North Carolina in Chapel Hill, where he studied molecular biology and human genetics.

Studying human genetics can be compared to studying a map of the components of the human body. Different genes in the body are responsible for different functions. Genes are passed on from one generation to the next, so some genes determine a person's skin color, others control a person's eye and hair color, and some cause diseases. The mid-1970s was an exciting time for the field of human genetics as scientists were starting to piece together how genes are involved with a variety of serious diseases. Isolating genes that cause a specific disorder has been an ongoing, important goal for geneticists. Along with paving the way for developing cures for these diseases, identifying the gene that causes the condition allows for the disease to be diagnosed while a fetus is still in the womb, or before a person shows symptoms of the disease.

A lab technician examines samples of purified DNA, as part of the Human Genome Project's effort to map the estimated 100,000 human genes.
Photograph by Elise Amendola. Reproduced by permission of AP/Wide World Photos.

Collins, who had been searching for a way to combine his love of science with his desire to help people, was hooked.

In 1977, Collins earned his medical degree with honors. He stayed in North Carolina to complete his internship and residency at North Carolina Memorial Hospital. In 1981, Collins accepted a fellowship in human genetics at Yale, where he continued his research into disease-causing genes. After finishing his fellowship in 1984, Collins was hired as an assistant professor of human genetics and internal medicine at the University of Michigan Medical School. His research projects were extremely successful, and Collins was promoted to full professor by 1991.

In 1989, Collins and his research team at Michigan discovered the gene that is responsible for cystic fibrosis, a disease in which the pancreas, lungs, and intestines become clogged with mucus. This achievement was not only important for cystic fibrosis research: it had an impact on the field of genetics, as well. Collins's team developed gene-identification tools known as positional cloning, which are comprised of a genetic map, a physical map, and a complete sequence. This method of gene identification was the first time scientists pinpointed the defective gene responsible for a disease even though they knew little about the gene product or how it caused the disease. Scientists all over the world now use the techniques developed in Collins's lab during this research.

Just a year later, using the same technique, Collins and his team discovered the gene for neurofibromatosis. This is a disease of the nervous system that causes disfiguring tumors on the face and other parts of the body. In 1993, in a collaborative effort with other teams from around the world, his team helped identify the gene for Huntington's disease, a disease of the central nervous system that causes a loss of muscle control and leads to either dementia or death.

Stunning success

As Collins continued with his quest to discover the genes that cause a variety of diseases, the National Institutes of Health (NIH) in Bethesda, Maryland, in 1992, offered him a job to serve as director of the National Human Genome Research Institute (NHGRI). As head of the NHGRI, Collins continued to work as a researcher; he and his team isolated the genes responsible for several different diseases, including the gene for ataxia telangiectasia (A-T), a neurological disorder, and prostate cancer. As head of the Human Genome Project (HGP), Collins also has been instrumental in helping scientists from around the world gain access to the huge amount of data at the NIH to help further their work studying genetic diseases such as Alzheimer's, colon cancer, diabetes, and breast and ovarian cancer. In addition to directing and taking part in these groundbreaking research projects, Collins was overseeing the Human Genome Project.

The Human Genome Project

The Human Genome Project is an international effort to map out the human chromosomes, pinpointing the location and details of all the genes and interconnecting segments. (Chromosomes are structures that contain genetic information in the nucleus, or center, of cells.) The HGP, too complex to be run by one scientist, or even one team of scientists, is a collaboration that spans the globe, combining expertise from scientists all over the world. A genome is the term for all the DNA (deoxyribonucleic acid, the constituent part of chromosomes that carries genetic information) and genes (segments or subunits of DNA) in a cell. DNA molecules are very long chains or units made of a combination of a simple sugar and a phosphate group. Attached at regular positions along this chain are nitrogen bases. Nitrogen bases are chemical compounds in which carbon, hydrogen, oxygen, and nitrogen atoms are arranged in rings. Four nitrogen bases occur in DNA: adenine (A), cytosine, (C), guanine (G), and thymine (T). The way in which nitrogen bases are arranged along a DNA molecule represents a kind of genetic code for the cell in which the molecule occurs.

The main goal of the HGP is to map the location, function, and exact sequence of the constituent chemical parts of the estimated 100,000 genes in the human body. From the very beginning, the scientists in the HGP have made all this information available to the public on a daily basis. Having this knowledge is already helping doctors and scientists figure out what causes a wide range of diseases. It may ultimately even allow inherited diseases to be prevented from occurring in future generations.

At the project's start in 1990, it was estimated that it would take about fifteen years to map the whole sequence of the human genome. In July 2000, several years ahead of schedule, it was announced that a draft of the sequence had been completed. The announcement was a joint one made by Collins and a competitor named Craig Venter, the founder of a company called Celera. After both HGP and Celera completed their "first drafts" of sequencing at roughly the same time, the two teams, with government pressure, coordinated future efforts. In the early twenty-first century, they were completing the work, bringing the sequence into its final finished form to be used for decades, maybe centuries. Most of the work of analyzing the sequence and determining what can be done with this wealth of information still lies ahead.

James Watson, left, and Francis Crick, discoverers of DNA structure. Their discovery led to the Human Genome Project, led by Francis Collins.
Reproduced by permission of AP/Wide World Photos.

Collins's apprehensions

Unlocking the mysteries of human genetic information can present many wonderful advantages, such as detecting and preventing the early onset of genetic diseases, and treating those diseases. But with more information there is also room for controversy. Collins is wary about how people will use the genetic information. He has voiced concern over the possibility of pregnancies being terminated not just because the fetus carries genes for a terminal illness, but because it carries a gene that predisposes it to obesity. This selective process worries many scientists and leads to further questions about the morality of such things as genetic manipulation. There are ethical, religious, and spiritual issues that complicate this matter. On the upside, however, there are benefits as well. A person who is genetically disposed to getting lung cancer, for example, may either never take up smoking or stop smoking a lot sooner than they would have without this prior knowledge.

Francis Crick and James Watson

British biologist **Francis Crick** (1916–) and American biologist **James Watson** (1928–; see entries in volume 1 and 3) shared the 1962 Nobel Prize in physiology or medicine for determining the structure of deoxyribonucleic acid (DNA), the carrier of genetic information. Watson and Crick, through their work with the structure of DNA, pioneered the field of genetic research and paved the way for projects such as the Human Genome Project. In fact, Watson was the first director of the Human Genome Project, and was followed in this role by Francis Collins.

Collins also has raised questions about privacy issues. One of his goals has been to ensure that someone having knowledge of a person's genetic information cannot use that information against that individual. For example, if an insurance company can tell by looking at someone's genetic code that the person might develop a life-threatening disease, that individual may be denied health insurance because the insurance company would deem him an expensive client. Collins emphasizes that just because we have a genetic predisposition to a disease does not guarantee that we will have that disease. In an Associated Press article Collins said, "We are all carrying around pre-existing conditions and we're learning more about how to find them. Pretty soon, we're all going to be uninsurable." Despite these concerns, Collins remains convinced that the future of genetic research will bring great benefits for mankind.

Further Reading

Collins, Francis S., and Ari Patrinos. "New Goals for the U.S. Human Genome Project: 1998–2003." *Science,* October 23, 1998, p. 682.

Collins, Francis S., and Karin G. Jegalian. "Deciphering the Code of Life." *Scientific American,* December 1999, p. 86.

Golden, Frederic, Michael D. Lemonick, and Dick Thompson. "The Race is Over." *Time,* July 3, 2000, p. 18.

Hayden, Thomas. "A Genome Milestone." *Newsweek,* July 3, 2000, p. 51.

"The Science Scoop." *Time for Kids,* October 5, 2001, Supplement, p. 6.

Sherrow, Victoria. *James Watson and Francis Crick: Decoding the Secrets of DNA.* San Diego, CA: Blackbirch, 1995.

Tennant, Agnieszka. "The Genome Doctor." *Christianity Today,* October 1, 2001, p. 42.

Jacques Cousteau

June 11, 1910
Saint-Andre-dé-Cubzac, France
June 25, 1997
Paris, France

update

French underwater explorer Jacques Cousteau led the way for countless oceanographers that followed him. Before he developed an innovative apparatus for breathing underwater and made great advances in underwater photography, few explorers had been able to experience and observe what lived deep in the sea. He not only inspired future oceanographers and marine biologists, he also made it possible for any person to be able to strap on scuba equipment and explore the sea. More important, however, Cousteau's documentaries and environmental organization, the Cousteau Society, alerted the public to the perils our oceans face from the hazards of pollution. **(See original entry on Cousteau in *Scientists*, volume 1.)**

"When you dive, you begin to feel that you're an angel."

Falling in love with the sea

On June 11, 1910, Jacques-Yves Cousteau was born in Saint-Andre-dé-Cubzac, France, to Elizabeth Duranthon and

Portrait reproduced by permission of Corbis Corporation.

87

Jacques Cousteau's invention of the aqualung, a device that allowed divers to breathe underwater for a little over an hour, marked the beginning of a new era in underwater exploration. His own underwater explorations have had a major impact on the public's awareness of the health of the world's oceans. His greatest contribution may be his educating the world, through his numerous books, film documentaries, and through the Cousteau Society, about the hazards of ocean pollution.

Daniel Cousteau. His father was a lawyer who represented American businesspeople in Europe and the United States and the family often traveled between Paris, France, and New York City. Jacques went to a boarding school as a teenager, then, in 1930, entered the French Naval Academy and graduated with a degree in engineering. While stationed aboard the cruiser *Dupleix* in the Mediterranean, he quickly fell in love with the sea. Having bought a home movie camera at thirteen, Cousteau began using goggles to see underwater and make movies under the waves. In 1937, Cousteau married Simone Melchoir and the couple later had two sons, Jean-Michel and Philippe.

The aqualung and Calypso

Cousteau loved to spend time underwater, but the goggles and other heavy equipment of the day, such as a diving suit with an air supply attached to a boat, limited his movement. He and an engineer friend named Emile Bagnan worked together to devise a small tank of compressed air with a mouthpiece through which a diver could breathe. The aqualung, as they called it, allowed divers to be completely mobile and breathe unassisted for a little more than an hour. (The U.S. Navy later renamed it scuba, for self-contained underwater breathing apparatus.)

At the end of World War II (1939–45), Cousteau convinced the French navy that his new invention could be put to an immediate practical use. He organized diving crews to remove mines, placed by the German occupying force during the war, that were blocking southern French ports. Cousteau remained in the French navy until 1956 and continued experimenting with underwater photography. He improved his equipment in order to make increasingly deeper dives. In the process, he developed an underwater camera that could operate up to 1,970 feet (600 meters) below the surface of the water, making some of the first photographs and films of life undersea.

An environmentalist

While still in the navy, in June 1950, Cousteau purchased a ship called the *Calypso*. He hired a crew to help refurbish it, and then they set off on an expedition of the Red Sea in 1951. They discovered underwater volcanic basins and identified previously unknown aquatic plant and animal species. In 1952, on their way back to land, Cousteau and his team found a Roman shipwreck loaded with treasure. The following year, Cousteau published *The Silent World,* an account of his *Calypso* trip that included underwater photography. The book made him internationally known and was later made into an award-winning film.

Cousteau continued with his underwater innovations and invented a small submarine he called a diving saucer. The saucer allowed him to spend extended periods of time diving and exploring life beneath the sea. By the 1960s, he became interested in finding ways to actually live underwater and he designed Conshelf, an underwater living environment where divers could spend several weeks at a time. The first one was finished in 1962 and two men stayed in it for a week. Conshelf 2 was completed in 1963 and five men lived underwater for a month. By 1965, Cousteau had developed a station that people could live in permanently.

During the 1960s, Cousteau realized that nuclear waste was being dumped in the Mediterranean Sea and took up environmental issues pertaining to the oceans of the world. In 1973, he founded the Cousteau Society, using the organization to call attention to the dangers of polluting the world's oceans, believing that the fate of the planet was at stake. He was one of the first people to show the public photographs of sea life entangled in nets and ocean debris.

With his fame, Cousteau was able to successfully use television to impart his message to the public. The show *The Undersea World of Jacques Cousteau,* which also featured his two sons, began being broadcast in 1968 and ran for eight seasons. Twelve one-hour episodes of *The Undersea Odyssey of the "Calypso"* followed in 1970. In all, he produced more than seventy documentaries, winning both Emmy and Academy Awards. Cousteau also published dozens of books throughout his lifetime. In addition to *The Silent World,* he also wrote *Jacques Cousteau's Calypso, Life and Death in a Coral Sea, Pharaohs of the Sea,* and many others.

Always active

Cousteau remained active in his later years. In 1990, at the age of eighty, he traveled with six school-age children, each chosen from a different continent, on an expedition to Antarctica to highlight the importance of protecting that unique environment. He was even working on building a new boat in which to adventure, called the *Calypso II,* when he died of heart failure in June 1997.

Cousteau received many awards during his life, including honorary degrees from several universities. In 1977, he was given the International Environmental Prize of the United Nations and he received the U.S. Presidential Medal of Freedom in 1985. Cousteau also received the James Smithson Bicentennial Medal in 1996 from the Smithsonian Institute. And, in April 2001, Cousteau was inducted into the National Wildlife Federation Conservation Hall of Fame for his lifetime commitment to protecting natural resources and the environment.

Further Reading

Cousteau, Jacques. *Jacques Cousteau's Calypso.* New York: Abrams, 1983.

Cousteau, Jacques. *Life and Death in a Coral Sea.* New York: Doubleday, 1971.

Cousteau, Jacques. *Pharaohs of the Sea.* New York: Abrams, 1975.

Cousteau, Jacques. *The Silent World.* New York: HarperCollins, 1953.

The Cousteau Society. http://www.cousteausociety.org/ (accessed on September 3, 2002).

Dutemple, Leslie. *A&E Biography: Jacques Cousteau.* Minneapolis, MN: Lerner, 2000.

Hopping, Lorraine Jean. *Jacques Cousteau: Saving One Seas.* New York: McGraw-Hill, 2000.

"Late Great Geographers." *Geographical Magazine,* February 2000, p. 91.

Markham, Lois. *Jacques-Yves Cousteau: Exploring the Wonders of the Deep.* Austin, TX: Raintree Steck-Vaughn, 1997.

Sobel, Rachel. "He Inspired Our Passion for the Oceans." *National Wildlife,* April/May 2001, p. 18.

René Geronimo Favaloro

1923
La Plata, Argentina
July 29, 2000
Buenos Aires, Argentina

update

I n 1967, surgeon René Favaloro performed a new technique, bypass surgery, on a patient suffering from atherosclerosis, the narrowing or blocking of arteries to the heart. The surgery was a success and demonstrated that bypass surgery could be a standard treatment for patients with restricted blood supply to the heart. Favaloro achieved worldwide recognition through his surgical work and respect through his dedication to providing the best health care to his native Argentineans. **(See original entry on Favaloro in *Scientists*, volume 6.)**

A talented physician

René Geronimo Favaloro was born in 1923 in La Plata, Argentina, to Jan and Ida Favaloro. He went to college and medical school at the University of La Plata, and earned his medical degree in 1949. Favaloro performed his internship and residency (school training at a hospital working in a specific

"I have always practiced medicine with a profound social pledge. . . . Every patient, paying or not, will continue receiving the same attention!"

Argentinean surgeon René Geronimo Favaloro proved that bypass surgery for certain types of heart patients could be used as a standard treatment for saving lives. Since his landmark operation in 1967, bypasses have been performed on millions of people. Favaloro also played a major role in training surgeons to perform bypass surgery through the Favaloro Foundation, one of the leading medical institutions in South America.

field for doctors) at Instituto General San Martin in La Plata, then practiced medicine in a remote part of Argentina for twelve years. When he became interested in learning more about the latest surgical techniques for heart patients, he went to the United States to visit the Cleveland Clinic in Ohio.

In 1962, doctors at the Cleveland Clinic were in the process of developing ways to help some heart patients by increasing the blood supply to the heart. In one method, called pericardial patch graft, a surgeon opens the wall of a blocked artery and "patches" it with a piece of the patient's leg vein in order to increase the size of the artery. The other technique was the mammary artery implant, in which one end of the mammary artery in the chest is inserted into the wall of the left ventricle of the heart, supplying the ventricle with blood to be pumped into the blood vessels.

Bypass shown as standard treatment

Favaloro studied the different methods being used and looked into another method, called a bypass, which had been performed twice, once in 1962 and again in 1964, both times in emergency situations. In bypass surgery, one end of the saphenous vein, removed from the patient's leg, is inserted into the aorta, the large artery above the heart. The other end is inserted into an artery that is below the obstructed area, thus bypassing the problem. Favaloro believed that the bypass method was superior to the pericardial patch and the mammary artery implant and set out to prove that bypass surgery was the best standard treatment for the appropriate patients.

In 1967, Favaloro performed the landmark surgery that illustrated his theory. The bypass procedure was done on a fifty-one-year-old woman in a nonemergency situation and was successful. Favaloro published his results in a 1968 paper that gained him worldwide recognition. Within just three years, Favaloro and other heart surgeons at the Cleveland Clinic had performed more than one thousand bypass operations with phenomenal success.

In 1970, Favaloro returned to Argentina to bring this life-saving technique to his native country. There he founded the Favaloro Foundation, which was dedicated to teaching surgeons how to perform bypass operations. Twenty years later, the foundation had grown into one of the finest medical institutions in South America, having trained more than three hundred surgeons.

A tragic end

During his lifetime, Favaloro earned the respect of the medical community around the world for both his surgical innovations and his commitment to teaching. Toward the end of his life, however, Favaloro seemed to have become increasingly distressed about the general state of health care in Argentina. Millions of Argentineans, who had traditionally received quality health care from union-related cooperatives, lost their health care altogether because of bank restructuring that allowed less funds for health care. In a decade, the national medicare system of Argentina went bankrupt. At first, Favaloro refused to turn away patients who could not afford to pay for medical care. But as time passed, he became utterly overwhelmed by the number of people he could not help. Adding to his worries, Favaloro's foundation was also failing financially, due to difficulties securing funds from the government to be reimbursed for their costs. According to a letter written by Favaloro to a friend, the foundation was owed close to $18 million.

In late June 2000, Favaloro was honored for his contribution to medicine at the opening of the Georges Pompidou European Hospital in Paris. Just a month later, on July 29, 2000, Favaloro was found dead in his apartment by a self-inflicted gunshot to the chest. The nation was deeply saddened at the loss of one of their heroes. In honor of Favaloro,

Argentina's President Fernando de la Rua declared a day of national mourning on July 31.

Further Reading

Barlow, Maude. "Conference on the Future of Health Care." *Canadian Health Coalition.* http://www.healthcoalition.ca/maude-sp.html (accessed on September 3, 2002).

Favaloro, René Geronimo. *The Challenging Dream of Heart Surgery: From the Pampas to Cleveland.* New York: Little Brown, 1994.

Iglesias-Rogers, Graciela. "Heart-Bypass Pioneer's Death Puts Argentine Health Care in Spotlight." *Lancet,* August 5, 2000, p. 492.

Carlos Finlay

December 3, 1833
Camaguey, Cuba
August 20, 1915
Havana, Cuba

arlos Finlay was a Cuban doctor and scientist who identified a specific mosquito as being responsible for the transmission of the deadly virus yellow fever. This disease was thought by most people to be contagious, passed on from person to person, not transmitted by insects. It took nearly twenty years for his theory to be proved, but once it was, a program ridding areas of Cuba of large mosquito populations dramatically reduced outbreaks of yellow fever. The techniques were soon adopted in other regions of the world. In 1933, one hundred years after his birth, Cuba issued a postage stamp in honor of Carlos Finlay.

Growing up in Cuba and abroad

Carlos Juan Finlay was born on December 3, 1833, in Camaguey, Cuba. His father, Edward Finlay, was a Scottish physician and his mother, Isabel de Barres, was French. When

"I understand . . . that nothing less than an absolutely inconvertible demonstration will be required before . . . my colleagues accept a theory so entirely at variance . . . about yellow fever."

Portrait reproduced by permission of Corbis Corporation.

Carlos Finlay was a Cuban doctor and scientist who identified the specific species of mosquito that was the carrier of a deadly illness called yellow fever. Yellow fever had long been thought to be a contagious virus because once it infected someone in a particular area a major epidemic, or outbreak, usually followed. His theory that mosquitoes were the cause of the disease was not supported by the scientific world for almost twenty years, until a team led by American Major Walter Reed was able to prove it through their own experimentation in Cuba. Identifying the mosquito as the carrier of yellow fever led to a sweeping effort to rid infested areas of the insect. This was extremely effective in eliminating the threat of future epidemics.

Carlos was still a baby, the family moved 300 miles to Cuba's capital city, Havana. There Edward owned a coffee plantation and Carlos grew up enjoying the natural beauty of their island environment. His Aunt Anna, Edward's sister, had been a schoolteacher in Scotland but had joined her brother in Cuba and gave Carlos his early schooling at home.

When Finlay was eleven, his parents sent him to France to further his education. He spent two years there, but was stricken with a case of cholera in 1846. (Cholera is a serious infectious [contagious] disease that can cause violent digestive symptoms such as chronic vomiting and diarrhea. Untreated, it can quickly result in the death of a patient.) Finlay went back home to Cuba to be with his family and recover from his illness. Because of the disease, he lost some of his ability to speak, but through therapy administered by his father he regained most of his ability. (As an adult, however, Finlay sometimes had trouble speaking, which was likely related to his short bout with cholera.)

In 1848, Finlay headed back to Europe with the intention of finishing his schooling in France. But France was going through turbulent times, suffering from an economic depression that caused riots and other difficulties there. Finlay instead spent some time in London, England, before returning to France to attend college in Rouen. Unfortunately, in 1851, Finlay became sick with a bacterial illness called typhoid fever. He again returned to Cuba while he recovered, but would soon make another move.

Medicine and marriage

Finlay decided he wanted to be a doctor. He was accepted at Jefferson Medical College in Philadelphia, Pennsylvania in 1853 and graduated in 1855. He then completed his studies at the University of Havana in Cuba. Finlay now had all the credentials needed to begin practicing medicine. He spent a few months working in Lima, Peru, Paris, France, and Matanzas, Cuba, before settling in Havana. Although he was a general practitioner, Finlay also had a specific interest in ophthalmic, or eye, surgery and focused on that whenever given the opportunity.

The following year, on October 16, 1865, Finlay married Adela Shine from Trinidad. The couple had a son named Carlos Eduardo who later would become a doctor.

Yellow fever and the mosquito

Beginning in about 1865, Finlay became interested in studying the cause of yellow fever. Yellow fever is a viral disease that can cause headaches, vomiting, and in more severe cases, bleeding from the mouth, nose, and eyes and, eventually, death. The disease was deadly most of the time and epidemics could spread throughout communities, killing many people in short amounts of time. Doctors and researchers who had begun to study yellow fever observed that there was a pattern. At first, there would be a few cases. Then two to three weeks later, there would be a major outbreak. There were several theories about the cause of yellow fever; some thought it was a result of unsanitary conditions, while others believed it was an extremely contagious type of flu virus.

In 1793, there had been a major yellow fever outbreak in Philadelphia, Pennsylvania. One noted physician, Benjamin Rush, later observed that there had been an unusually large number of mosquitoes in the city at that time. In 1795, there was another outbreak, this time in New York City. Again, it was noticed that mosquitoes had been plentiful. Latin America's hot, damp climate was a perfect environment for mosquitoes, and Cuba was no exception. The island had been hit many times in its history with outbreaks of yellow fever. Finlay began to look at the mosquito as a carrier of the dreaded disease.

This yellow fever cage in Panama shows how patients with the disease were often isolated because they were considered contagious.
Reproduced by permission of Corbis Corporation.

In addition to his work as a physician, Finlay began studying mosquitoes. He observed different species and conducted experiments to determine which was the primary disease carrier. Between 1865 and 1881, Finlay published ten papers on the subject. He believed he had identified the particular species of mosquito responsible for yellow fever: *Aedes aegypti.* (American doctor Joshua Nott had published an earlier mosquito theory in 1848, but Finlay was the first person to identify one specific species of mosquito as the carrier.)

In February 1881, Finlay traveled to Washington, D.C., to give a talk about his mosquito theory at the International Sanitary Conference. Finlay then presented his work to the Havana Academy of Science a few months later, reading his paper "The Mosquito Hypothetically Considered as the Agent of Transmission of Yellow Fever." Unfortunately, his break-through was met with skepticism. Many scientists still strongly believed that yellow fever was contagious due to its tendency to spread so rapidly.

Finlay continued to conduct experiments for the next two decades. Although he was confident in his theory, he was not able to produce enough hard evidence to prove it. A few other scientists had similar ideas that supported Finlay's. British and Italian scientists had made a connection between insects and malaria, which supported the notion that insects could be a carrier of disease. Also, American doctor Henry Rose Carter had done research he believed confirmed earlier observations that there was a delay period of approximately two to three weeks between the first time a yellow fever case shows up and all the cases that then follow. He reasoned that this time frame would fit with a mosquito biting a person with the virus, having it incubate in its system, and then transmitting it to another person with another bite. Nonetheless, nothing more was done to definitively prove Finlay's theory for almost twenty years after his 1881 presentation.

The Reed Commission

In 1898, American troops were sent to Cuba to fight in the Spanish-American War. As U.S soldiers began to die from yellow fever, the American army's surgeon general, George Miller Sternberg, sent a team to investigate and determine what caused this disease once and for all. Major **Walter Reed** (1851–1902; see entry in volume 6), a doctor and a scientist, was in charge of the team.

The Reed Commission, joined by Henry Rose Carter, began their work in Cuba in June 1900. Finlay had already been assisting the Americans in a medical capacity from Cuba, as well as reinforcing his mosquito theory, before being asked to help study yellow fever patients with the Reed Commission. Reed's group first ruled out a recent theory, put forth by the Italian scientist Guiseppe Sanarelli, that the cause of yellow fever was a germ, which Sanarelli called *Bacillus icteroides*. The commission tested eighteen yellow fever patients for

Major Walter Reed was an American surgeon who led the Reed Commission that worked with Finlay in Cuba to find the cause of yellow fever.

Reproduced by permission of Corbis Corporation.

Bacillus icteroides and did not detect any of the bacterium in these patients.

Reed's team then learned of a yellow fever outbreak in a town called Pinar del Rio, about one hundred miles from Havana. Upon their arrival, Reed's group noticed a few key things that led them to rule out the idea of yellow fever being a contagious disease. First, bedding and clothing were used both by patients who had yellow fever and those who did not. If the disease were contagious, these items would have been contaminated and the disease would have spread. Second, a prisoner in a jail set apart from the town was also sick, but none of the other prisoners or guards who came in contact with him were ill. That suggested to Reed that the prisoner did not catch the disease from anyone else.

With their observations at Pinar del Rio, the earlier link between mosquitoes and malaria, and Carter's research, Reed began to think the culprit could very well be the mosquito. He decided it was time to reconsider Finlay's theory.

Reed proves Finlay right

The team had no research animals at its disposal and was being encouraged to determine the cause of the disease in a timely manner. Therefore, Reed's group made the dramatic decision to use human volunteers in their experiments, including themselves. In August 1900, Finlay supplied the team with mosquito eggs. The mosquitoes grew and were allowed to feed on blood the researchers had tainted with yellow fever. These mosquitoes were allowed to bite some of the scientists, as well as other volunteers. When those bitten did not immediately become ill, the scientists realized that they had not allowed for an incubation period in the mosquito, as Carter had proposed.

The experiment was redone, with Finlay again supplying the mosquito eggs. This time, a soldier who had not been exposed to yellow fever allowed himself to be bitten by one of the mosquitoes carrying the disease. The soldier did indeed become ill. The Reed Commission had the first piece of scientific evidence that proved that the mosquito was indeed transmitting yellow fever and that the virus was not contagious.

In November 1900, the commission established a research station to conduct more experiments. They had two buildings, one called the "infected clothing building" and the other the "infected mosquito building." In the clothing building, volunteers used items that had been dirtied by yellow fever patients and contained many of their germs. Nobody became ill, confirming that the germs were not contagious.

The infected mosquito building was divided in two by a screen through which mosquitoes could not travel but contagious germs certainly could. Volunteers on one side shared the space with mosquitoes that had bitten yellow fever patients; volunteers on the other side were protected from the mosquitoes. Almost all of the people bitten by mosquitoes contracted yellow fever, while none of the volunteers on the other side became sick. In 1901, Reed's team published their results in the *Journal of the American Medical Association*. Their experiments proved what Finlay had known to be true for nearly twenty years. That same year, a program was implemented to rid the area of mosquitoes. Within ninety days, yellow fever was absent from Havana for the first time in 150 years.

New respect and admiration

Finlay had been unwavering in his belief of his mosquito theory and waited a very long time to reap the benefits. In 1901, the Liverpool School of Tropical Medicine awarded him the Mary Kingsley medal. Jefferson Medical College, where he had attended medical school, inducted him into the prestigious College of Physicians of Philadelphia. In 1902, the Cuban government made him the president of the Superior Board of Health, as well as Cuba's chief health officer, a position he held until his retirement in 1909. The Finlay Institute for Investigations in Tropical Medicine was also created in Cuba. And in 1903, he was elected president of the American Public Health Association.

Finlay died in Havana on August 20, 1915 at the age of eighty-two. Seventeen years after his death, and one hundred years after his birth, Cuba issued a postage stamp in his honor.

Further Reading

Bilchik, Gloria Shur. "In War and Peace." *AHA News,* October 26, 1998, p. 7.

finlay-online.com. http://www.finlay-online.com/welcome/whowasdrfinlay.htm (accessed on September 3, 2002).

McCarthy, Michael. "A Century of the US Army Yellow Fever Research." *Lancet,* June 2, 2001, p. 1772.

Sumption, Christine. *Carlos Finlay.* Austin, TX: Raintree Steck-Vaughn, 1989.

Writer, James V. "Did the Mosquito Do It?" *American History,* January/February 1997, p. 44.

Judah Folkman

February 24, 1933
Cleveland, Ohio

J udah Folkman is an American doctor and scientist who has spent most of his career working on a treatment for cancer. His efforts have greatly enhanced what we know about tumors and how they grow. Folkman discovered that angiogenesis, or the growth of new blood vessels, is necessary for tumors to grow. His theory that there must be a way to prevent the growth of these vessels led to the discovery of substances that do just that, called angiogenesis inhibitors. There is still much work to be done to figure out how effective these inhibitors can be in humans, but Folkman's work has brought the world closer to finding a treatment for cancer.

"You have to think ahead. Science goes where you imagine it."

A boy's dream

Moses Judah Folkman was born on February 24, 1933, in Cleveland, Ohio, to Jerome Folkman, a rabbi, and Bessie Folkman. As a child, Judah, his sister Joy, and his brother David

Judah Folkman has been called the man who will cure cancer. Folkman's research efforts have given the scientific world a wealth of knowledge regarding how cancerous tumors grow and how they might eventually be treated. His work has shown that tumors need a blood supply created by angiogenesis, or new blood vessel growth, in order to thrive and grow. He theorized that if an "off switch," or angiogenesis inhibitor, could be found to eliminate the flow of blood to a tumor, it could either be reduced or eliminated. The first two of many off switches, endostatin and angiostatin, were discovered in Folkman's laboratory. Several specific inhibitors have been identified and are at various stages of testing in cancer patients. Time, and continued research, will eventually tell if one or more of the angiogenesis inhibitors can effectively treat cancer.

often went with their father to visit sick people in the hospital. Judah saw first-hand the importance of doctors and dreamed of becoming a surgeon. For a bar mitzvah present, Judah asked his grandfather to buy him an expensive microscope rather than the car his grandfather was planning to give him. (A bar mitzvah is a ceremony in which a thirteen-year-old Jewish boy is admitted as an adult into the religious community.) Microscope in hand, Judah set up a small laboratory in his parents' basement.

Folkman's talent for science was evident in high school when he won a prize for an astonishing science project. With a toy refrigerator and bicycle pump, he kept a rat's heart beating outside of its body for more than half an hour. After high school graduation, Folkman attended Ohio State University as a pre-med undergraduate student, where he began to study cancer and how to treat it. He even a co-wrote scientific papers about a new way to treat cancer of the liver. Folkman graduated in 1953 with high academic honors after just three years.

A shining medical career begins

Only twenty years old, Folkman was then admitted to Harvard Medical School. While there, he helped design one of the first pacemakers, an electronic device that helps to control the rhythm of the heart in patients with heart disorders. In 1957, Folkman received his medical degree.

Folkman then went on to do his internship at Massachusetts General Hospital in Boston, followed by a surgical residency there. He was known as a hardworking, dedicated, and compassionate doctor who frequently stayed at the hospital long after his shift was over to comfort a patient or family member in need.

In 1960, Folkman moved to Bethesda, Maryland, to work at the National Naval Medical Center as a lieutenant in the U.S. Navy. That same year, he married Paula Prial. The couple later had two daughters. In Bethesda, Folkman performed research on substitutes for blood in transfusions. He also worked on a project to create artificial glands that could be placed in a body so time-release drugs within them could be distributed to the targeted area. This work led to the later development of Norplant, a birth-control method that involves implanting devices under the skin that release hormones into the system that inhibit ovulation or the release of eggs from the ovaries.

Also at Bethesda, Folkman had a major breakthrough in oncology, or the study of tumors. He and a colleague, Frederich Becker, removed the thyroid gland from a rabbit and introduced cancer cells into the gland. Small tumors developed in the gland, but they did not continue to grow. When they implanted these tumors into mice, however, they did grow. Folkman and Becker reasoned that the tumors needed to be fed by an organism's blood in order to develop further. This was the beginning of an idea that Folkman would base his career on: angiogenesis.

Returning to Harvard

In 1962, Folkman moved back to Boston and resumed a surgical residency at Massachusetts General. Also in 1962, he was hired as an assistant surgeon at Boston City Hospital and as a surgery instructor at Harvard University Medical School. Folkman had a reputation as a technically skilled doctor and was promoted to associate professor in surgery in 1967. With rapid success, that same year he became a full professor in surgery. Beginning in 1968, he also served as a senior surgeon at the Children's Hospital Medical Center in Boston.

During the late 1960s, Folkman continued his research on cancer tumors. Using rabbits again, he implanted tumors in two specific locations. The first was near the iris of the eye, where there is a large supply of blood. The second was behind the cornea of the eye, where there is no blood supply. The

Interferon is an angiogenesis inhibitor that helps prevent the growth of new blood vessels and the spread of disease.
Photograph by Zeva Oelbaum. Reproduced by permission of Corbis Corporation.

tumors behind the cornea did not grow, while the tumors near the iris got bigger. Indeed, the tumors near the blood-fed iris sparked the growth of new blood vessels. Folkman's findings again supported his theory that tumors need a blood supply in order to grow and he also discovered that the tumor depended on the new growth of blood vessels, called angiogenesis, to feed the growth of the tumor. Folkman termed this "angiogenesis dependency"; "angio" means blood vessel and "genesis" means to create. He believed that if scientists could find a way to stop the growth of the new blood vessels, the growth of the tumor could also be stopped. Although his study was published in the respected *New England Journal of Medicine* in 1971, the scientific community did not believe his data was strong enough and met his results with great skepticism.

In 1974, Folkman received a twelve-year, $23-million grant, or donation, from the Monsanto Company, an agricultural company, that allowed him to fund further studies. He wanted to determine the molecule that "turned on" the cells that are used to grow blood vessels. For the next seven years, he worked tirelessly to do his research and also uphold his nearly full-time responsibilities as a surgeon. In 1981, he made the decision to give up his position as chief surgeon at Children's Hospital in Boston and was made director of the Surgical Research Laboratories there.

Research results improve

Folkman finally achieved a breakthrough in his struggle to definitively prove the connection between tumors and angiogenesis in early 1983. Two members of the Folkman group, Michael Klagsbrun and Yuen Shing, identified the substance a certain tumor was producing that was responsible for prompting blood vessels to grow. The substance is a protein called a Tumor Angiogenesis Factor (TAF), also nicknamed "on switches." (These proteins, of which fourteen have since been discovered, are now known as angiogenic factors.) TAF is the substance that causes tumors to become enlarged, and it also causes them to spread to other parts of the body. Folkman was now certain that if a way to block the blood supply from

Donald E. Ingber

Donald Ingber discovered many different kinds of angiogenesis inhibitors.
Reproduced courtesy of Donald Ingber.

Don Ingber is the scientist in Judah Folkman's laboratory at Children's Hospital in Boston who discovered the "off switch," or angiogenesis inhibitor, that stops cancer growth. Ingber was born in East Meadow, New York, in May 1956, and attended public schools before entering Yale University in New Haven, Connecticut. At Yale, he worked toward several degrees simultaneously. First, Ingber received a bachelor's degree and a master's degree in molecular biophysics and biochemistry. This was followed by a medical degree from the Yale University School of Medicine combined with a doctorate in cell biology from the graduate school. In 1984, Ingber went to Harvard University to perform postdoctoral work with Judah Folkman. Harvard then hired him as faculty, where he works as a Professor of Pathology at Harvard Medical School and in the surgery department at Children's Hospital in Boston.

In addition to his work with Folkman with angiogenesis inhibitors, Ingber has undertaken extensive work with the structure of cells. He combined his interest in cell biology with his interest in sculpture to create a model of a cell using wooden dowels (tubes) and elastic cords that can be flattened and released. He then mimicked this experiment using living cells to investigate the many shapes in which cells can be distorted and how this distortion affects what happens to the cells. Ingber's initial idea—to connect a model of a mechanical structure to living cells—has resulted in scientists being able to predict different cell behaviors.

the tumor could be determined, science would be closer to successfully treating cancer.

Then something significant occurred in the lab. In 1985, blood vessel cells the team was working with were accidentally contaminated by yeast. The yeast did not kill the cells, but it did stop them from growing. Donald E. Ingber, a scientist working in Folkman's lab, had discovered a fungus that was, in effect, the "off switch" they were looking for. Ingber was responsible for much of the work that resulted in discovering several more of these off switches, or angiogenesis inhibitors. A chemical company was able to use Ingber's work to create the first angiogenesis inhibitor, called TNP-470, used in human clinical trials to stop cancer growth. Over the next decade several more angiogenesis inhibitors were discovered by other scientists. Some of the inhibitors were tested on people, but only a few were shown to work, and those few were only effective with weaker strains of cancer cells.

Front-page news

In Folkman's lab in 1994, Michael O'Reilly found a more powerful natural inhibitor of angiogenesis called angiostatin. Two years later, a second one, endostatin, was found. These were the most powerful inhibitors to date. Both worked to slow or stop the progression of tumors in mice and did not cause any side effects, as some of the earlier inhibitors had.

Then something happened to put Folkman's work on the map. American biologist **James Watson** (1928–; see entry in volume 3), who won the Nobel Prize with **Francis Crick** (1916–; see entry in volume 1) for discovering the structure of DNA, reportedly made a comment that "Judah is going to cure cancer in two years." Suddenly, on May 3, 1998, Folkman's work with endostatin and angiostatin, which had not been tested in humans, was announced to the world on the front page of the *New York Times*. Folkman himself criticized the attention, telling *People* and *U.S. News & World Report* magazines that month, "If you have cancer and you're a mouse, we can take good care of you."

From that moment on, Folkman and his lab were in the spotlight. His office was flooded with phone calls from people who wanted angiostatin to treat their cancer. But skepticism soon returned as the National Cancer Institute discovered that their scientists could not reproduce the results Folkman's team had achieved. Skepticism was then followed by renewed excitement as other scientists found that endostatin did shrink tumors in mice. Scientists went back and forth trying to prove and disprove Folkman's results.

In the meantime, drug companies are working to develop angiogenesis inhibitor drugs that they hope will eventually be used to treat cancer. In fact, there is so much attention to this area of testing and research that a nonprofit organization, called the Angiogenesis Foundation, was established to track the progress of the field. In February 2001, there were nearly twenty of these drugs in clinical trials. While there is no longer much doubt that Folkman's overall theory that tumors need a blood supply to grow is correct, developing the right drug and determining the right dose to effectively treat tumors has yet to be established. Folkman's research, however, has led scientists down an exciting path that might lead to an effective treatment for cancer.

Further Reading

Boyce, Nell. "High Hopes, Unmet Promises." *U.S. News & World Report,* April 1, 2002, p. 60.

Brownlee, Shannon. "They Called His Theory Ridiculous: Now It's Revolutionizing Cancer Treatment." *U.S. News & World Report,* December 9, 1996, p. 82.

Brownlee, Shannon, Nancy Shute, and Laura Tangley. "Killing Cancer." *U.S. News & World Report,* May 18, 1998, p. 56.

"Dr. Judah Folkman." *Biography,* December 1998, p. 54.

Fields-Meyer, Thomas, and Joseph V. Tirella. "Hope for a Cure?" *People,* May 25, 1998, p. 119.

Folkman, Judah. "Fighting Cancer by Attacking Its Blood Supply." *Scientific American,* September 1996, p. 150.

Ingber, Donald E. "The Architecture of Life." *Scientific American,* January 1998.

Kalb, Claudia. "Folkman Looks Ahead: The Controversial Pioneer of Angiogenesis Is Back on the Map—and Now His Theories Are Being Tested on Humans." *Newsweek,* February 19, 2001, p. 44.

Kalb, Claudia. "Hype, Hope, Cancer." *Newsweek,* December 28, 1998–January 4, 1999, p. 73.

Stipp, David. "A New Way to Attack Cancer." *Fortune,* May 28, 2000, p. 165.

Tetsuya Theodore Fujita

October 23, 1920
Kitakyushu, Japan
November 19, 1998
Chicago, Illinois

update

Meteorologist Theodore Fujita made a major impact on both the meteorological world and general society. In addition to developing the Fujita scale to measure the intensity of tornadoes, Fujita also identified dangerous winds called microbursts as a source of peril for low-flying aircraft. Because of his work, Doppler radar systems that can detect these violent winds are now used at airports and have been successful at preventing many airplane crashes. **(See original entry on Fujita in *Scientists*, volume 1.)**

Japanese-born American meteorologist

Tetsuya Fujita was born in Kitakyushu, Japan, on October 23, 1920, to Yoshie (Kanesue) Fujita and Tomojiro Fujita, a schoolteacher. He studied engineering at the Meji College of Technology, later called the Kyushu Institute of Technology, and graduated in 1943. Two years later, while working as an

"There was an insight he had, this gut feeling. He often had ideas way before the rest of us could even imagine them."

—Jim Wilson, senior scientist at the National Center for Atmospheric Research in Boulder, Colorado, who worked with Fujita

Portrait reproduced by permission of AP/Wide World Photos.

Meteorologist Tetsuya Theodore Fujita devised the Fujita scale for measuring the intensity of tornadoes, ranging from F-0 (very weak) to F-6 (inconceivable). Fujita also discovered microbursts, strong bursts of downward winds that have caused many plane crashes. Through his research and the employment of Doppler radar, airports are now equipped to warn pilots of these winds and prevent airline accidents.

assistant professor of physics, Fujita witnessed the devastation caused by the atomic bombs dropped by the United States on the Japanese cities of Hiroshima and Nagasaki at the close of World War II (1939–45). At both of these bomb sites he calculated how high above the ground the bombs had exploded to create unique starburst patterns on the ground. These starburst patterns were similar to patterns he would later see related to weather phenomena.

In 1948, Fujita married Tatsuko Hatano and they later had a son named Kazuya. A year later, Fujita began working on his doctorate degree in atmospheric science at Tokyo University in addition to teaching at Kyushu. In his research he was influenced by the work of another atmospheric scientist, Horace R. Byers, who was on the faculty at the University of Chicago in Illinois. After completing his doctorate program in 1953, Fujita accepted an invitation to be a visiting research associate at the University of Chicago and traveled to the United States.

Fujita became a senior meteorologist, or a scientist who studies the atmosphere and its phenomena as well as weather and its forecasting, at the university and was promoted to associate professor in 1962. In 1965, he became a full professor, and three years later, he became an American citizen, adopting the first name Theodore to use in the United States. In 1968, Fujita divorced his first wife and a year later married Sumiko Yamamoto.

The F Scale and microbursts

At the University of Chicago in 1971, Fujita developed the Fujita Tornado Damage Scale, or "F Scale," a system of measuring tornado strength that correlates ground damage to wind speed. It is a six-point system that operates on an F-0 (very weak) to F-6 (inconceivable) scale and is similar to the

Richter scale created by **Charles F. Richter** (1900–1985; see entry in volume 3), that measures the strength of earthquakes. The F Scale earned Fujita the nickname "Mr. Tornado."

A few years later, Fujita embarked on another course of study. In a tragic accident on June 24, 1975, Eastern Airlines Flight 66 crashed at New York's Kennedy Airport during a thunderstorm, killing 120 people. It was suspected that winds were involved, but speeds of only 6 knots had been registered at the airport. (A knot is a unit of speed equal to one nautical mile per hour used especially by ships and aircraft.) Fujita was called in as an expert to investigate. He analyzed the winds, looked at satellite and radar data, and charted the flight paths from Flight 66 as well as the other planes that had landed safely during the storm.

Fujita discovered that Flight 66 had crashed because it had been caught by small but powerful downdrafts, or downward currents of air, that he called "downbursts" and microbursts. Fujita coined the term downburst for the powerful downdrafts that strike the ground and deflect in all directions, causing danger for low-flying aircraft. Meteorologists knew by the mid-1970s that severe storms produce downdrafts. However, because they assumed those downdrafts lost most of their force before they hit the ground and therefore did not cause much damage, the phenomenon was largely ignored. Fujita began research to prove his thesis that downdraft is a significant weather phenomenon and was eventually able to show that downdrafts cause wind shear, which poses a particular hazard in aviation.

Air safety has improved dramatically because of Fujita's research, which led to the development of Doppler radar. (The Doppler effect is a change in frequency with which sound or light waves reach an observer when both the source and the observer are in motion. The Doppler effect explains, for example, why the sound of a train grows louder as it approaches and then softens once it has gone by. Doppler radar systems use the Doppler effect to measure wind velocity). Doppler radar is so sensitive it actually picks up particles of debris in the air that are as fine as dust. Movements of these particles are tracked to measure shifts in wind velocity. By the mid-1990s, the National Weather Service and the U.S. Air Force together had installed 137 Doppler systems, essentially blanketing the continental United States. Because of these radar systems, which give aviators twenty to twenty-five minutes' warning of approaching tornadoes, there has already been a decrease in airline accidents.

Award-winning scientist

In 1988, Fujita became director of the University of Chicago's Wind Research Laboratory and held that position until his death in 1998. In 1995, his health began to fail, and on November 19, 1998, at the age of seventy-eight, Fujita died in his sleep.

Further Reading

Frank, James. "Mr. Tornado," *Chicago Tribune,* May 10, 1990.

"The Fujita Scale." *Tornado Project Online.* http://www. tornadoproject.com (accessed on September 3, 2002).

"'Mr. Tornado,' Ted Fujita, dies at 78." *USA Today,* November 19, 1998.

Rosenfeld, Jeff. "Mr. Tornado: The Life and Career of Ted Fujita." *Weatherwise,* May–June 1999, p. 18.

Taubes, Gary. "Ted Fujita: On the Tornado's Tail." *Discover,* May 1983, pp. 48–53.

Williams, Jack. *The Weather Book: An Easy to Understand Guide to the U.S.A.'s Weather.* New York: Vintage Books, 1992, pp. 122–23.

Charles Martin Hall

December 6, 1863
Thompson, Ohio
December 27, 1914
Daytona Beach, Florida

harles Martin Hall was an American chemist known for developing a process to produce aluminum in a cost-effective way. At the time of his discovery, aluminum was considered a semiprecious metal that cost about $100 per pound. Once Hall's process was patented and production of aluminum was streamlined at his company, the Aluminum Company of America (ALCOA), the price of aluminum plummeted to $0.18 per pound. The ready availability of aluminum and its low cost had a dramatic impact on the world of manufacturing, making the metal available for general use. Today, aluminum is used in many different industries, including aviation, automobile, aerospace, construction, and packaging. Hall's discovery made him a multimillionaire and affected people's lives across the globe.

Charles Martin Hall's method of producing aluminum cheaply brought the cost of aluminum down from about $100 per pound to $0.18 per pound.

A passion for chemistry

Charles Martin Hall was born on December 6, 1863, in Thompson, Ohio, to Sophronia and Herman Hall. Both of his

IMPACT

Charles Martin Hall's work had a tremendous impact on nearly every major category of mass production. Before he discovered how to produce aluminum in a cost-effective way, it was considered a semiprecious metal and was very expensive. Once Hall's process was patented and his company, the Aluminum Company of America (ALCOA), was producing aluminum, the price of metal dropped almost $100. This made Hall an extremely wealthy man and, more importantly, it made aluminum accessible for general use. Aluminum is one of the world's most important metals because it is lightweight but strong (when alloyed with copper or magnesium), doesn't corrode easily, and is a good conductor of heat. Aluminum has countless commercial uses, including in the automotive, aviation, and aerospace industries; cookware; packaging, such as soda cans and foil wrap; and construction equipment. One of its most significant uses is in the aluminum-clad cables used for high-tension electric lines.

parents were graduates of Oberlin College, and in 1873 they moved back to Oberlin, Ohio, so their seven children could have the opportunity to attend Oberlin as well.

Hall was a bright child who did well at Oberlin High School. He loved to read old chemistry books and perform scientific experiments. Hall did odd jobs such as cleaning yards around his neighborhood to earn the money to buy test tubes and other inexpensive equipment he could use in the mini-laboratory he built on the third floor of his parents' house. After starting a small fire, his parents made Hall conduct his experiments in the woodshed off the back of the house. In 1880, he was admitted to Oberlin College and studied chemistry with Frank Fanning Jewett, an American chemist who had performed extensive research on the metal aluminum.

Aluminum is abundant in nature, but it is always found in combination with other elements. It is one of the world's most important metals because it is lightweight but strong (when alloyed with copper or magnesium), doesn't corrode easily, and is a good conductor of heat. Jewett had studied aluminum with German chemist Friedrich Wöhler (1800–1882), who had isolated aluminum as a metal in 1827. But Wöhler's method was inefficient and expensive. Other chemists in Europe also had been developing ways to isolate aluminum, but their methods were also too costly.

Some historians believe that a comment Jewett had made about how successful the person who invented a cost-effective way to produce aluminum would be sparked Hall's interest in that metal. Others claim that Hall had been interested in aluminum since reading about it in high school. Either way, Hall was still in college when he began to develop his ideas for producing aluminum cheaply.

Determination proves fruitful

After graduating with a degree in chemistry in 1885, Hall did not look for work in industry but pursued his experiments in his laboratory at home. Jewett continued to offer encouragement and support.

Hall was certain that the key to isolating aluminum was by using electrolysis. Electrolysis is a process by which electrical energy is used to produce a chemical change.

For example, to isolate, or breakdown, a metal compound into its separate parts an electric current is passed through an ore (a mineral compound). The main natural source of aluminum, aluminum oxide, is a very stable compound, which makes it difficult to break apart. You can't get aluminum out of aluminum oxide just by heating the compound—you need more energy than heat can provide.

Hall built a furnace capable of reaching the high temperatures needed to melt a variety of different substances. Next, he began his search for the solvent capable of dissolving aluminum oxide. (A solvent is a liquid that is capable of dissolving another substance.) The solvent would have to breakdown aluminum oxide into its basest components, thus isolating aluminum. First Hall tried the mineral fluorspar, then potassium fluoride, sodium fluoride, and aluminum fluoride. None of these solvents were successful.

The ultimate success

Then, on February 9, 1886, while experimenting with cryolite, Hall discovered that the mineral, a good conductor when melted, was an excellent solvent for aluminum oxide. On February 16, 1886, he conducted the electrolysis experiment. His solution of aluminum oxide in molten cryolite was contained in a clay pot. Electric current was then passed

Paul Louis-Toussaint Héroult

Paul Louis-Toussaint Héroult was born on April 10, 1863, in Thury-Harcourt, Calvaedos, France. Like Charles Martin Hall, Héroult became interested in the process of producing aluminum as a young man after reading about the struggles chemists had encountered finding a way to make the metal in an inexpensive way. As a student, he experimented with different techniques and, in doing so, accidentally isolated aluminum by electrolysis. Coincidentally, he did so at virtually the same time as Hall.

Héroult filed his patent a few months earlier than Hall did, which raised a patent dispute that lasted several years before it was finally settled in Hall's favor. Their methods were different, but their overall results were the same. Although a conflict arose, Hall and Héroult became good friends and the process the two men discovered is often referred to as the Hall-Héroult process. Paul Louis-Toussaint Héroult died on May 9, 1914.

French scientist Paul Héroult discovered how to isolate aluminum at virtually the same time as Charles Martin Hall.
Reproduced by permission of Corbis Corporation.

through electrodes placed in the solution and the mixture was cooled and hardened. (An electrode is a conductor through which an electric current enters or leaves a liquid or gas.). Hall hypothesized, or made an educated guess, that once he cracked open the substance, he would find aluminum pellets inside. But when he smashed it open, he saw only a grayish deposit on one of the electrodes.

Hall tried to determine what had gone wrong. He repeated the experiment several times and continued to get the same disappointing results. Hall then theorized that the problem had to do with material being drawn out of the clay pot that held his mixture. He fashioned a liner for the pot made of graphite, the same material the electrodes were made of,

which would not cause the material to be drawn out, and repeated his experiment.

On February 23, 1886, Hall once again cracked open the cooled substance. This time, his efforts paid off: he found silvery pellets of aluminum. Hall was only twenty-two years old at the time, having graduated a mere eight months before making this monumental discovery. He now set out to determine how to capitalize on his discovery as efficiently as he had resolved to produce aluminum in his laboratory.

The road to fame and fortune

Hall knew that his invention could bring him enormous wealth, considering industry's need for aluminum's many uses, but he needed to protect his discovery with a patent. A patent is a grant made by the government that assures the inventor the exclusive right to manufacture, use, and sell an invention for a stated period of time. He also needed to find investors to provide financing to build a company dedicated to producing aluminum. It took him four months to raise enough money to hire a lawyer to file the patent for him. He applied for a patent on July 9, 1886, for "The Process of Reducing Aluminum by Electrolysis," but the patent was not granted until a dispute was settled. A French chemist named Paul Louis-Toussaint Héroult (1863–1914) had nearly simultaneously developed the same process for producing aluminum. Héroult had filed his French patent just a few months earlier than Hall, in April 1886. After Hall was able to produce proof as to the exact date of his discovery, he was awarded a U.S. patent. (Today, it is often called the Hall-Héroult process in honor of both chemists' work.)

It took Hall about two years of demonstrating the qualities of both his process and his product to secure financial backing. He finally found the support he needed in Alfred E. Hunt (1855–1899). Hunt was a metallurgist, or someone who specializes in the technology of extracting metals from their ores, refining them for use, and creating useful objects from the metals. With Hunt's money, in 1888, the Pittsburgh Reduction Company was founded. The first factory, in Pittsburgh, Pennsylvania, began producing aluminum in November 1888. Soon more plants were set up, in New Kensington, Pennsylvania, and Niagara, New York. Hall was named vice-president of the company in 1890.

Hall's process quickly changed aluminum's status from a semiprecious metal to a common one by bringing the price per pound down dramatically. Before the Hall-Héroult process, the cost of aluminum was the same as the cost of silver, about $100. By 1914, the price had plummeted to a fraction of a dollar per pound, about $0.18. Aluminum suddenly became available for an enormous variety of uses. The Pittsburgh Reduction Company was renamed the Aluminum Company of America (ALCOA) in 1907. Hall continued researching and developing further refinements to his process throughout his lifetime. In 1911, he was awarded the Perkin Medal for outstanding achievement in chemistry, and in 1916, he was inducted into the National Inventors Hall of Fame.

Hall died in Daytona Beach, Florida, on December 27, 1914, at the age of fifty-one. In his will, he left about one-third of his estate to Oberlin College. He had realized his dream of becoming wealthy from his discovery. In the early twenty-first century, ALCOA was the world's leading aluminum company.

Further Reading

"It all starts with dirt." *Alcoa.com.* http://www.alcoa.com/global/en/about_alcoa/dirt.asp (accessed on September 3, 2002).

"Charles Martin Hall and the Electrolytic Process for Refining Aluminum." *Oberlin College History Website.* http://www.oberlin.edu/~chem/history/cmh/cmharticle.html (accessed on September 3, 2002).

Daintith, John, Sarah Mitchell, and Elizabeth Tootill, eds. *A Biographical Encyclopedia of Scientists,* Vols. 1 and 2. New York: Facts on File, 1981.

Muir, Hazel, ed. *Larousse Dictionary of Scientists.* New York: Larousse, 1994.

Yale-Peabody, Diane. "Charles Is Cooking Something Out There." *Cricket,* May 1992, p. 12.

Leland Hartwell

October 30, 1939
Los Angeles, California

Leland Hartwell is an American geneticist who has vastly expanded our knowledge of how cells are regulated and how they divide and multiply. He discovered the class of genes (coded segments of DNA molecules that carry instructions for the formation, functioning, and transmission of specific traits) that control the cell division cycle and another set of genes that monitor the progress and stability of the cycle during different phases. His work with yeast cells, which are similar to human cells, may help scientists determine methods for detecting cancer at earlier stages and new ways of treating cancer patients.

"Forget the pressure to be productive; work on whatever captures your interest."

Discovering the scientist within

Leland H. Hartwell was born on October 30, 1939, in Los Angeles, California. Although there were no clear signs that he would grow up to be an award-winning scientist, he did like to

Portrait reproduced by permission of AP/Wide World Photos.

Leland Hartwell moved the study of the cell cycle forward with his discovery of genes that regulate the cell cycle. In 2001, he shared the Nobel Prize with British scientists Tim Hunt and Paul Nurse. All three scientists devoted their careers to understanding how cells divide and how to stop the growth of genetically damaged cells. Because of their work, drug companies began to determine ways to kill cancer cells by finding ways to force the cells to stop dividing. It is hoped that the work of Hartwell, Hunt, and Nurse will lead to powerful new treatments for cancer.

collect butterflies and research his specimens in the library. He was not an outstanding student in his first years of high school and belonged to a car club called the Sinbads. Then Hartwell's high school physics teacher got him interested in science by giving him difficult but fun problems to solve.

Hartwell's first real awareness that he loved science came during his years as a college undergraduate at the California Institute of Technology (Cal Tech) in Pasadena, California. He participated in laboratory research and was intrigued by it. "I discovered a whole fabulous world of science that I really didn't even know existed," Hartwell said in the February 1999 *American Society of Cell Biology Newsletter.* Hartwell started out studying physics at Cal Tech, but changed his focus to biology after taking a class about DNA (deoxyribonucleic acid, the carrier of genetic information). He graduated in 1961 with a bachelor's degree in science.

Gaining experience

After college, Hartwell was admitted to the doctoral program at the Massachusetts Institute of Technology (MIT) in Cambridge, Massachusetts. In 1964, he earned his Ph.D. in biology from MIT. Hartwell then continued his studies for a year at the Salk Institute for Biological Studies in La Jolla, California. He studied cell division in mammals with scientist Renato Dulbecco (1914–), who won the 1975 Nobel Prize in physiology or medicine for his discoveries concerning the interaction between tumor viruses and the genetic material of the cell. Hartwell's research focused on how viruses that cause cancer interact with the host cell, or the cell that supports the growth and development of the cancer that has infected it.

In 1965, Hartwell was hired as an assistant professor at the University of California at Irvine, where he stayed for

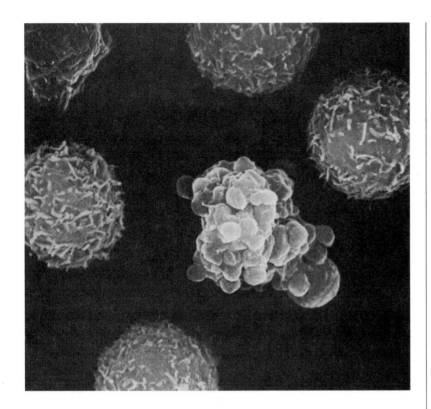

This image shows the death of a cell, which was studied by Leland Hartwell in his work with the cell cycle.
Reproduced by permission of Phototake.

three years. While at Irvine, Hartwell set out to find an organism that would be simpler to experiment on than animal or human cells yet still have the structural complexity of a human cell. He hoped that his findings on the simpler organism would significantly impact our understanding of higher organisms, from animals to humans. He chose yeast, a single-celled fungus that divides quickly, in his cell division research. Yeast cells reproduce by cell division, in which the nucleus, or center, of a cell, which contains DNA that is passed on from generation to generation, splits to produce two identical cells. As a young scientist, this was a risky choice, because most scientists did not see yeast as a good model for human cells.

In 1968, Hartwell moved to Seattle, Washington, where he became an associate professor at the University of Washington, a school known for its genetic research program. Hartwell believed it was the best place for him to focus his research efforts and was still a member of that faculty in 2002.

All the pieces of a puzzle

In the early 1970s, at Washington, Hartwell began a series of experiments intended to look at what happens during the life cycle of a cell. He worked with cells from the yeast *Saccharomyces cerevisiae,* the same yeast that makes it possible for bread dough to rise. Through his experiments, Hartwell discovered the genes responsible for cell division. These genes are called cell division cycle (CDC) genes and Hartwell identified more than twenty of them.

Among the CDC genes Hartwell studied was CDC28, a gene that, he discovered, controls the point at which a cell makes a duplicate copy of its DNA before dividing, called replication. Replication is the first part of the cell division process and Hartwell termed this stage START. He also theorized that the cell division cycle of yeast was related to the cell division cycle of humans.

A few years after Hartwell's initial experiments, British biologist Paul Nurse (1949–), the director-general of the Imperial Cancer Research Fund's Cell Cycle Laboratory, used a yeast called *Schizosaccharomyces pombe* and some of Hartwell's techniques, from papers Hartwell had published, in his own study of the genetics of cell division. Nurse successfully identified a cell division gene called CDC2, which controls the beginning and ending of mitosis, the process by which the nucleus of a cell divides into nuclei that have the same number of chromosomes. A chromosome consists of the body's genetic material DNA, along with a small amount of protein. The preservation of chromosome number is accomplished through the replication of the entire set of chromosomes just prior to mitosis. In 1987, Nurse also discovered in his research that the START gene acts the same in a human cell—it begins the cell division process—as when it is put into a yeast cell, proving Hartwell's theories about yeast cells.

The more Hartwell and Nurse learned about CDC genes, the more it seemed clear that there was an important link between CDC2 and CDC28. Both of these genes had a specific protein, or a very large molecule consisting of long chains of smaller units known as amino acids, in common.

They theorized that this protein controlled both mitosis and replication. How could one gene control different parts of the cell cycle? It would take a third scientist to help pull the different pieces together and solve the puzzle.

In the early 1980s, another British biologist with the Imperial Cancer Research Fund, Timothy Hunt (1943–), discovered proteins that are both formed and broken down during each cell cycle. He named them "cyclins" because their concentrations rise and fall throughout the cell cycle. The cyclins were found to interact with CDC2 and CDC28 to regulate both replication and mitosis.

Cell division cycles and cancer

Interested in finding out what impact his cell division research could have on cancer research, in 1984, Hartwell performed research for a year at the Fred Hutchinson Cancer

Paul Nurse, left, and Tim Hunt, after learning of their Nobel Prize for medicine in 2001, which they shared with Leland Hartwell for their studies of cell cycles.

Photograph by Alastair Grant. Reproduced by permission of AP/Wide World Photos.

Research Center in Seattle. At about this same time, experiments being done in Hartwell's lab at the University of Washington began to show that certain genes, which Hartwell called "checkpoints," determined whether the cell division process was progressing normally. If the checkpoint genes identified abnormalities in a cell, they halted the process of cell division long enough to repair the problem.

But when an abnormality occurs in the checkpoint genes themselves, these genes may lose the ability to halt the process and the cell continues dividing, allowing the unstable genetic material, such as cancer cells, to reproduce. Thus a defective checkpoint can lead to the spread of human cancer. Hartwell's description of checkpoint genes has led other scientists to explore how checkpoints might be used to develop treatments and therapies for cancer by finding ways to force the cells to stop dividing.

In 1996, the Fred Hutchinson Cancer Research Center hired Hartwell to become its senior scientific advisor. The following year he was made its president and director and continued his research on how to stop the growth of genetically damaged cells. Hartwell hopes his work will help to find a way of preventing cancer, or at least diagnosing it at much earlier stages.

The Nobel Prize

Hartwell has received several awards for his work, including the Albert Lasker Basic Medical Research Award in 1998, the American Cancer Society Medal of Honor Basic Research Award in 1999, and the Leopold Griffuel Prize in 2000. For their work in understanding the cell division cycle, Hartwell, Nurse, and Hunt were awarded medical science's highest honor on October 8, 2001, the Nobel Prize in physiology or medicine.

Further Reading

Batistick, Mike. "Hartwell, Leland H." *Current Biography,* November 1999.

Foster, Alecia. "Nobel Prize Winner Remembers School Days." *Glendale News-Press,* October 26, 2001.

Frankish, Helen. "Nobel Prize Awarded to US and UK Cancer Researchers." *Lancet,* October 13, 2001, p. 1243.

Fred Hutchinson Cancer Research Center. http://www.fhcrc.org/ (accessed on September 3, 2002).

"Lee Hartwell." *Lancet,* October 28, 2000, p. 1534.

Paulson, Tom. "It's Now Dr. Hartwell, Nobel Laureate." *Seattle Post-Intelligencer,* October 9, 2001.

Werner Heisenberg

December 5, 1901
Würzburg, Germany
February 1, 1976
Munich, Germany

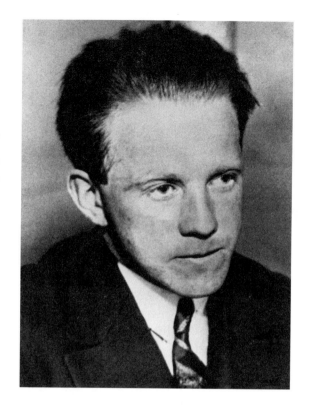

erner Heisenberg was a German physicist who was best known for his refinement of quantum mechanics and the development of the uncertainty principle. In 1932, he was awarded the Nobel Prize in physics for his work in quantum mechanics and his contribution to atomic theory. During World War II (1939–45), Heisenberg headed the German effort to build an atomic bomb. There has been much speculation and controversy regarding whether Heisenberg was helping or hindering the Nazi effort to build a bomb. Despite this controversy, Heisenberg is globally recognized for his scientific contributions.

"The interaction between observer and object causes uncontrollable and large changes in the system being observed."

Son of a professor

Werner Karl Heisenberg was born on December 5, 1901, in Würzburg, Germany, to Annie Wecklein Heisenberg and August Heisenberg. August taught Greek language and litera-

German physicist Werner Heisenberg won the 1932 Nobel Prize in physics for his contributions to quantum mechanics and atomic theory. He developed the uncertainty principle, which became a fundamental law of nature. Heisenberg came under public scrutiny after World War II for his role in helping the German Nazi Party develop an atomic bomb. Although his morality has been questioned, it remains a mystery whether he was following orders and developing the bomb for Germany or purposely stalling their progress. Regardless, his scientific contributions have been recognized around the globe.

ture at the University of Würzburg, and when Karl was nine years old, his father was hired as a professor at the University of Munich. The family moved to Munich and Heisenberg attended the Maximilian Gymnasium, a school where his maternal grandfather was the headmaster.

In 1918, World War I (1914–18) interrupted Heisenberg's education. He was sent to work on a farm in Bavaria to help harvest crops. After the war ended, Heisenberg returned to Munich, where he became involved in a youth movement called the Bund Deutscher Neupfadfinder, or New Boy Scouts. This group believed that German society had deteriorated during World War I and needed to be rebuilt through direct experience of nature, music, and thought.

In 1920, Heisenberg finished his studies at the Maximilian Gymnasium and enrolled at the University of Munich. He had shown a talent for mathematics at an early age and originally chose that as his focus. Over time, however, he switched his major to physics, and studied with Arnold Sommerfeld (1868–1951), a well-known German physicist at the university.

Becoming a physicist

Heisenberg's connection with Sommerfeld not only introduced him to the world of physics, it also led him to study with a group of scientists who were leaders in their field. Among them were Italian-born American physicist **Enrico Fermi** (1901–1954; see entry in volume 1), British physicist Max Born (1882–1970), and Danish physicist **Niels Bohr** (1885–1962; see entry in volume 1).

At Munich, Heisenberg began to work on unresolved problems regarding Bohr's model of the atom, which utilized the fairly new concept of quantum theory. An atom is the smallest component of an element having the chemical properties of the element. Quantum theory basically states that atoms consist of a positive nucleus surrounded by negative electrons that orbit the nucleus. The electrons are held in their orbits by electrical attraction, and the energies of those electrons occur in fixed quantities.

Quantum theory, although sophisticated, had a few flaws, including an inadequate explanation of how light is given off and absorbed by atoms. Heisenberg was intrigued by this theory and began to examine the flaws more closely, hoping to resolve them. He studied a phenomenon called the Zeeman effect, the splitting of spectral lines, which had been observed but not explained. Spectral lines are lights of a single frequency, or wavelength, which are emitted by an atom when an electron changes its energy level. Because the energy levels of the electron vary from element to element, scientists can determine the chemical composition of an object from a distance by examining its spectrum. Heisenberg published a series of papers on the Zeeman effect, two of which were written with Sommerfeld, that were well respected by physicists.

After Sommerfeld took a position at the University of Wisconsin in 1922, Heisenberg transferred to the University of Göttingen, where he studied with Max Born. Heisenberg returned to Munich the following year to complete his doctorate, then returned to Göttingen to teach classes and work with Born. Meanwhile, Niels Bohr, who led the Institute for Theoretical Physics at the University of Copenhagen, in Denmark, was also interested in Heisenberg's research with atomic theory. In 1924, Heisenberg received a Rockefeller Grant that enabled him to work with Bohr at the University of Copenhagen. In Copenhagen, Heisenberg immersed himself in the most recent studies of atomic theory, most of which had been developed by German physicist and Nobel Prize-laureate **Max Planck** (1858–1947; see entry in volume 3), Bohr, and Sommerfeld.

Matrix mechanics

Prior to the development of quantum theory, scientists approached the study of natural phenomena through the methodology developed by British physicist and mathematician **Isaac Newton** (1642–1727; see entry in volume 4). Newton believed that the physical conditions of the universe could be explained with precise descriptions on a macroscopic level that would not only detail current conditions but also predict future ones. The term macroscopic refers to properties that can be observed with the five human senses, aided or unaided. But the methods used by Newton, which held true for events at the macroscopic level, were essentially worthless when dealing with submicroscopic phenomena. Submicroscopic phenomena, which includes something as small as the movement of an electron in an atom, involves objects and events that are too small to be seen even with the very best microscopes. As a result, physicists essentially had to start over in thinking about the ways they studied nature. Heisenberg soon developed a method to deal with the problems of the submicroscopic world.

In June 1925, Heisenberg devised a new approach to the problem of the Zeeman effect in particular and of atomic theory in general. Physicists had devoted too much effort, he said, to devising pictorial models that might have some physical reality. A better approach, he suggested, would be to work strictly with experimental data and to determine the mathematical implications of that data. In order to pursue this approach, Heisenberg devised a system that came to be known as matrix mechanics. Although, as he later learned, the mathematics of this technique was already familiar to professional mathematicians, its application to the problems of atomic physics was entirely new.

With the help of Born and Born's assistant, Pascual Jordan, Heisenberg, only twenty-three years old, published a scientific paper in November 1925 detailing his idea of matrix mechanics. Although some physicists were uncomfortable with the idea of not having a physical model to relate to, Heisenberg's work brought him widespread recognition in the scientific world and launched a new era of atomic physics. Six

months after the paper was published, Heisenberg left Göttingen to become Bohr's assistant at Copenhagen and a lecturer in theoretical physics.

The uncertainty principle

In February 1927, Heisenberg was studying the properties of an electron in its orbit around the nucleus. It occurred to

Werner Heisenberg, center right, talks with other scientists at the Second United Nations International Atomic Energy Conference.

Reproduced by permission of Corbis Corporation.

him that the very act of measuring an electron's properties by shining gamma rays (short electromagnetic wavelengths that come from the nuclei of atoms during radioactive decay) on it would disturb the electron in its orbit; the act of observing the electron, therefore, altered its behavior, and objectivity was lost. Out of this realization, he developed a fundamental principle of physics called the uncertainty principle. According to the uncertainty principle, one can measure the position of a particle or its momentum with as much precision as desired. However, the more precise one of these measurements becomes, the less precise the other will be. Heisenberg wrote in *The Physical Principles of the Quantum Theory,* that "the interaction between observer and object causes uncontrollable and large changes in the system being observed" thus leading to errors and uncertainty. The principle was quickly and widely accepted by most, though not all, physicists, who soon acknowledged the concept as a fundamental law of nature.

In October 1927, Heisenberg was appointed full professor of theoretical physics at the University of Leipzig, in Leipzig, Germany, at the young age of twenty-five. After the neutron was discovered in 1932, Heisenberg proposed a model of the nucleus that consisted of protons and neutrons rather than protons and electrons, as favored by some physicists. Heisenberg's scientific research decreased however and he spent much of his time teaching and managing administrative responsibilities that came with his position In Leipzig. In 1932, Heisenberg was awarded the Nobel Prize in physics for his refined theory of quantum mechanics and his contributions to atomic theory.

War and marriage

Adolf Hitler, the chancellor of Germany since 1933, declared himself that nation's supreme ruler in 1934 when German President Paul von Hindenburg died. Hitler led the Nazi Party in Germany, which believed in a powerful government that had complete control over society and the economy. The Nazis also believed themselves to be a superior race and persecuted minorities, especially the Jewish people. At first, Heisenberg and his colleagues resisted Hitler's efforts to "purify" and nationalize German science, but the forces they faced were too great. Heisenberg's position was especially tenuous since the Nazis regarded theoretical physics (as opposed to experimental physics) as a suspect, "Jewish" science. In 1935, an invitation from Munich for Heisenberg to succeed his former teacher Sommerfeld was met with violent opposition from German political leaders and professional colleagues. Any hope that Heisenberg may have had of accepting the Munich offer was dashed and, for a time, even his personal safety was at risk.

At the beginning of World War II (1939–45), the Nazi government recognized Heisenberg's value and made him director of the German atomic bomb project. For the next five and a half years, all of his efforts were devoted to this project. Questions have since been raised as to the morality of Heisenberg's decision. To this day, it is unclear whether he was actually helping the Nazis or if he was purposely trying to figure out a way to stall their research, as a few historians have suggested.

When the war came to an end in 1945, Heisenberg and his bomb research team were captured in a remote region of southern Germany, where they had been sent to be safe from Allied bomb attacks. After a six-month imprisonment in England, Heisenberg was allowed to return to Göttingen, where he re-established the Kaiser Wilhelm Institute for Physics and renamed it the Max Planck Institute in honor of his colleague and friend, the originator of quantum theory. In the postwar years, Heisenberg became particularly interested in the search for a unified field theory, which would link all physical fields, such as gravitation and electromagnetism. He continued with his research until retiring in 1970. In 1971, he published his autobiography, *Physics and Beyond*. Werner Heisenberg died on February 1, 1976, in Munich and was survived by his wife, Elisabeth, whom he had married in 1937. He also left seven children, four daughters and three sons.

Further Reading

Austin, D. Brian. *Great Thinkers of the Western World*. New York: HarperCollins, 1992, pp. 530–6.

Bernstein, Jeremy. "What Did Heisenberg Tell Bohr About the Bomb?" *Scientific American,* May 1995, p. 92.

Collins, Graham P. "Atomic Dead Letter." *Scientific American,* June 2000, p. 34.

Hayden, Thomas. "A Human Uncertainty Principle." *U.S. News & World Report,* February 18, 2002, p. 64.

Heisenberg, Werner. *Physics and Beyond.* New York: Harper & Row, 1971.

"Werner Heisenberg." *American Institute of Physics.* http://www.aip.org/history/heisenberg/p01.htm (accessed June 18, 2002).

"Werner Karl Heisenberg—Biography." *Nobel e-Museum.* http://www.nobel.se/physics/laureates/1932/heisenberg-bio.html (accessed on September 3, 2002).

Thor Heyerdahl

October 6, 1914
Larvik, Norway
April 18, 2002
near Colla Michari, Italy

update

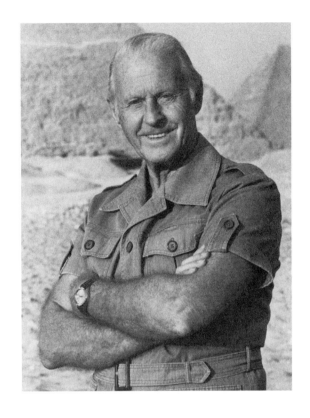

Norwegian explorer and anthropologist Thor Heyerdahl stunned the world when he embarked on a daring adventure across the Pacific Ocean in 1947. Setting sail on a raft made of balsa wood called the *Kon-Tiki,* he traveled 4,300 miles (6,919 kilometers) from Peru to the Polynesian island chain of Tuamotu to prove that South Americans may have made such a migration thousands of years before. Heyerdahl's *Kon-Tiki* trip, as well as his other expeditions, opened up the possibility that prehistoric travel by sea allowed early cultures to interact more than previously thought. **(See original entry on Heyerdahl in *Scientists,* volume 2.)**

The adventure begins

Thor Heyerdahl was born on October 6, 1914, in Larvik, Norway. His father owned a brewery while his mother was a museum director. Heyerdahl studied biology, geography, and

"We seem to believe the ocean is endless, but we use it like a sewer."

Portrait reproduced by permission of Reuters NewMedia Inc./Corbis Corporation.

141

Norwegian explorer Thor Heyerdahl challenged established theories of anthropology by conducting several ocean voyages to show that it was possible for certain ancient peoples, such as the pre-Incas and Mesopotamians, to have traveled by boat, reaching far-off destinations that influenced their cultures. The scientific community did not embrace his work, but his adventures were the material of best-selling books that delighted the world.

zoology at the University of Oslo, but left college in 1936 to travel to Fatu Hiva, in the French Polynesian Marquesas islands, with his new bride, Liv Coucheron Torp Heyerdahl. (They later divorced and Heyerdahl married his second wife, Yvonne Dedekam-Simonsen Heyerdahl, whom he also later divorced.)

Heyerdahl and his wife lived on Fatu Hiva for a year, immersing themselves in the culture, language, flora, fauna, and myths of the island. Heyerdahl was particularly intrigued by the island's legend of the sun god Tiki, which was very similar to a prehistoric South American myth about a figure named Kon-Tiki. He wondered if there were a relationship between the two figures that might link these geographically separated cultures.

Heyerdahl was also curious about the currents and winds that affected Fatu Hiva. He had noticed that they moved from east to west, from South America toward Polynesia. This puzzled him because the accepted theory of Polynesian migration was that Asian people had drifted eastward over the water to reach Polynesia. Heyerdahl began to develop a theory of his own that explored the possibility that the ancient people of South America had built wooden boats and traveled from the Pacific to Polynesia, and therefore had an impact on Polynesian culture.

Gathering evidence for his theory

During the 1930s and 1940s, Heyerdahl studied ancient civilizations in North America, South America, and Polynesia. He found carvings and statues that were similar in form on both sides of the Pacific Ocean. He explored the Kon-Tiki legend and compared it to other Polynesian myths. Although he found striking similarities, the anthropological community held that the first Polynesian settlers had traveled from the west. They were not to be swayed by an adventurer without the proper credentials.

Heyerdahl decided to plan an expedition to prove that it was possible for Peruvians to have settled in Polynesia. He built a replica of a pre-Inca vessel out of native Peruvian balsa logs and reeds and, in April 1947, he and five others set sail. The trip took 101 days as the crew traveled over 4,300 miles (6,919 kilometers) across the Pacific on the 40-square-foot (4-square-meters) raft equipped with a sail. Finally, they crashed onto a coral reef off the Polynesian island chain of Tuamotu.

After news of his journey became known, Heyerdahl became a celebrity and hero. He published a book about the expedition, *Kon-Tiki: Across the Pacific by Raft,* that became an international bestseller. It was translated into sixty-five languages and a documentary film based on his trip won an Academy Award. His voyage, however, did not win over the scientific community, which questioned, if Heyerdahl's theory were correct, why the travelers had not settled in the Galapagos Islands instead, since they would have arrived there sooner.

The Galapagos and beyond

Heyerdahl's next target, not surprisingly, became the Galapagos Islands. He traveled there in 1953 with two archaeologists to begin an in-depth study of fossils and other remains. The team found evidence, in the form of pottery shards and other artifacts, which did support the notion that South Americans had traveled to the Galapagos on several occasions but probably did not find adequate water supplies needed for settlement.

In 1955 and 1956, Heyerdahl concentrated on the mysteries that surround Easter Island and the island's statues carved by unknown artists. Easter Island is located 2,300 miles (3,701 kilometers) west of Chile and is the closest Polynesian island to South America. Heyerdahl traveled there with five archaeologists and determined, with carbon-dating techniques, that humans had visited Easter Island about one thousand years earlier than experts had thought. (Carbon-dating, or radiocarbon dating, is the process by which scientists measure the decay of the natural radioactive isotope carbon 14, which almost all organisms ingest while they are alive, to estimate how long it has been since an animal or plant died.)

Over the next decade, Heyerdahl lectured, wrote articles, and conducted research to support his theories. Although he did convince some scientists, most did not believe that his research was accurate. But Heyerdahl continued his work and turned his attention to the possible path of migration from Egypt to Peru. Although anthropologists had long noted cultural similarities, they did not believe that it would have been possible for such a migration to exist because the ancient Egyptians did not have the materials needed to make boats that would survive a trip across the Atlantic.

Heyerdahl sets sail again

Heyerdahl decided to once again prove the skeptics wrong. Again, he built a replica of a vessel, this time using materials that would have been available in Egypt at the time. His 50-foot (15-meter) long raft of papyrus, a tall, grasslike water plant, set sail from Morocco in May 1969 headed for the Caribbean. He named it the *Ra,* after the Egyptian sun god and the Polynesian word for sun. Heyerdahl and his six-member crew traveled a distance of 2,700 miles (4,344 kilometers) across the Atlantic, over eight weeks, but they had to abandon ship 600 miles (965 kilometers) from Barbados because of heavy seas.

Ten months later, Heyerdahl tried again with a boat that was lighter, shorter, and stronger. The *Ra II* reached Barbados in 57 days, after traveling 3,200 miles (5,149 kilometers). Heyerdahl had proven with this successful journey that it was possible that ancient Egyptian civilizations had crossed the oceans in search of new lands.

Heyerdahl continued with this pursuit in 1977, theorizing that ancient Mesopotamians (ancient peoples who lived in the region between the Tigris and Euphrates rivers—modern-day Turkey and Iraq—and founded the first known urban civilization) may have traveled as far as India. He sailed a 60-foot (18-meter) reed boat across the Indian Ocean to prove his point. Heyerdahl also conducted archeological research on the Maldives islands in the Indian Ocean and suggested that they were a frequent stopover for prehistoric traders traveling between China, India, and Africa. And in the late 1980s, he organized a large project to study twenty-six pre-Incan pyramids in Peru.

An explorer's life

Heyerdahl did not slow down as he approached older age. In 1995, at eighty-one, he stirred up the scientific waters again when he announced that he had evidence that Christopher Columbus had reached America in 1477 instead of the widely accepted date of 1492. In 1999, he proposed a theory that Norwegian explorer Leif Eriksson had sailed to North America a thousand years earlier than was believed.

In 1996, Heyerdahl had published a book called *Green Was the Earth on the Seventh Day*, in which he discusses the journeys he took during his life. That same year, he married his third wife, Jacqueline Beer Heyerdahl. In March 2002, Heyerdahl was vacationing in Italy when he became ill. Diagnosed with a terminal form of brain cancer, he died in Italy, on April 18, 2002.

Heyerdahl had the spirit of an explorer his entire life. Within his last few months, he traveled to Samoa, Cuba, and Norway. He even organized an excavation in Russia designed to uncover evidence that Odin, a mythological Norwegian god, was actually a real king. He was in the process of writing a book on that subject during the last months of his life.

Further Reading

Heyerdahl, Thor. *Aku-Aku: The Secret of Easter Island.* Chicago, IL: Rand McNally, 1958. Reprint, New York: Ballantine Books, 1974.

Heyerdahl, Thor. *Green Was the Earth on the Seventh Day.* New York: Random House, 1996.

Heyerdahl, Thor. *Kon-Tiki: Across the Pacific by Raft.* Chicago, IL: Rand McNally, 1950.

McWilliam, Fiona. "Sailing into the Past." *Geographical Magazine,* September 1995, p. 32.

Westman, Paul. *Thor Heyerdahl: Across the Seas of Time.* Minneapolis, MN: Dillon Press, 1982.

Wilford, John Noble. "Thor Heyerdahl Dies at 87; His Voyage on Kon-Tiki Argued for Ancient Mariners." *New York Times,* April 19, 2002.

George H. Hitchings

April 18, 1905
Hoquiam, Washington
February 27, 1998
Chapel Hill, North Carolina

Gertrude Belle Elion

January 23, 1918
New York, New York
February 21, 1999
Chapel Hill, North Carolina

update

George Hitchings and Gertrude Elion were American biochemists who contributed dramatically to the field of drug research. By employing an innovative technique termed "rational" drug design, they succeeded in producing a vast array of drugs useful in treating such illnesses as childhood leukemia, gout, malaria, herpes, and AIDS. Their work also enabled transplant patients to better accept donor organs without their bodies rejecting the organs. Hitchings and Elion received the 1988 Nobel Prize in physiology or medicine in honor of their achievements. **(See original entry on Hitchings and Elion in *Scientists*, volume 2.)**

The path to partnership

George Herbert Hitchings, Jr., was born on April 18, 1905, in Hoquiam, Washington, to George Herbert Hitchings, Sr., and Lillian H. Belle Hitchings. His father's early death

> *"I am incredibly blessed to have been involved for well over four decades in a field that continues to become more exciting with every passing year."*
>
> —*George H. Hitchings*

ertrude Bell Elion and George H. Hitchings were an enormously successful scientific team that produced a wide variety of drugs to treat infections and diseases. Their first major achievement was the development of a drug to treat childhood leukemia called 6-mercaptopurine (6MP). Their studies of 6MP led to the discovery of azathioprine, which prevents rejection of transplanted organs and helps treat severe rheumatoid arthritis. Hitchings and Elion received the 1988 Nobel Prize for their scientific contributions.

when George Jr. was only twelve and his admiration for the work of the renowned French chemist **Louis Pasteur** (1822–1895; see entry in volume 3) sparked his interest in medicine. Hitchings went to the University of Washington in Seattle for both his bachelor's and his master's degrees, finishing both by 1928. He was then accepted as a doctoral student at Harvard University, earning his doctorate in 1933. For his doctorate, he focused on the chemical change of nucleic acids, the chemicals that make up deoxyribonucleic acid (DNA), the carrier of genetic information. In 1942 he took a position with pharmaceutical company Burroughs Wellcome, now known as Glaxo Wellcome. In 1967, he was named vice president of research.

Gertrude Belle Elion was born on January 23, 1918, in New York City, to Robert Elion and Bertha Cohen. Like Hitchings, she also was interested in medicine from a young age and vowed to help fight cancer after watching her grandfather suffer from the disease. She attended Hunter College, in New York City, on an academic scholarship and studied chemistry.

Elion earned her bachelor's degree at the young age of nineteen. In 1941, she received her master's degree in chemistry from New York University. As a woman in the 1940s, Elion had trouble finding work in her field. She had a variety of jobs, including one as a chemist for a food company, but did not find any of them challenging. When World War II (1939–45) began and so many men became soldiers and went overseas, jobs for women became more plentiful. Elion was hired to work in Hitchings's lab at Burroughs Wellcome in June 1944. She was very successful in the company, being promoted to Hitchings's previous positions as he reached higher ones.

Developing rational drug design

Prior to the work that Hitchings and Elion did together at Burroughs, researchers who created new drugs did so by modifying natural products. But Hitchings and Elion had an innovative, unique approach. They identified the agents of various diseases, whether they were cancer cells, bacteria, viruses, or other carriers, and studied the differences between the metabolism (the highly integrated network of chemical reactions by which living cells grow and sustain themselves) of the disease-causing cells and normal body cells. They focused on how nucleic acids are used by disease-causing cells in order to thrive and grow. In this way, Hitchings and Elion reasoned, they could determine how to wipe out the diseased tissue without harming healthy tissue. This method was later termed "rational" drug design.

Hitchings and Elion looked at the chemical pathways by which nucleic acids combine, or are synthesized, with other substances. Two types of nucleic acids that interfere with DNA synthesis are purines and pyrimidines. With chemical synthesis, they produced compounds similar to purines and pyrimidines in the laboratory. (Chemical synthesis is the process of building up a desired compound from simpler and readily available components.) These compounds are effective at killing diseased cells, such as cancer cells, as they try to divide. This effect provides the basis for the cancer treatment known as chemotherapy.

Hitchings's and Elion's first major success using this approach came in 1951 when they developed 6-mercaptopurine (6MP), similar to purine. Working in collaboration with scientists at Sloan-Kettering Institute in New York City, they perfected the drug for use in treating childhood leukemia, a disease that attacks the white blood cells. It is still used in the early twenty-first century, along with thioguanine, another compound effective against leukemia that the two scientists also produced together.

Their approach has a major impact

For the next several decades, Hitchings and Elion worked together to produce an impressive list of drugs to fight disease.

They made a derivative of 6MP, called azathioprine, which blocks the body's rejection of foreign tissues. Azathioprine, in combination with other drugs, helps transplant patients avoid rejecting donor organs and is useful in treating severe cases of rheumatoid arthritis. Hitchings and Elion also produced allopurinol, which treats gout; an antiviral drug called acyclovir to treat infections from the herpes virus; and pyrimethamine to fight malaria. The drug trimethoprim that they created is used for bacterial infections, including a form of pneumonia, which is the leading cause of death for people with acquired immunodeficiency syndrome (AIDS).

Rational drug design had a major impact on the pharmaceutical field as well, giving other scientists effective methods and tools for their own research. For example, researchers who had been trained by Elion and Hitchings developed azidothymidine (AZT) in 1984, which was the first drug successful in treating AIDS. Four years later, Hitchings and Elion shared the Nobel Prize in physiology or medicine with British chemist James W. Black for their body of work.

Maintaining active lives

Throughout his life, Hitchings was devoted to charitable causes. From 1974 to 1990, he served as president of the Burroughs Wellcome Fund, a charitable organization dedicated to supporting research in the biomedical sciences. The fund also supports research museums and libraries related to this field. Also, Hitchings donated his Nobel Prize award money to the Triangle Community Foundation, which he founded in 1983. This foundation assists battered women, as well as funds health care and camp fees for people who cannot afford them.

Hitchings died on February 27, 1998. He left behind his second wife, Joyce Shaver Hitchings, whom he married just months before receiving the Nobel Prize. (He was married to his first wife, Beverly Reimer Hitchings, for fifty-two years before she passed away in 1985.)

Elion retired from Burroughs in 1983, and later took a part-time teaching position at Duke University in Durham,

North Carolina. She also served as president of the American Association for Cancer Research and was a member of the National Cancer Advisory Board. In 1991, Elion was awarded the National Medal of Science and became the first woman inducted into the National Inventors Hall of Fame. She also held a spot in the National Women's Hall of Fame. Elion died in Chapel Hill, North Carolina, on February 21, 1999. Several months after her death the documentary film *Me & Isaac Newton,* in which great scientists—including Elion—talk about what inspires them, was released. The film was dedicated to Elion.

Further Reading

Altman, Lawrence K. "Gertrude Elion, Drug Developer, Dies at 81." *New York Times,* February 23, 1999.

Bertsch, Sharon McGrayne. *Nobel Prize Women in Science: Their Lives, Struggles, and Momentous Discoveries.* Secaucus, NJ: Carol Publishing Group, 1993.

Cockrell, Eddie. "Film Reviews." *Variety,* October 18, 1999, p. 41.

Colvin, Michael. "Gertrude Belle Elion (1918–1999)." *Science,* May 28, 1999, p. 1480.

Raju, Tonse N. K. "The Nobel Chronicles." *Lancet,* March 18, 2000, p. 1022.

Ernest Lawrence

August 8, 1901
Canton, South Dakota
August 27, 1958
Palo Alto, California

Ernest Lawrence's invention of the cyclotron, a high-speed particle accelerator, launched a new era in the study of nuclear physics. With this innovation, scientists are better able to study and understand the structure of the atom. Since the cyclotron's introduction in the early 1930s, the machines have been enlarged and improved upon and are now a major tool for nuclear physicists around the world. Lawrence's achievements were recognized in 1939 when he was awarded the Nobel Prize in physics. Both during and after World War II (1939–45), Lawrence was at the forefront of research on nuclear weapons and was in favor of the United States being a major nuclear force.

"I had the remarkable good fortune of observing that this apparatus [the cyclotron] was rather more successful than we had expected."

An interest in physics

Ernest Orlando Lawrence was born on August 8, 1901, in Canton, South Dakota. His father, Carl Gustav Lawrence, was

Portrait reproduced courtesy of Library of Congress.

an educator who later became South Dakota's superintendent of public education and president of a teacher's college. His mother, Gunda Jacobson Lawrence, was also a teacher. Ernest's parents instilled a strong sense of loyalty, responsibility, and integrity in him. He was a good student, with an interest in science from an early age. He graduated from public high school at age sixteen and entered St. Olaf's College in Minnesota in 1918. The following year, he transferred to the University of South Dakota, where he began studying medicine but changed his focus to physics. He graduated with high honors in 1922.

After earning his bachelor's degree, Lawrence enrolled at the University of Minnesota graduate school and earned a master's degree in physics in 1923, studying with the physicist W. F. G. Swann. When Swann took a position at the University of Chicago, Lawrence followed him to Chicago to continue with his doctoral studies. When Swann left Chicago to go to Yale University, Lawrence followed his mentor again. In 1925, while at Yale, Lawrence completed his doctorate.

Lawrence stayed at Yale for three more years, first as a research fellow and then as an assistant professor. At Yale, he met Mary Kimberly Blumer, who was the daughter of the Yale Medical School's dean. The two were married on May 14, 1932, and later had six children. In 1928, Lawrence accepted an offer for a higher-level position at the University of California at Berkeley (UCB).

The cyclotron

Lawrence had not been at UCB long when he came up with the idea for what would become the cyclotron. One night, Lawrence came across a scientific article written in German, which he was not able to read. However, he was able to understand the diagrams and equations in the article, and determined that the author, a Norwegian engineer, was describing a device to speed up, or accelerate, parts of the atoms, of which all forms of matter and energy are composed. A particle accelerator would allow the known subatomic particles, protons and electrons, to accelerate to very high velocities. The purpose of doing this was to cause the particles to collide with atomic nuclei (center of the atoms) and blast the nuclei apart in order to learn more about the composition and structure of atoms.

Lawrence quickly saw the flaw in the design of the particle accelerator in the article. It was rectangular in shape, and would have to be extremely long to allow the particles to reach high enough speeds to be smashed. Lawrence believed he could solve this design flaw by building a circular accelerator. He made two semicircular, hollow chambers and placed them back-to-back in a vacuum chamber with a small gap in between them. (A vacuum chamber is a chamber completely empty of matter or particles.) When particles such as protons were placed in the center of the cyclotron, a magnetic field forced them to travel in a circular path. Each time a particle went by, the magnetic field pushed it again. All of these small pushes increased the speed of the particle as it spiraled toward the rim of the can. When it approached the rim, the particle was made to hit a target—a nucleus. The goal was to achieve a high-enough speed to smash apart a nucleus upon contact. Two graduate students, Niels E. Edlefsen and M. Stanley Livingston, helped Lawrence build the first cyclotron, which took two years to complete.

The first cyclotron was only 4.5 inches (11 centimeters) in diameter. Lawrence and his team were fortunate enough to convince the Federal Telegraph Company to donate a huge eighty-ton magnet that was no longer in use. With this magnet, and a bigger cyclotron chamber, Lawrence could impart a great deal of energy onto

≋IMPACT≋

American physicist Ernest Lawrence earned worldwide recognition, as well as the 1939 Nobel Prize in physics, for his invention of the cyclotron. Also known as a particle accelerator, a cyclotron forces subatomic particles, the "pieces" of an atom, such as protons and electrons, to speed up to very high velocities and to collide with the nucleus (center) of an atom, smashing the nucleus apart, which enabled scientists to learn more about the composition and structure of atoms. With the cyclotron, Lawrence could impart a great deal of energy onto particles, measured in millions of electron volts and he and his team were able to measure how much energy is needed to bind the nucleus of an atom together. Lawrence's new machine issued in a new era of nuclear physics that included the development of nuclear weapons. He is also known for fostering the idea of big-group science, in which large numbers of scientists collaborate as a team to focus on large issues

particles, measured in millions of electron volts. Lawrence realized that future cyclotrons would need to be larger in order to further increase the speed of acceleration and increase the energy produced. The next accelerator Lawrence built, in 1932, was 9.8 inches (25 centimeters) in diameter and produced particles with energies in excess of one million electron volts. Three more cyclotrons were constructed, each bigger than the one built before it. A 27-inch (68-centimeter) model was built and later expanded to 37 inches (94 centimeters) by 1937. By 1939, a 60-inch (152-centimeter) cyclotron was in operation. In 1940, a 184-inch (467-centimeter) model was approved to be built, but construction of this cyclotron was put on hold until the end of World War II.

Lawrence worked tirelessly and drew other scientists to his project, encouraging a group approach that was relatively new to physics. The UCB team grew in size to include more students and colleagues and became a major center of research for particle physics, the branch of physics concerned with the study of the constitution, properties, and interactions of elementary particles. By the end of the 1930s, other laboratories were constructing particle accelerators. There were more than fifty either being built or being used in labs around the world. In 1939, for his invention and development of the cyclotron, Lawrence was honored with the Nobel Prize in physics.

Radioactive isotopes and the bomb

In 1936, UCB created the Radiation Laboratory and appointed Lawrence its director. In 1932, Lawrence and his team were able to disintegrate a lithium nucleus. As they smashed other nuclei, they were able to measure how much energy is needed to bind the nucleus of an atom together. In other experiments they bombarded other elements to obtain radioactive isotopes of carbon, iodine, and uranium. (Isotopes are one of two or more atoms of a chemical element that have the same structure but different physical properties. Radioactivity is the property possessed by some elements or isotopes of spontaneously emitting energetic particles by disintegration of their atomic nuclei.) One of the radioactive isotopes discovered was plutonium, an element that was crucial to the development of the atomic bomb.

World War II had begun in September 1939 when German leader Adolph Hitler invaded Poland. It was known that Germany was working on an atomic bomb that would wreak mass destruction. In a hope to build and use the weapon first,

President Franklin D. Roosevelt created a U.S. atomic research program, known as the Manhattan Project, that employed some of the United States' best physicists.

During the war, the Radiation Laboratory, led by Lawrence, played an important part in developing the bomb. The bomb, scientists determined, would be powered by nuclear fission, the process in which an atomic nucleus is split, resulting in the release of huge amounts of energy. This marked an important shift in the importance of Lawrence's work. Prior to the perceived need for nuclear weapons and the scientific know-how to produce them, the work Lawrence and other scientists were doing was for the sake of research: to find out what would happen if a particle accelerator *could* split the atom. Suddenly, with a war in progress and the Germans threatening to build and unleash an atomic bomb, there was more at stake. Now the science was being put to a specific use, a use that became extremely controversial in nature. Lawrence was in favor of the United States increasing its nuclear power. Other scientists, many of whom also worked on these bomb projects during the war, were not in favor of building nuclear weapons.

The U.S. scientists ultimately won the race, creating two bombs that the U.S. military dropped on Japan, in Hiroshima and Nagasaki, to end the war in August 1945. The bombs caused widespread human devastation, killing close to a million people, some dying immediately and others taking years to die from exposure to the cancer-causing radiation from the bomb. **Robert Oppenheimer** (1904–1967; see entry in volume 2), who had been a colleague of Lawrence's and then had gone to Los Alamos, New Mexico, to direct the laboratory where the first atomic bomb was made, was certain that research related to nuclear weapons should be stopped before the world was destroyed by nuclear weapons. Lawrence disagreed, as did Congress and much of the American public at the time.

When the Soviets detonated an atomic bomb in 1949, Lawrence and others felt it was time to increase research efforts again. (Though the Unites States and the Soviet Union were allies during WWII, after the war the former allies engaged in a cold war that lasted for more than forty years in which both sides tried to prove their military might.) After receiving government approval and funding, Lawrence and Hungarian-born physicist Edward Teller (1908–) started a radiation laboratory in 1952 called the Livermore Lab devoted to research on nuclear weapons. In other parts of the country, other research laboratories similar in focus followed, such as the Brookhaven National Laboratory in Long Island, New York and the Fermi National Accelerator Laboratory in Geneva, Illinois. During the 1950s, Lawrence oversaw operations in the nuclear research laboratories he had helped to fashion. His original cyclotron had been superseded by newer and faster ones designed by other scientists, but he continued to show his inventiveness, both in nuclear physics and in applied physics. He even designed a novel type of color television picture tube. Lawrence was also busy as a government consultant on nuclear-energy issues for the Eisenhower administration. In the summer of 1958 he attended a conference in Geneva on the possibility of detecting violations of nuclear test agreements. During his stay there, he suffered a relapse from an intestinal ulcer he had. He returned to California for an operation, from which he did not survive. Lawrence died on August 27, 1958.

Lawrence was extremely well respected and was awarded numerous honorary degrees from different universities. In 1946, he was given the Medal of Merit. In 1957, a year before his death, Lawrence received the Enrico Fermi Award, the highest U.S. honor given in physics, named after Italian physicist **Enrico Fermi** (1901–1954; see entry in volume 1). He also earned the Faraday Medal, the National Academy of Sciences Comstock Prize, the Royal Society's Hughes Medal, and many others.

In 1961, a chemical element discovered at UCB was named lawrencium (Lw) in honor of Lawrence. The Radiation Laboratory where he worked is now called the Lawrence Berkeley Laboratory and the laboratory that was built in Livermore has also been renamed and is now known as the Lawrence Livermore National Laboratory.

Further Reading

Bankston, John. *Edward Teller and the Development of the Hydrogen Bomb.* Elkton, MD: Mitchell Lane, 2001.

Brown, Andrew P. "Liverpool and Berkeley: The Chadwick-Lawerence Letters." *Physics Today,* May 1996, p. 34.

Cohen, Daniel. *The Manhattan Project.* Brookfield, CT: Twenty-First Century Books, 1999.

Davis, Nuel Pharr. *Lawrence and Oppenheimer.* New York: Simon & Schuster, 1968.

"Ernest Orlando Lawrence—Biography." *Nobel e-Museum.* http://www.nobel.se/physics/laureates/1939/lawrence-bio.html (accessed on September 3, 2002).

Mary Leakey

February 6, 1913
London, England
December 9, 1996
Nairobi, Kenya

Richard Leakey

December 19, 1944
Nairobi, Kenya

update

Leakey is the best-known name in the field of paleoanthropology, or the study of mammal fossils. The husband and wife team of Louis and Mary Leakey discovered the remains of prehistoric humans at the Olduvai Gorge in Tanzania in Africa. Later, their son Richard unearthed major anthropological finds at Lake Turkana, which lies along the border of Kenya and Ethiopia. The work of this family has expanded the world's knowledge of how humans have evolved over time and what the conditions were on Earth during that evolution. **(See original entry on the Leakeys in *Scientists*, volume 2.)**

A famous collaboration

Mary Douglas Nicol was born on February 6, 1913, in London, England. Her father, Erskine (Edward) Nicol, was an artist who traveled often, and he took his daughter Mary on several occasions to see ancient ruins and monuments, such as the

"Given the chance, I'd rather be in a tent than in a house."

—Mary Leakey

Portrait of Mary Leakey reproduced by permission of AP/Wide World Photos.

161

Mary and Richard Leakey have both played major roles in revealing the complexity of the pre-history of human beings. Their combined anthropological work has expanded the world's knowledge of the stages of human evolution and the conditions under which they occurred.

cave paintings in Dordogne, France. While in France, Mary developed a love of pre-history that led her to a career in archaeology.

When Mary was twenty years old, she met a well-known archaeologist named Louis Leakey, who had seen Mary's illustrations of Egyptian stone tools in articles published about her work. Leakey asked her to help illustrate his 1934 book *Adam's Ancestors*. The two fell in love, and after he divorced his wife in 1936, Louis and Mary were married.

The Leakeys spent most of their time in Africa for the next few years, conducting various archaeological digs, or excavations. In 1939, when World War II erupted, Louis Leakey joined the British military near Nairobi, Kenya. During the war, Mary continued her work and the couple had three children: Jonathan, Richard, and Deborah, who died in infancy. Mary's digs were very productive, turning up thousands of stone tools from various periods, the bones of some extinct animals, and samples of Iron Age pottery that date back to sometime before 1000 B.C.E.

After the war ended in 1945, Louis became the director of the Coryndon Museum in Nairobi. The Leakeys continued their fieldwork and, in 1948, Mary made a discovery that brought the couple worldwide attention. She unearthed a fossilized skull and other bones that were determined to be that of an apelike creature between twenty-five and forty million years old, called *Proconsul africanus*. This was the first evidence that humans may have originated in east Africa, not Asia, as most scientists had thought. The following year, in 1949, Mary gave birth to her third son, Philip.

More archaeological finds

The Leakeys continued to dig in east Africa, especially at the site of the Olduvai Gorge. On July 17, 1959, Mary spotted some molar teeth sticking out of a small slope. After days of careful excavating with dental picks and brushes, a complete skull was unearthed. The skull was approximately 1.75 million years old, nearly twice as old as scientists had previously estimated the human species' age to be. The public attention the discovery received led to the National Geographic Society providing funding for the Leakeys' work. They remained at Olduvai year-round, making further discoveries in the early 1960s that led to their belief that humans existed in Africa as far as two million years ago.

Louis died from a heart attack in 1972 and Mary went on with her work at Olduvai throughout the 1970s and early 1980s. In 1978, she discovered a well-preserved set of footprints that seem to have been made by two adults and a child. They were located about 30 miles (48 kilometers) from Olduvai, on the Serengeti Plain in Tanzania. Amazingly, the footprints, estimated to be about 3.6 million years old, were as clear as if they had been made that day. The prints showed that these prehistoric humans walked upright. In 1982, after losing the sight in one of her eyes, Leakey cut back on her fieldwork, eventually moving to Nairobi. She died peacefully, at the age of eighty-three, on December 9, 1996. Mary Leakey was respected for being a patient and dedicated scientist. During her life, she was given many honorary degrees from colleges and received medals from the Geological Society of London, the National Geographic Society, and the Royal Swedish Academy.

Continuing the legacy

Mary and Louis's son Richard had shown an interest in his parents' work from the time he was a small boy. He worked as a safari guide as a young man instead of finishing high school. By 1963, Richard decided he needed to complete his education and finished his high school requirements in London before returning to Africa to work on an expedition with his father. Richard was confident and bold and, while attending a 1968 business meeting with his father, asked the National Geographic Society to fund a project for him. They agreed to give the twenty-three-year-old the money he needed to conduct an investigation along the shores of Lake Turkana in Kenya.

Almost immediately, Richard displayed signs that he had inherited what many people called "Leakey's luck." He uncovered an abundant amount of fossil evidence, including crude tools and humanlike remains. By 1971, his research indicated that three different kinds of early humanlike species coexisted in east Africa about two to three million years ago. Leakey quickly landed in the scientific spotlight, with some scientists bothered by his lack of academic training. His fame even disturbed his father, who had dominated the field of African anthropology. The two later made amends before Louis's death.

Richard continued to discover evidence at Turkana of several different types of humans coexisting there. In 1975, he found a skull that was about 1.5 million years old. By 1977, he was on the cover of *Time* magazine and his work was covered in *National Geographic* magazine on more than one occasion. In addition to his fieldwork, Leakey was very active as an environmentalist. He directed the National Museums of Kenya for twenty years, from 1969 to 1989. In 1989, he became the head of the Kenya Department of Wildlife Services, through which he greatly reduced the amount of poaching, or illegal hunting, that was endangering elephants and other African animals. In June 1993, Leakey lost both his legs in an airplane crash and now uses artificial limbs to walk.

Since Leakey left his Department of Wildlife post in 1994, he has been involved in the democratic movement in Kenya as well as continuing to spend time on environmental concerns. His wife, Maeve Leakey, is also following in the family's tradition, having identified new humanlike species in 1995 and 2001. Their daughter Louise studied geology and zoology, and has gone on to organize digs. It seems the Leakey legacy will continue for years to come.

Further Reading

Begley, Sharon. "Witness to the Creation." *Newsweek,* December 23, 1996, p. 74.

"Can He Save the Elephants?" *New York Times Magazine,* January 7, 1990.

Leakey, Mary. *Disclosing the Past.* New York: Doubleday, 1984.

Leakey, Richard. *One Life: an Autobiography.* Salem, NH: Salem House, 1984.

Linden, Eugene, and Andrea Dorfman. "Richard the Lionhearted." *Time,* July 19, 1993, p. 51.

Morell, Virginia. *Ancestral Passions: The Leakey Family and the Quest for Humankind's Beginnings.* New York: Simon & Schuster, 1995.

Neill, Michael, et al. "African Queen." *People,* December 23, 1996, p. 102.

Wilford, John Noble. "Mary Leakey, 83, Dies; Traced Human Dawn." *New York Times,* December 10, 1996.

Leon Lederman

July 15, 1922
New York, New York

Leon Lederman is an American physicist and educator with an impressive career that spans more than five decades. He was awarded the 1988 Nobel Prize in physics for developing a way to isolate subatomic particles called neutrinos. Through this method, which he developed with physicists Melvin Schwartz and Jack Steinberger between 1959 and 1962, a previously unknown neutrino, called a muon, was discovered. Lederman continued his research in particle physics and went on to direct Columbia University's Nevis Laboratory. From 1979 to 1989, he was the director of the Fermi National Accelerator Laboratory. Lederman retired from research and devoted himself to teaching and in 1991 became President of the American Association for the Advancement of Science. In addition to being a professor of physics, he has founded two schools dedicated to the teaching of science and mathematics.

"There are five billion people living on this planet, and at the moment of discovery, you are the only one in the world to know this new bit of information."

From chemistry to physics

Leon Max Lederman was born in New York City on July 15, 1922. Both of his parents, Morris Lederman and Minna Rosenberg, were Russian immigrants and his father operated a laundry service. Leon went to public schools while growing up and later attended the City College of New York. He majored in chemistry but became fascinated with physics during his time there. After Lederman graduated from City College in 1943, he spent three years in the U.S. Army. On September 19, 1945, he married Florence Gordon and the couple later had three children. When his service in the army was over, Lederman was accepted at Columbia University graduate school to study physics.

At Columbia's Nevis Laboratory in Irvington, New York, Lederman joined a group of physicists who were building a cyclotron, a high-energy particle accelerator. A particle accelerator forces subatomic particles—the "pieces" of an atom, such as protons and electrons—to speed up to very high velocities, collide with the nucleus (center) of an atom, and smash the nucleus apart. Through this process scientists are able to learn about the structure and composition of atoms, which make up all forms of matter.

Lederman and another physicist named John Tinlot developed ways to make the Nevis accelerator more powerful. Lederman also built a cloud chamber, a device filled with saturated clean air that allows scientists to view the curved paths of subatomic particles by the trail of water droplets they leave in their wake. With a cloud chamber, physicists can also determine the particles' momentum. In his doctoral research, Lederman used the new Columbia accelerator to measure the lifetimes of two different kinds of pions, a type of meson or fundamental particle that the machine produced in abundance. After receiving his doctorate from Columbia in 1951, he began teaching physics at that school and working at Nevis.

Muons

It is not uncommon for physicists to collaborate with other scientists at different labs, and from 1950 through 1970 Lederman conducted experiments at a number of different facilities, including the Fermi National Accelerator Laboratory in Batavia, Illinois, the CERN Laboratory in Switzerland, and the Brookhaven Laboratory in Upton, New York.

From 1959 to 1962, Lederman conducted research on neutrinos with physicists Melvin Schwartz and Jack Steinberger at Brookhaven. Neutrinos are subatomic particles without a detected mass or an electric charge. They interact very weakly with matter, making it easy for them to penetrate practically anything. Yet, neutrinos have a large amount of energy and momentum. All of these characteristics make neutrinos extremely difficult to detect.

In the experiments, Lederman, Schwartz, and Steinberger fired a beam of protons at a block of beryllium metal, producing a blast of subatomic debris, including neutrinos. A 40-foot (12-meter) -thick barrier of steel plates culled from a battleship in the process of demolition absorbed all particles but the neutrinos. After eight months of shooting protons, the scientists found that some fifty-six neutrinos had betrayed their existence in the accelerator's ten-ton particle detector, the result of two different kinds of interactions involving the weak force, a fundamental physical force responsible for particle decay processes in radioactivity. One of the particles, the electron neutrino, had been known to physicists already. But the scientists also found the elusive muon neutrino, produced only during high-energy collisions.

Their discovery of the muon neutrino provided the foundation for what became known as the standard model of the atom: that there are two kinds of neutrinos, one intimately associated with electrons and the other with muons. As another milestone, Lederman, Schwartz, and Steinberger were the first scientists to create a neutrino beam in a laboratory. Using a neutrino-beam technique quickly became the standard method of isolating neutrinos in laboratories all over the world. In 1988, Lederman shared the Nobel Prize in physics with Schwartz and Steinberger for their work together.

Leon Lederman was awarded the Nobel Prize for developing a way to isolate neutrinos, like this spherical halo of neutrinos surrounding the Milky Way galaxy.

Lederman was promoted to professor at Columbia in 1958. In 1961, he was made director of the Nevis Laboratory while continuing to teach and perform research. In 1977, Lederman's group discovered another new particle called the bottom quark. (A quark is the smallest known building block of matter.) Lederman was also active on issues that pertained to physics, participating on such committees as the Advisory Committee to the U.S. Atomic Energy Commission from 1966 to 1970. In 1965, President Lyndon B. Johnson (1908–1973) recognized Lederman's achievements with the National Medal of Science. Lederman left Nevis in 1979 to become the director of the Fermi National Accelerator Laboratory, also known as Fermilab.

The Tevatron and the SSC

Lederman ran the Fermilab from 1979 to 1989. He was a well-liked, humorous leader who could maintain a casual style while being extremely productive. At Fermilab, he oversaw the creation and utilization of the Tevatron, the highest-energy particle accelerator in the world. The Tevatron weighs 4,500 tons (4,082 metric tons) and consists of an enormous underground ring, 4 miles (over 6 kilometers) in circumference. With this accelerator, scientists can mimic the believed state of the universe just after the Big Bang, giving researchers new insights into the most fundamental particles of the universe. (In astronomy, the Big Bang theory states that the universe resulted from a cosmic explosion that occurred about thirteen billion years ago.) Scientists travel from around the world to conduct experiments using the Tevatron.

Although Lederman was often busy with responsibilities in addition to his research, such as lending his name and time to the Fermilab's Lederman Science Center, which provides science education programs for teachers, the excitement of discovery never faded for him. In a 1988 *Chicago Tribune Magazine* article, he was quoted as saying, "Most of the magic moments of discovery—the times when you get goose bumps on goose bumps—occur when you're out in an experimental shed at 4 A.M., staying awake with gallons of coffee. There are five billion people living on this planet, and at the moment of discovery, you are the only one in the world to know this new bit of information."

In the late 1970s, the High Energy Physics Advisory Panel (HEPAP), of which Lederman was a founding member, and the U.S. Department of Energy proposed an even larger, more powerful accelerator than the Tevatron called the Superconducting Super Collider (SSC). Lederman, and other scientists, were outspoken supporters of this project, and Lederman hoped that when the project was approved, it would be built at the Fermilab. In November 1988, even though the Fermilab was one of seven finalists considered to host this project, the Texas Accelerator Center near Dallas was chosen as the site.

The SSC was a controversial project, because of its $6 billion price tag as well as questions about what kind of practical applications this machine would have. Lederman remained an outspoken voice in favor of the project. He firmly believed, along with many other scientists, that the SSC was needed to further our understanding of the fundamental structure of nature. Others argued that the project was too costly to support without a clear focus of what the machine could be used for. The objectors won out, and in 1993, the U.S. House of Representatives voted to halt production of the SSC after 14 miles (23 kilometers) of the tunnel had already been completed.

A masterful teacher

In 1989, Lederman decided to devote himself full-time to teaching and accepted a position as a professor of physics at the University of Chicago, where he taught a course called Physics for Poets. That same year, he was appointed Chairman of the State of Illinois Governor's Science Advisory Committee. He then became Pritzker Professor of Science at the Illinois Institute of Technology. From 1990 to 1991, he also served as president of the American Association for the Advancement of Science.

Throughout Lederman's career he was committed to furthering education. He founded a residential public high school for gifted students called the Illinois Mathematics and Science Academy. One result of that program has been the 2001 publication of a book by fifteen of Lederman's students, *Portraits of Great American Scientists*. Lederman also created the Teachers Academy for Mathematics and Science, helping primary school teachers attain additional skills, as well as a boost of enthusiasm, to enrich their abilities to teach science and math. He was active on that board of directors, as well as on many other science and education-related boards including the Chicago Museum of Science and Industry, the Council of American Science Writers, and the Secretary of Energy Advisory Board.

In addition to winning the Nobel Prize, Lederman has received numerous other awards, including the Wolf Prize in Physics and the Elliot Cresson Medal of the Franklin Institute. In 1992, he was honored with the U.S. Department of Energy's Enrico Fermi Award, which was presented to him for a lifetime of achievement in nuclear energy by President Bill Clinton at the White House in Washington, D.C.

Further Reading

Lederman, Leon, and Dick Teresi. *The God Particle: If the Universe Is the Answer, What Is the Question?* New York: Bantum/Dell, 1994.

Lederman, Leon, ed. *Portraits of Great American Scientists.* Amherst, NY: Prometheus Books, 2001.

"Lederman Wins Fermi Award." *Bulletin of the Atomic Scientists,* September 1993, p. 7.

"Leon M. Lederman—Autobiography." *Nobel e-Museum.* http://www.nobel.se/physics/laureates/1988/lederman-autobio.html (accessed on September 3, 2002).

Spotts, Peter N. "Leon Lederman." *Christian Science Monitor,* February 25, 1997, p. 10.

Weinberg, Steven. *Dreams of a Final Theory.* New York: Vintage Books, 1994.

Stanley Prusiner

May 28, 1942
Des Moines, Iowa

American neurologist Stanley Prusiner is the discoverer of prions, a previously unknown cause of infectious disease. The prion, a shortened term for proteinaceous infectious particle, is believed to bring about certain degenerative brain diseases that eat away at tissue in the brain. Prior to Prusiner's discovery, the only known agents of infectious disease were fungi, parasites, bacteria, and viruses. Many scientists doubted his work and believed he coined the term prion in order to grab media attention, causing his discovery to be met with criticism. As time progressed, however, his theory gained wider acceptance and earned him the highest award in science, the Nobel Prize, in 1997.

An interest in medical research

Stanley Prusiner was born on May 28, 1942, in Des Moines, Iowa. World War II (1939–45) had begun and Stanley's father, Lawrence, was drafted into the U.S. Navy. The

"The amazing properties of the . . . 'slow virus' captivated my imagination and I began to think that defining the molecular structure of this elusive agent might be a wonderful project."

Portrait reproduced by permission of AP/Wide World Photos.

175

Stanley Prusiner is an American neurologist who discovered a previously unknown infectious agent he called a prion, or proteinaceous infectious particle. Prior to his work, known agents included viruses, fungi, bacteria, and parasites. All of these disease-causing organisms have genetic material that allows them to reproduce themselves, further infecting a body. A protein was not generally known to have this capability, but Prusiner theorized that the prion protein did. As Prusiner and other scientists further researched prions, more of the scientific community became convinced that he was right. Prusiner's work has been instrumental in the fight against mad cow disease and Creutzfeldt-Jakob disease and in 1997, he was awarded the Nobel Prize in physiology or medicine. Since there are similarities between the loss of brain function in prion diseases and in Alzheimer's disease, Prusiner's research may also lead to a deeper understanding about other diseases of the brain, including Alzheimer's.

family moved to Boston, Massachusetts, so Lawrence could train for naval duty. After Lawrence Prusiner shipped out, Stanley and his mother Miriam moved to Cincinnati, Ohio, to be near Stanley's maternal grandmother, Mollie Spigel.

After the war ended in 1945, Stanley's father returned home and the Prusiner family returned to Des Moines, Iowa, where Miriam gave birth to another son, Paul. In 1952, the family returned to Cincinnati, where Lawrence worked as an architect. Stanley attended Walnut Hills High School, then went on to the University of Pennsylvania, in Philadelphia.

Prusiner majored in chemistry at the University of Pennsylvania, and took architecture, philosophy, economics, and additional science courses. He also made time to be on the university's rowing team. A research project Prusiner started after his junior year led him on a new path of scientific research. He studied hypothermia, a dangerous condition that occurs when body temperature falls below 95°F (35°C), with Sidney Wolfson, a faculty member in the Department of Surgery. Their work together lasted until Prusiner graduated from college in 1964.

Because of Prusiner's strong interest in science and how much he enjoyed his research experience with Wolfson, he decided to pursue medical school at the University of Pennsylvania. During medical school, Prusiner again became involved in research projects, traveling to Stockholm, Sweden, during his fourth year. From his research experiences, Prusiner knew he was interested both in medicine and biomedical research. He received his medical degree from Penn in 1968.

Prusiner then moved to California to undertake a medical internship at the University of California at San Francisco (UCSF). While in San Francisco, he met Sandy Turk, a high school math teacher. The two were married in 1970 and they later had two daughters, Helen and Leah. The opportunity to perform biomedical research at the National Institutes of Health (NIH) moved Prusiner once again, this time to Bethesda, Maryland. He spent three years working in a laboratory and gaining valuable research experience conducting experiments, analyzing data, organizing information clearly, and writing scientific papers. Then Prusiner returned to USCF and began his residency (school training for doctors through an internship at a hospital) to study neurology (the nervous system and its disorders). It was a move that changed the course of Prusiner's scientific life.

A scientific mission

Prusiner began his residency in July 1972. Just two months later, he encountered a patient who had a profound effect on his scientific interests. The patient was suffering from a rare brain disease called Creutzfeldt-Jakob disease (CJD). At the time, scientists were not sure what caused this disease, which led to dementia and eventual death.

Immediately, Prusiner wanted to study CJD. He learned that there were a few other illnesses that affected the brain and whose origins had yet to be explained, such as bovine spongiform encephalopathy, also called mad cow disease; scrapies, which affects sheep; and kuru, a disease that affects the Fore people of New Guinea. These are all spongiform encephalopathies, or diseases that cause the brain to become riddled with sponge-like holes, and were thought to be infections caused by some type of "slow virus," which would take years and sometimes decades to incubate the host. While doing his residency, Prusiner read scientific papers and developed ideas for experiments that might lead him to the cause of these diseases.

In 1974, Prusiner was hired as an assistant professor at UCSF, where he had the opportunity to act on his ideas. He set up his own laboratory there and studied mice and hamsters that had diseased tissue transplanted into their brain. Prusiner tried for years with little success to isolate the chemical agent that was causing the degeneration of the brain tissue. He was confident that persistence would pay off and eventually it did.

The discovery of prions

The experiments Prusiner had performed over the years kept pointing him in the direction of proteins as the cause of the infections of the brain tissue. (Proteins are very large molecules consisting of long chains of smaller units known as amino acids.) By 1981, Prusiner was convinced by his data that a protein was the causative agent in these brain diseases. He termed these agents prions, short for "proteinaceous infectious particles." In April 1982, he announced this discovery in an article in the scientific journal *Science.* His paper was met with much controversy, as scientists who had been studying the same diseases were certain the cause was a nucleic acid and not some previously unknown entity. Though Prusiner was doubted and criticized by many of his colleagues, he did not waver in his certainty.

Prusiner and his research team conducted more experiments to further support his initial findings. Over the next two years, Prusiner's lab determined the specific protein that was the prion. He called it a protease resistant protein, or PrP. Their work showed that PrP exists in two forms, harmless and disease-causing, and that it exists in all animals. Furthermore, the disease-causing PrP can transform the benign, or harmless, form into a destructive form. As the infected animal or human gets sicker, more and more of the harmless prions are reshaped into infectious ones. Unlike a virus that enters a system, the prions have been in the body since birth and, therefore, the body's immune system does not attack them. Eventually, the disease-causing prions destroy parts of the brain.

Some scientists did not believe that prions could cause this kind of destruction because proteins have never been known to be able to multiply like viruses or bacteria because they lack the

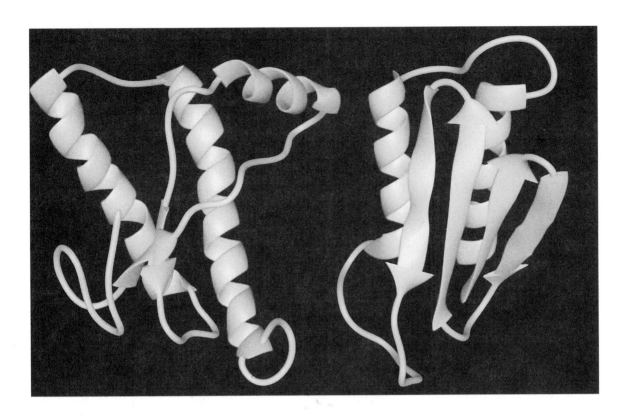

genetic material to do so. Other scientists tried to disprove Prusiner's theory altogether, but were not successful. Some scientists, especially Prusiner, believed that prions were at work in patients with Alzheimer's disease, a degenerative disease of the central nervous system, with symptoms of mental deterioration. (Although Alzheimer's is a degenerative disease, it is not infectious, making it different from the other prion diseases.) Still, Prusiner was criticized for what many saw as a lack of hard data to support his theory and a 1986 article in *Discover* magazine painted him in a very unflattering light.

But by the early 1990s, Prusiner's theories had gained acceptance from many people in the scientific community. By 1992, he had demonstrated that diseases caused by prions can be inherited, transmitted within species, or occur spontaneously. More significant, Prusiner was credited with identifying a previously unknown infectious agent. Prions joined the group of known infectious agents, bacteria, viruses, fungi, and parasites.

Widespread recognition and continued criticism

Although Prusiner's critics remained, he began to be rewarded for his scientific efforts. In 1991, the American Academy of Neurology awarded him the Potamkin Prize for Alzheimer's Disease Research. The following year he was given the Charles A. Dana Award for Pioneering Achievements in Health. Prusiner received the Gairdner Foundation Award for Outstanding Achievement in Medical Science in 1993 and the Albert Lasker Award for Basic Medical Research in 1994. Two years later, he was awarded the Wolf Prize in Medicine.

In October 1997, the scientific world was again buzzing with controversy. At the age of fifty-five, Prusiner was awarded the Nobel Prize in physiology or medicine. The award caused quite a stir as Prusiner still had many critics who believed his theory about prions was never definitively proven. Prusiner was not bothered by the controversy. In an autobiography for Nobel e-museum he wrote, "While it is quite reasonable for scientists to be skeptical of new ideas . . . the best science often emerges from situations where results carefully obtained do not fit with the accepted paradigms [standards]."

Further Reading

Altman, Lawrence K. "U.S. Scientist Wins Nobel Prize for Controversial Work." *New York Times,* October 7, 1997.

Koerner, Brendan I. "This Year's Nobel Laureates." *U.S. News & World Report,* October 20, 1997, p. 18.

Raju, Tonse N. K. "The Nobel Chronicles." *Lancet,* July 15, 2000, p. 260.

Rogers, Adam. "Science of War, War of Science." *Newsweek,* October 20, 1997, p. 51.

"Still A Lot to Learn: Nobel Prize in Medicine." *The Economist,* October 11, 1997, p. 104.

Taubes, Gary. "The Game of the Name is Fame. But is it Science?" *Discover,* December 1986, p. 28.

William Ramsay

October 2, 1852
Glasgow, Scotland
July 23, 1916
Buckinghamshire, England

William Ramsay was a Scottish chemist who became known throughout the world for the discoveries that he made with other scientists in the field of inorganic chemistry, the branch of chemistry that studies all of the elements except for carbon. He was awarded the Nobel Prize in chemistry in 1904 for his work in determining the previously unknown inert gaseous elements argon, xenon, neon, krypton, helium, and radon.

Becoming a chemist

William Ramsay was born in Glasgow, Scotland, on October 2, 1852, to Catherine and William Ramsay, a civil engineer. Young William did not show any interest in science as a boy. When he entered the University of Glasgow at the young age of fourteen, he was mainly focused on studying literature, the arts, and mathematics. He gradually became

"The discoveries which have gained for me the supreme honour of the Nobel Prize for chemistry appear to me to have been the result of causes only partially within my control."

Scottish chemist William Ramsay received the Nobel Prize in chemistry in 1904 for his work discovering the previously unknown inert gaseous elements argon, radon, xenon, neon, helium, and krypton. He was a talented chemist who spent most of his career collaborating with his colleagues. He worked with John William Strutt (1842–1919, also known as Lord Rayleigh) to discover argon and later collaborated with Maurice Travers to discover xenon, neon, and krypton.

interested in science, however, and began to attend scientific lectures.

After finishing his undergraduate work in 1869, Ramsay went to work as an apprentice (a person working without pay in return for instruction in a craft or trade) for a local chemist named Robert Tatlock. In 1871, Ramsay traveled to Germany to begin a doctoral program in chemistry at the University of Tübingen, working with a well-known chemist named Rudolf Fittig. Ramsay's thesis project was on a white crystalline substance called orthotoluic acid and completed his doctorate at the age of nineteen.

Ramsay returned to Scotland in 1872 and was hired as a research assistant in chemistry at Anderson College, later called the Royal Technical College, in Glasgow. His research was in organic chemistry, the study of the compounds of carbon, natural or synthesized (man-made). (All living organisms are composed of carbon.) Two years later, Ramsay began similar work in the chemistry department at the University of Glasgow. He worked there until 1880 when he secured a job as a professor in chemistry at Bristol University in Bristol, England. The following year Ramsay married Margaret Stevenson Buchanan and the couple later had two children, one son and one daughter.

The discovery of argon

Ramsay stayed at Bristol for seven years, at which point he took a position as professor of chemistry at University College in London in 1887. A few years later, he started working in the field of inorganic chemistry. He began collaborating with another chemist and physicist, John William Strutt (1842–1919; also known as Lord Rayleigh), to prove that a previously unknown gas existed in the atmosphere. Although Ramsay and Rayleigh were at two different universities, they jointly set out to determine why nitrogen extracted from the air, called atmospheric nitrogen, is heavier than nitrogen that is a by-product of certain chemical reactions, known as chemically pure nitrogen.

While experimenting in August 1894, Ramsay removed all of the nitrogen and oxygen from a sample of air by burning magnesium metal, which reacts with both the nitrogen and the oxygen and dispels them. What was left was a small bubble of gas that was not destroyed in the reaction. Ramsay then asked another scientist, William Crookes, to analyze the gas for him with an instrument called a spectroscope. A spectroscope splits the light given off by an element into its component colors so that the various elements present within that object can be identified. The result of that analysis was a set of spectral lines that had never been seen before—the gas bubble was clearly a new element. Ramsay and Rayleigh named it "argon," derived from the Greek word for "lazy," because the gas was inert, or did not react with other elements to form compounds. Ramsay also realized that argon most likely belonged to an unknown family of inert gases. Inert gases, also known as rare or noble gases, are unreactive gases that form few compounds with other elements. Soon after Ramsay announced his discovery of argon, his new focus became discovering other inert gases similar to argon.

Ramsay heard about another inert gas that had been discovered by the American chemist William Hillebrand. To see if Hillebrand's gas might also be argon, Ramsay heated a sample of the mineral clevite in sulfuric acid and had the gas produced tested by spectroscopic analysis. The results of that analysis showed that the gas was not argon, but it did have the same spectral lines as those of an element discovered in the Sun in 1868 by Pierre Janssen and Joseph Lockyer, an element they had named helium. Ramsay's research showed that helium also existed on the Earth.

Over the next few years, Ramsay looked for the remaining missing inert gases in various minerals, always without success. Then in 1898 he decided on another approach. He and a colleague, Morris Travers, prepared fifteen liters of liquid

argon, which they then allowed to evaporate very slowly. Eventually they identified three more new gases, krypton, neon, and xenon, which they announced to the world on June 6, June 16, and September 8, 1898, respectively.

Awards and honors

Ramsay was extremely respectful of the scientists he worked with and was always certain to give them credit for their work. Because of his scientific discoveries, he was made a fellow of the Royal Society in 1888, was awarded the 1895 Davy Medal of the Royal Society, and was given the August Wilhelm von Hoffmann Medal of the German Chemical Society in 1903.

In 1902, Ramsay was knighted, and became known as Sir William Ramsay. Two years later, in 1904, he was awarded the Nobel Prize in chemistry for his work in discovering the inert gases argon, radon, neon, xenon, helium, and krypton. Even after he retired from his position as Chair of Inorganic Chemistry at University College in London in 1913, Ramsay continued to conduct experiments at his home. He died three years later on July 23, 1916.

Further Reading

"Chemical Achievers: William Ramsay." *Chemical Heritage Foundation.* http://www.chemheritage.org/Educational Services/chemach/ppt/wr.html (accessed on September 3, 2002).

Lindsay, Robert Bruce. *Lord Rayleigh—The Man and His Work.* Tarrytown, NY: Pergamon Press, 1970.

"Sir William Ramsay—Biography." *Nobel e-Museum.* http://www.nobel.se/chemistry/laureates/1904/ramsay-bio.html (accessed on September 3, 2002).

Sally Ride

May 26, 1951
Encino, California

S ally Ride is an American physicist whose early interest in mathematics and science evolved into a career in aeronautics. Entering the National Aeronautics and Space Administration (NASA) as an astronaut candidate in 1978, Ride trained to become an astronaut and worked as part of the ground crew for two shuttle missions before being given the opportunity to travel into space. On June 18, 1983, on board the space shuttle *Challenger*, Ride became the first American woman to ever fly in space.

"Our future lies with today's kids and tomorrow's space exploration."

An athlete and scholar

Sally Kristen Ride was born on May 26, 1951, in Encino, California, a suburb of Los Angeles. She was the first of two daughters of Joyce and Dale Ride, who was a political science professor at Santa Monica Community College. Sally was interested in sports from a young age and the boys in her neighbor-

ally Ride is the first American woman to have traveled in space. She achieved this honor on June 18, 1983, aboard the space shuttle *Challenger.* She functioned as the flight engineer on that mission, as well as on her second flight in the *Challenger* in 1984. When the *Challenger* exploded upon a launch in 1986, Ride served on the committee that investigated the disaster. After leaving NASA the following year, Ride took a position as director of the California Space Institute and taught physics at the University of California in San Diego. Today, Ride still teaches physics, writes children's books about space, and gives public speeches.

hood often picked her first to play on their teams. As a teenager she was a nationally ranked tennis player and was awarded a partial scholarship to a private high school called Westlake School for Girls.

At Westlake, Ride developed an interest in science. She graduated near the top of her class in 1969, then enrolled at Swarthmore College in Pennsylvania to study physics and to play tennis. But she missed the warm California weather, which allowed her to play tennis year-round, and after a few semesters at Swarthmore, Ride transferred to Stanford University in Palo Alto, California. There she studied astronomy (the science that deals with the study of the Sun, Moon, planets, stars, and other celestial bodies), physics (the science that explores the physical properties and composition of objects and the forces that affect them), and astrophysics (the branch of astronomy that deals with the physical processes, such as energy generation, that occur in stars, galaxies, and interstellar space). She also loved to study Shakespeare.

In 1973, she graduated from Stanford with a bachelor of arts degree in English and a bachelor of science degree in Physics. Ride also earned a master's degree in physics in 1975 and a doctorate in astrophysics in 1978 from Stanford. While finishing her work for her doctorate, Ride had applied to be an astronaut.

Perfect timing

Ride's timing to apply to the space program could not have been better. In 1978, the same year she finished her doctorate, NASA allowed women to apply to be astronauts for the first time. (The Soviet space program had led the way for women astronauts when cosmonaut Valentina Tereshkova became the first woman in space in 1963.) NASA engineers also began making changes to spacecrafts allowing for the difference in body sizes between men and women.

NASA received more than eight thousand applications, more than one thousand from women, for the astronaut program. Of the thirty-five people accepted into the program, six were women and Ride was one of them. She reported for duty in July 1978 to train as a mission specialist for the Space Transportation System (STS) program. As a mission specialist, Ride learned all about the shuttle systems and how to perform specific scientific tasks unrelated to the actual flying of the spacecraft. The space shuttle is a reusable spacecraft that takes off like a rocket, travels around Earth like a spacecraft, and then lands once again like a glider. American shuttles have operated with two major goals: to conduct scientific experiments in a zero-gravity environment, and to launch, capture, repair, and release satellites.

Ride studied navigation, physics, astronomy, mathematics, meteorology, and computers. She also obtained a jet pilot's license and underwent training in the shuttle simulator, a machine NASA uses to imitate the feeling of being inside a shuttle in space without ever leaving the ground. She went through other rigorous training exercises as well. To become familiar with the feeling of weightlessness, Ride learned how to move underwater while wearing a space suit. She also practiced doing different tasks in a special plane NASA used that could provide trainees with a short free-fall to simulate weightlessness. In addition, Ride and the other members of her program underwent physical training to ready their bodies for potential space flight. Ride ran, played tennis, and trained with weights to prepare herself.

When Ride finished her initial training, she made the transition from astronaut-candidate to astronaut. As an astronaut, she could be selected to go on an actual space flight. She then began the second phase of her astronaut education, during which each astronaut becomes an expert in one aspect of the shuttle. Ride's specialization was with the Remote Manipulator System (RMS), a 50-foot-long (15-meter-long) robotic arm used to grasp and maneuver objects outside the shuttle. She studied how to control and operate the arm in every possible situation and learned to perform corrective procedures, on a satellite for instance, should they become necessary in space. In addition to specializing, Ride also had to learn to operate all the instruments of the shuttle.

The beginning of many firsts

In April 1981, Ride received her first chance to participate in a space shuttle mission. John Young and Robert Crippen flew the first U.S. shuttle, called the *Columbia*. Ride flew in the T-38 chase plane that accompanied the shuttle back down from the atmosphere to the landing site.

For the second and third *Columbia* flights, in November 1981 and March 1982, Ride functioned as the capcom, or capsule communicator. The capcom is the person who talks to the astronauts in the shuttle, relaying information and instructions from mission control to the shuttle crews. The capcom has one of the most important jobs in the shuttle program and has to understand every aspect of the mission. Ride was the first woman to perform this crucial task.

In April 1982, NASA announced the names of the astronauts who were scheduled to fly the seventh shuttle mission and Ride was one of them. But before she became the first female to fly in space, Ride married Steven Hawley, an astronaut, in a quiet family ceremony that she flew herself to in a jet plane. On July 26, 1982, the couple became the first astronauts to ever marry each other during active duty.

First woman in space

Ride spent many hours studying the mission details and practicing tasks in the simulator that she would be responsible for in space to prepare for her upcoming flight. There was a lot of media attention surrounding Ride's historic moment as the first woman in space, but she was focused on the mission, not the media. In a *Time* magazine article released a few days

The space shuttle *Challenger*, with Sally Ride on board, before its launch at Kennedy Space Center, in Cape Canaveral, Florida, in 1983.

before *Challenger* was launched, she was quoted as saying, "It's too bad that society isn't to the point yet where the country could just send up a woman astronaut and nobody would think twice about it." As far as Ride was concerned, she was the same as any other astronaut.

The *Challenger* space shuttle, STS-7, carried the largest crew ever aboard a shuttle—four astronauts and a doctor.

More than one-half million people watched in Cape Canaveral, Florida, on June 18, 1983, when *Challenger* was launched, carrying the first American woman ever to travel into space and, at the age of thirty-two, the youngest American ever to fly in space.

Ride's job aboard *Challenger* was flight engineer. She monitored all the control signals, assisting the pilot and commander. She and another member of the crew, John Fabian, were responsible for conducting a number of experiments, including monitoring how certain crystals grow and watching the behavior of an ant colony in space. This mission was also the chance for Ride to use her expertise with the robotic arm, which was one of the reasons she was chosen for the mission. The Shuttle Pallet Satellite (SPAS), a small laboratory with a television camera, accompanied *Challenger.* Ride was in charge of releasing the satellite and retrieving it a short time later. It was the first time the robotic arm was used in space to deploy and retrieve a satellite. *Challenger* orbited Earth for six days before landing safely at Edwards Air Force Base in California.

Another mission and a tragedy

Upon her return, the American public treated Ride as a hero. People wore T-shirts with her face on them, and newspapers and magazines across the country publicized her success. Though she received a flurry of invitations to speak and made several public appearances on NASA's behalf, she continued to be focused on the next mission.

Ride was given the chance for a second trip into space on October 5, 1984. This time there were two female astronauts aboard the shuttle *Challenger,* Ride and Kathryn Sullivan. Ride served as the flight engineer again, and achieved another milestone: it was the first time a mission specialist, male or female, had made a second shuttle flight. Ride again worked the robotic arm, this time using it to rid the exterior of the shuttle of some ice and readjusting a radar antenna.

While Ride was getting ready for her third mission into space, tragedy struck. On January 28, 1986, the *Challenger*

Female astronaut Shannon Lucid has logged over 3000 hours in space.
Reproduced by permission of AP/ Wide World Photos.

Shannon Lucid set the record in 1996 for spending more time in space than any other American astronaut. She was born Shannon Wells in Shanghai, China, on January 14, 1943, during World War II (1939–45). Her parents, Joseph and Myrtle Wells, were Baptist missionaries working in China. During Shannon's first year of life, her family was put into a prisoner of war camp in Japan. They were returned to the United States as part of a prisoner exchange, but returned to China after the war. When Shannon was six, they moved back to the United States again, settling in Bethany, Oklahoma, where she spent the rest of her childhood.

Shannon was always interested in math and science, and wanted to grow up to be a rocket scientist. After she earned a bachelor's degree in chemistry in 1963 from the University of Oklahoma, she worked as a research assistant and lab technician. She married Michael Lucid in 1968 and returned to the University of Oklahoma that same year. She earned a master's degree in science in 1970 and a doctorate in biochemistry in 1973. Lucid applied to NASA's astronaut-training program. It was the first time NASA had opened the application process to women and Lucid joined Sally Ride in this first class.

On June 17, 1985, Lucid made her first trip into space aboard the space shuttle *Discovery,* and since then she has logged more flight hours in orbit than any woman in the world. In 1996, after being aboard the Russian *Mir* space station for five months, she set the record for longest period of time ever spent by a U.S. astronaut in space. (This record was broken in June 2002 by U.S. astronauts Daniel Bursch and Carl Walz who spent more than 195 days in space.) In February 2002, Lucid was chosen to be NASA's chief scientist. She was also given the Congressional Space Medal of Honor by the President George W. Bush, becoming the first woman to earn that award.

was launched once again. This time there were seven crew members, including two women: Michael Smith, Richard Scobee, Ronald McNair, Ellison Onizuka, Gregory Jarvis, Judith Resnik, and Christa McAuliffe. Just seventy-three seconds after launch, the shuttle exploded and all members on board died.

Ride was devastated and joined an investigation, called the Presidential Commission, to determine what had gone wrong. The problem, it was discovered, was with a handful of faulty rubber O-rings that were used as seals on the shuttle. Furthermore, it appeared that it was known that the O-rings could pose a problem, but NASA had delayed replacing the O-rings. The shuttle program was put on hold while changes were made at NASA in an effort to reassess their programs.

Time for a change

Because of Ride's involvement with the *Challenger* investigation, she moved to NASA headquarters in Washington, D.C., and became assistant to the NASA administrator for long-range planning. In this position, Ride published a report, *Leadership and America's Future in Space,* in which she made suggestions for the future of the NASA space program.

Ride also branched out in her activities. She traveled and gave talks about being an astronaut. In 1986, she co-wrote her first children's book, *To Space and Back.* The following year, she left NASA and moved back to California to work at Stanford University's Center for International Security and Arms Control. In 1989, Ride was hired as the director of the California Space Institute and as a professor of physics at the University of California at San Diego.

Ride has been honored for her achievements with several awards. She was given National Spaceflight Medals in 1983 and 1984. In June 1985, she received the Lindbergh Eagle Award and in 1988 was inducted into the National Women's Hall of Fame. Ride's second book for children, *Voyager: An Adventure to the Edge of the Solar System,* was published in 1992. Four years later, Ride left the California Space Institute, but continued to teach physics at the University of California, write books for children, and be involved with different organizations that supported girls interested in math, science, and technology.

Further Reading

Bredeson, Carmen. *Shannon Lucid: Space Ambassador.* Brookfield, CT: Millbrook Press, 1998.

Camp, Carole Ann. *Sally Ride: First American Woman in Space.* Springfield, NJ: Enslow, 1997.

"Female Frontiers. Meet: Sally Ride, First American Woman in Space." *NASA Quest.* http://quest.arc.nasa.gov/space/frontiers/ride.html (accessed on September 3, 2002).

Golden, Frederic, Sam Allis, and Jerry Hannifin. "Sally's Joy Ride into the Sky: The First American Woman to Fly in Space Shows She Has Got the Right Stuff." *Time,* June 13, 1983, p. 56.

Kramer, Barbara. *Sally Ride: A Space Biography.* Springfield, NJ: Enslow, 1998.

Ride, Sally, and Susan Okie. *To Space and Back.* New York: Lothrop, Lee & Shepard, 1986.

Ride, Sally, and Tam O'Shaughnessy. *The Mystery of Mars.* New York: Crown, 1999.

Ride, Sally, and Tam O'Shaughnessy. *The Third Planet: Exploring Earth from Space.* New York: Crown, 1994.

Ride, Sally, and Tam O'Shaughnessy. *Voyager: An Adventure to the Edge of the Solar System.* New York: Crown, 1992.

George Westinghouse

October 6, 1846
Central Bridge, New York

March 12, 1914
New York, New York

George Westinghouse was an American industrialist and inventor who invented, or improved upon, hundreds of devices. He had to his credit 361 patents, or the exclusive right to manufacture, use, and sell an invention of one's making. His major achievements include improving the braking system of trains by inventing the air brake; redesigning railway signaling systems to reduce the number of train accidents; supplying natural gas and electricity to people in a safe manner; and converting the immense power of water at Niagara Falls into electrical energy. To keep the profit from his various inventions separate from one another, he organized several different companies throughout his lifetime. Some of these were the Westinghouse Air Brake Company, the Philadelphia Company, the Union Switch and Signal Company, the Westinghouse Machine Company, and the Westinghouse Electric Company. Despite his providing the United States with alternating current electricity and several inventions to make railroad transportation safer and more convenient, late in his life Westinghouse lost most of his fortune.

"If someday they say of me that in my work I have contributed something to the welfare and happiness of my fellow men, I shall be satisfied."

George Westinghouse was a brilliant inventor who secured more than 350 patents for his designs and inventions. He vastly improved the safety of America's railway systems with his invention of the air brake and gave the world safe but powerful electricity in the form of alternating current. He also made it possible for natural gas to be piped safely into homes with a new piping system. When a light switch is turned on or a train pulls gently into a station, most of the engineering involved is directly related to Westinghouse's ideas.

A budding inventor

George Westinghouse was born on October 6, 1846, in Central Bridge, New York. His parents, George and Emmeline Vedder Westinghouse, had ten children and George was their seventh child. George Sr. was a farmer, carpenter, and mechanic. He was also an inventor in his own right, having received seven patents for farm machines that he had designed. When George Jr. was ten years old, the family moved to Schenectady, New York, where his father opened his own machine shop called George Westinghouse & Company. His father was a good businessman and it didn't take long for the company, which manufactured agricultural machinery, to do well.

George Jr. was not a very good student, but he loved to spend time in his father's machine shop, often sneaking out of school in order to do so. In 1859, when George Jr. was just thirteen years old, he began working at his father's company. He assisted the other workers by handing them parts they needed, cleaning and oiling machines, and sweeping the floor. George Jr. had a natural talent for machinery and quickly learned how to take things apart and rebuild them, and how to read blueprints, or the plans of an invention. One day, George Sr. asked his son to cut a large pile of metal pipes into pieces of equal length, a job that should have taken a few days. Instead of doing the job by hand, George Jr. surprised everyone by designing a cutting machine that helped him to measure and cut each piece. He was finished within a few hours.

The Civil War and college

When the Civil War broke out in 1861, Westinghouse wanted to join the war but he was too young. (The Civil War pitted the North against the South in the United States over the

issue of slavery.) He made one attempt to leave home to join the fighting, but his father brought him back home. In 1863, when he was seventeen, Westinghouse joined the Sixteenth New York Volunteer Cavalry. A year later, he transferred to the navy as an assistant engineer. (Two of his older brothers had already joined the army. One of them, Albert, was killed in action.)

The Westinghouse Electric Plant, where many of George Westinghouse's numerous inventions were created.
Reproduced by permission of Corbis Corporation.

When his naval duties were finished in June 1865, Westinghouse returned home and enrolled at Union College in Schenectady to study engineering. But Westinghouse, as he always had been in school, was bored. Instead of concentrating on his class work, he worked at improving a rotary engine, any of various engines in which power is applied to vanes or similar parts constrained to move in a circular path. On October 31, 1865, Westinghouse was awarded his first patent, for a small steam-powered rotary engine. It was the first of hundreds of patents he would earn in his lifetime. Instead of remaining in college to learn about other people's ideas, Westinghouse left Union College to pursue the many ideas he had for his inventions. He returned to work at his father's company, where he could devote his time to inventing.

Trains play a major role

The late 1800s were the beginning of the Industrial Revolution in America, a time of major change in the economy and society because of the increased use of machinery to create products. The nation was growing quickly, goods became more readily available, and communication and transportation became extremely important. This was one of the most exciting times in American history to be an inventor as the nation was eager to embrace mechanical innovations. The telephone and radio were already bringing people closer together, as were the railroads. Trains were a major fascination for Westinghouse, and as he spent more time on them traveling to and from his home, he thought of ways to vastly improve the railroads.

In 1866, Westinghouse was a passenger on a train that was stopped due to an accident ahead of them. Some cars had derailed, or come off the tracks, and Westinghouse watched as the workers struggled to get them back on. This gave him an idea for the car replacer, a small piece of track that could be carried on a train to use in just such an emergency. When a car became derailed, the car replacer was laid down in front of the car's wheels. Then the car could be slid onto the replacer, which then guided the car back on the track. No more heavy lifting was required. Westinghouse earned a patent for this invention in February 1867. Later that same year, on August 8, he married Marguerite Erskine Walker who, ironically, he had met on a train.

Trains continued to be the inspiration for several more of Westinghouse's patented inventions. He greatly improved the frog, a segment of train track that allows one section of the railway to cross over another, by designing one made from long-lasting steel that could be turned over once one side was worn.

While traveling on another train delayed by an accident on the tracks ahead, Westinghouse was struck with another new idea. At the time, railroad workers used hand brakes to stop each individual car. Westinghouse came up with a plan that would allow the whole train to be stopped at once by the locomotive engineer. According to the specifications for this new invention, pipes would run the length of the train, attached to an air pump powered by the train's engine. When the engineer turned a valve, air was sent through the pipes into cylinders (chambers in which a piston moves up and down, as in an engine or pump) that pushed the brakes against the wheels, slowing down the train. On April 13, 1869, Westinghouse received a patent for his air brake, and it would eventually be used on the majority of the world's railroads. At the age of twenty-two, he organized the Westinghouse Air Brake Company in 1869 with himself acting as president. Throughout his life, Westinghouse continued to make improvements to the air brake and received many more patents related to his design.

A well drilled in the yard of Westinghouse's home led to several dozen inventions for the control and distribution of natural gas. Natural gas is a power source that is found in wells in the ground. In 1884 and 1885, Westinghouse developed ways to regulate the flow of gas and prevent gas leaks, which could cause dangerous explosions, with a new piping system. He applied for patents for his designs, and soon founded the Philadelphia Company to help give area residents safe access to natural gas.

Electrifying new ideas

Though Westinghouse was making a very good living off of his many inventions, it would be his ideas related to harnessing electricity that would make him a very wealthy man. There are two different kinds of electrical current: direct current (DC) and alternating current (AC). Direct current always involves the movement of electrons from a region of high negative charge to one of lower negative charge. The electric current produced by batteries is direct current. If a current changes direction repeatedly it is called an alternating current. In 1882, **Thomas Edison** (1847–1931; see entry in volume 1) already had begun to build electrical power stations and provide people with electricity using direct current. With this method, he needed many stations because each one could only service about 1 square mile (2.59 square kilometers). Westinghouse's plan was very different from Edison's.

Westinghouse believed that using alternating current was the only efficient, cost-effective way to supply the masses with electrical power. He gathered some of the best engineers and purchased the American rights to an alternating current transformer that had been designed by French engineer Lucian Gaulard and British engineer John D. Gibbs. The Westinghouse engineers improved upon Gaulard and Gibbs's design for use in the United States.

The Westinghouse team tested their alternating-current system on the towns of Great Barrington, Massachusetts, and Lawrenceville, Pennsylvania, and successfully powered their lights. On January 8, 1886, Westinghouse opened the Westinghouse Electric Company, later known as the Westinghouse Electric and Manufacturing Company. By 1890, the Westinghouse Electric Company had three hundred alternating-current power stations in the United States. Westinghouse had succeeded in providing electricity to much larger areas, and at a lower cost, than Edison's company had.

The only thing lacking in Westinghouse's plan was a safe and efficient way to power motors. Westinghouse's company only powered electric lights. Problems with power surges (sudden increases of too much power) had to be solved before the alternating-current system could be used to power motors. (Power surges, depending upon the voltage level reached, can cause hardware disturbances and damage sensitive equipment.) A Hungarian engineer named **Nikola Tesla** (1856–1943; see entry in volume 1) developed a generator (a machine that converts mechanical energy into electrical energy) that made it possible to power motors using alternating current. Ironically, Tesla had been working for Westinghouse's rival, Edison, but the two had parted ways over a financial dispute. Westinghouse bought the patents Tesla had obtained for his machine and hired him.

In 1893, Westinghouse got his chance to show the world the usefulness of alternating-current electricity when his company was hired to supply and design the electrical lighting for the World's Columbian Exposition in Chicago, Illinois. Westinghouse's success at the event—a spectacular display of 250,000 lights—earned him a contract to build three huge generators to harness the immense power from the water at Niagara Falls into electrical energy. Water is an energy source that has the ability to drive generators at the very high speeds at which they operate most efficiently.

Nikola Tesla, an employee of George Westinghouse, invented an alternating-current motor that could power motors as well as lights.

Reproduced by permission of Corbis Corporation.

A national treasure

In the early 1900s, the various Westinghouse companies were worth about $120 million and employed approximately 50,000 workers. By 1904, there were nine Westinghouse companies in the U.S., one in Canada, and five in Europe. But the United States began to suffer economic problems at the beginning of the 1900s, and hard times fell on the Westinghouse Electric Company as well. In 1907, the company's value had dropped so low that it was easily bought by another company, and by 1911 George Westinghouse had severed all ties with his companies, which he had lost control of.

Westinghouse's health began to suffer in 1913. Although he was confined to a wheelchair in his last days, Westinghouse continued to make sketches of his ideas. He died on March 12, 1914, at the age of sixty-seven. Westinghouse, because he was a Civil War veteran, was buried in Arlington National Cemetery in Arlington, Virginia, where hundreds of thousands of U.S. soldiers are buried.

Further Reading

Dommermuth-Costa, Carol. *Nikola Tesla: A Spark of Genius.* Minneapolis, MN: Lerner, 1994.

Prout, Henry G. *A Life of George Westinghouse.* New York: Arno Press, 1972.

Ravage, Barbara. *George Westinghouse: A Genius for Invention.* Austin, TX: Raintree Steck-Vaughn, 1997.

Ryback, James P. "AC or DC?" *Popular Electronics,* September 1994, p. 42.

Wicks, Frank. "How George Westinghouse Changed the World." *Mechanical Engineering,* October 1996, p. 74.

Robert B. Woodward

April 10, 1917
Boston, Massachusetts
July 8, 1979
Cambridge, Massachusetts

R obert B. Woodward was an American chemist who determined the structure of such organic chemical compounds as penicillin and strychnine. Woodward was also known for his remarkable ability to chemically synthesize, or artificially create, many complex organic substances such as quinine, cholesterol, and cortisone. To honor his work in organic synthesis, Woodward received the Nobel Prize in chemistry in 1965.

"In considering the development of a plan for the synthesis of any complicated substance, it is always desirable to look at the problem from an entirely fresh point of view."

Portrait reproduced by permission of Corbis Corporation.

A brilliant young man

Robert Burns Woodward was born on April 10, 1917, in Boston, Massachusetts. His father, Arthur Chester Woodward, died the following year during a flu epidemic, leaving Robert's mother, Margaret Burns, to raise him. From a very early age, Robert was exceptionally smart. He graduated from public high school at sixteen and was admitted to the Massachusetts

American chemist Robert Woodward determined the chemical structure of many substances found in nature and produced them synthetically in the laboratory. This process provided the scientific and medical world with less expensive and more consistent substances that have a wide range of uses. Some of the substances Woodward synthesized include quinine, used to treat malaria; tetracycline antibiotics, used to fight infection; reserpine, the first tranquilizer used effectively in the treatment of mental illnesses; and cephalosporin C, an antibiotic. Woodward was awarded the 1965 Nobel Prize in chemistry for his outstanding contribution to the field of chemical synthesis.

Institute of Technology (MIT). There, a teacher remarked that Woodward knew as much chemistry entering college as most of the students finishing college.

Even though he had a natural talent for chemistry, Woodward had trouble following the rules. He was asked to leave MIT because he did not attend classes regularly and only showed up to take exams. After agreeing to comply with MIT's requirements, he was allowed to return and to spend less time in classes while he conducted experiments in the laboratory. In June 1936, he earned his bachelor's degree from MIT. A year later, at just twenty years old, he earned a doctorate from the same institution. Woodward was such an impressive student that an article about his achievements ran in the *Boston Globe* on June 8, 1937. Chemistry Professor James Norris said of him: "We had no [other] student like him in the department. Woodward is brilliant but, unlike some scholars, he will not burn out suddenly. We are convinced that he will make a distinguished name for himself in the scientific world." Woodward was married in 1938 to Irja Pullman, and after that marriage ended, in 1946 to Eudoxia Muller, having a total of three daughters and one son.

Quickly successful

After a brief job teaching at the University of Illinois, Woodward was hired as a research assistant at Harvard University's organic chemistry department. In 1941, Harvard offered Woodward a teaching position in the chemistry department. He also began his work with synthesizing compounds in the laboratory. Chemical synthesis is the process of building a desired compound from simpler and readily available compo-

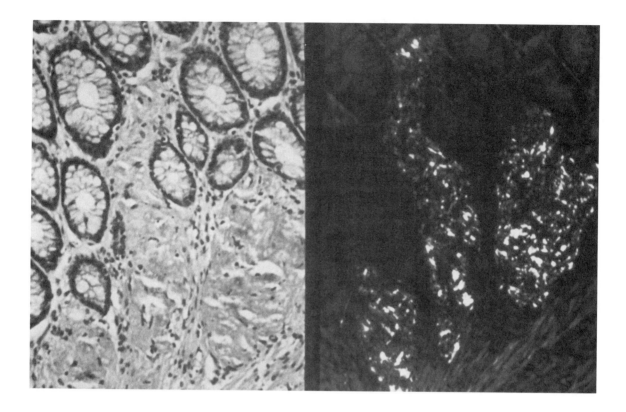

nents. Synthesizing a natural product in the laboratory is desirable because the synthetic version can offer a less expensive and more consistent alternative than the natural product. Also, synthetic products can be modified to make a pharmaceutical (drug) more potent and less toxic (poisonous).

Chemical synthesis, however, is not a simple process. Biochemical molecules exhibit not only a particular bonding pattern of atoms, but also a certain arrangement of those atoms in space. The study of the spatial arrangements of molecules is called stereochemistry, and the individual configurations of a molecule are called its stereoisomers. Sometimes the same molecule may have many different stereoisomers; only one of those, however, will be biologically relevant. Consequently, a synthesis scheme must consider the basic reaction conditions that will bond two atoms together to form a compound, as well as determine how to ensure that the reaction positions the atoms properly to obtain the correct stereoisomer.

Cholesterol crystals, whose structure was determined by Robert B. Woodward.

Photograph by Lester V. Bergman. Reproduced by permission of Corbis Corporation.

In 1944, Woodward, with the help of chemist William E. Doering, successfully synthesized quinine, a drug used to treat malaria and other illnesses. (Malaria is a parasitic disease transmitted by mosquitoes that can cause fever, headache, vomiting, and sometimes death.) This discovery, made during World War II (1939–45), was extremely important in helping treat American soldiers who were fighting in tropical regions where malaria cases were abundant. That same year, Woodward was promoted to assistant professor at Harvard and became involved with the British-American effort during World War II to synthesize penicillin by creating a theory of penicillin's chemical structure. Penicillin, found in nature's *Penicillium* fungus, is an important antibiotic used to treat infections and illnesses.

In 1946, Woodward was promoted to associate professor at Harvard. The following year, he and chemist C. H. Schramm created an artificial protein (a very large molecule consisting of long chains of smaller units known as amino acids) that was later used in the plastics industry. By 1947, Woodward had determined the structure of strychnine, a poison that comes from a certain type of plant seed. Woodward quickly earned the respect of fellow chemists with his impressive talent for synthesizing difficult compounds and determining the structures of others.

On a roll

Woodward was just as successful throughout the 1950s and 1960s. Harvard made Woodward a full professor in 1950 and in 1951, he and his colleagues succeeded at synthesizing two steroids, cortisone and cholesterol. (Steroids are drugs that stimulate the adrenal glands [which in turn secrete hormones, or chemical messengers that regulate various bodily functions] and are highly effective in treating asthma and allergies but also have many side effects.) Cortisone had been found to provide relief for patients with rheumatoid arthritis. Woodward's other accomplishments in synthesis include strychnine (1954), a poison isolated from the *Strychnos* species and often used to kill rats; colchicine (1963), a toxic natural product found in

Roald Hoffmann

Roald Hoffman developed a set of rules for chemists based on quantum mechanics with Robert B. Woodward.

Reproduced courtesy of Roald Hoffman.

Roald Hoffmann is a scientist who became known worldwide for his work with Robert Woodward on the Woodward-Hoffman rules, based on quantum mechanics, which explain whether a particular overlap is likely or even possible for the orbitals of two reacting species. He was born in Poland in 1937. As a Jewish child in Europe during World War II (1939–45), Hoffmann left his home with his family in order to escape the German Nazis who were forcing Jewish people from their homes and taking them to death camps. The Nazis promoted a powerful government that had complete control over society and also believed themselves to be a superior race. They persecuted minorities, especially the Jewish people, and began to systematically kill the Jews of Europe. While hiding in the attic of a schoolhouse, the young Hoffmann began to read science books he found there. After spending time in a refugee camp in Germany, he moved to the United States with his family in 1949. Even with the challenge of learning a new language, Hoffman was an outstanding student and excelled at Stuyvesant High School in New York City.

Hoffmann received his bachelor's degree from Columbia University in New York City in 1958. He then obtained both his master's degree in 1960 and doctorate in 1962 from Harvard University. Hoffmann joined the faculty at Cornell University in 1965 where he met Robert Woodward and began working with him on the Woodward-Hoffmann rules. The Woodward-Hoffmann rules, based on quantum mechanics, accounted for the failure of certain compounds to form from apparently appropriate starting materials and helped chemists successfully synthesize molecules.

In 1981, Hoffmann was awarded the Nobel Prize in chemistry for the Woodward-Hoffmann rules and received the National Medal of Science in 1983.

autumn crocus; and lysergic acid (1954) and reserpine (1956), both psychoactive substances. Reserpine, a tranquilizer found naturally in the Indian snake root plant *Rauwolfia,* was widely used to treat mental illness and was one of the first genuinely effective psychiatric medicines. In 1960, after four years of work, Woodward synthesized chlorophyll, the light-energy-capturing pigment in green plants, and in 1962 he accomplished the total synthesis of a tetracycline antibiotic, used to fight infection.

In 1960, Woodward undertook his most difficult synthesis project, working on creating the vitamin B_{12}. While still at Harvard, Woodward traveled often to Switzerland to work on projects at the Woodward Institute, which had been established for him in 1963 at the headquarters of a corporation called CIBA-Geigy. For more than a decade, with help from colleagues at Harvard and in Switzerland, he studied the vitamin's structure and worked on its synthesis. Although their synthesis did not turn out to be a practical source of the vitamin, it was considered a true masterpiece of chemical construction, and it helped other scientists understand similar compounds.

Physical chemists assume that certain areas around an atom or molecule are more likely to contain electrons than other areas. These areas of probability, called orbitals, are described visually as having specific shapes and orientations relative to the rest of the atom or molecule. Woodward and Roald Hoffmann of Cornell University established the Woodward-Hoffmann rules based on quantum mechanics, which state that a chemical reaction will not occur if the symmetry or alignment of the orbitals of the combined atoms or molecules is not maintained during that reaction. In 1970, Woodward and Hoffmann published their work on the subject, *The Conservation of Orbital Symmetry;* Woodward by that time had demonstrated repeatedly by his own startling successes at synthesis that the rules worked.

In 1964, Woodward was awarded the National Medal of Science. The following year, he received the Nobel Prize in chemistry for his enormous contributions to the field of chemical synthesis. Also in 1965 Woodward and his Swiss collaborators synthesized Cephalosporin C, an important antibiotic. He helped start two organic chemistry journals, *Tetrahedron Letters* and *Tetrahedron,* served on the boards of several science organizations, and received awards and honorary degrees from many countries, including the Davy Medal (1959) and the Copley Medal (1978), both from the Royal Society of Britain. On July 8, 1979, Woodward died in his Cambridge home at the age of sixty-two from a heart attack. Until the end of his life, he had worked on the synthesis of the antibiotic erythromycin.

Further Reading

Hoffmann, Roald. *Gaps and Verges: Poems.* Orlando, FL: University of Central Florida, 1990.

Hoffmann, Roald. *The Same and Not the Same.* New York: Columbia University Press, 1995.

Lord, Lew. "Take the Chaucer." *U.S. News & World Report,* March 14, 1988.

"Robert Burns Woodward—Biography." *Nobel e-Museum.* http://www.nobel.se/chemistry/laureates/1965/woodward-bio.html (accessed on September 3, 2002).

Cumulative Index to Volumes 1-7

Italic type indicates volume numbers; **boldface** type indicates entries and their page numbers; (ill.) indicates illustrations.

*Eugenie Clark.
Reproduced by permission
of Ms. Eugenie Clark.*

Altman, Sidney *1:* 91
Aluminum *7:* 117–23, 121 (ill.)
Aluminum Company of America
   (ALCOA) *7:* 117, 122, 123
Alvarez, Luis *1:* **7–14,** 7 (ill.),
   11 (ill.)
Alvarez, Walter *1:* 9, 13
Alvariño, Angeles *1:* **15–18**
Alzheimer, Alois *6:* 64
Alzheimer's disease *5:* 73;
   6: 62–64; *7:* 179
*American Ephemeris and Nautical
   Almanac 4:* 172
American Red Cross *1:* 233,
   235–36
American Revolution *3:* 772, 774
Ames, Bruce N. *1:* **19–23,**
   19 (ill.)
Ames test *1:* 19–21
Amino acids *4:* 137, 201
Analytical engine *1:* 37, 40–42;
   7: 46–50
Analytical Institutions 5: 4–5
Analytical psychology *2:* 541
Andersen, Dorothy *5:* **7–13,**
   7 (ill.)
*And Keep Your Powder Dry: An
   Anthropologist Looks at
   America 2:* 636–37
Andreessen, Marc *5:* **14–20,**
   14 (ill.)
Andrews, Thomas *2:* 655
Aneroid barometer *6:* 106,
   106 (ill.)
Angiogenesis inhibitors *7:* 105,
   107 (ill.), 108–11
Angiography *6:* 49, 51
Angiostatin *7:* 110
Angus 1: 50
Animal conservation *4:* 92, 94,
   96, 98
Animal ecology *6:* 40–42
*Animal Ecology and Evolution
   6:* 43
*The Animal Kingdom, Distributed
   According to Its Organization
   1:* 206; *4:* 161
Animal psychology *4:* 3
Animals, ethical treatment of
   2: 411, 413

An Anthropologist on Mars 3: 830
Anthropology *4:* 66; *5:* 170,
   173–74; *7:* 27, 29–34, 161–65
Anthropology, forensic *5:* 171, 173
Antibiotics *6:* 9
Antigens *6:* 96
Antimatter *4:* 188
Antinuclear movement
   1: 124–26, 128
Antiproton *4:* 188
Apollo *4:* 14, 29
Apollo 11 4: 29
Apollo space program *4:* 24, 29,
   30; *5:* 151, 153
Apple I *2:* 510
Apple II *2:* 510–11
Apple Computer Inc. *2:* 508,
   510–11
Appleton, Edward *3:* 941–42
Aqualung *7:* 88
Archimedes *4:* 101, 106; *5:* 44
Argo-Jason system *1:* 49–50
Argonne National Laboratories
   1: 290
Aristarchus of Samos *4:* 50
Aristotle *1:* 206; *4:* 101–03, 106,
   160, 178; *6:* **11–16,** 11 (ill.)
Arkwright, Richard *1:* 24–29,
   24 (ill.)
Army Ballistic Missile Agency
   (ABMA) *4:* 26, 28
Arp, Halton *1:* 121
Arrhenius, Svante *1:* **30–36,**
   30 (ill.)
Arrhythmias *3:* 929–31
Arrow (race car) *4:* 84
Arsenic *4:* 112, 114
Arteriosclerosis *6:* 51
Articulata 4: 161
Artificial heart *2:* 502–05; *7:* 21,
   23 (ill.)
Artificial intelligence *2:* 665–69;
   4: 229, 230, 233; *6:* 147
Artificial radioactivity *4:* 117,
   119, 122; *6:* 179
Artificial satellites *3:* 920
Asbestos *6:* 76
Asclepigenia *6:* 83
Asilomer Conference *3:* 872
Assembly line *4:* 80, 82, 85

Astatine *4:* 188

Aston, Francis *4:* 226

Astrology *6:* 28, 159

Astronomical unit *4:* 132; *7:* 63

Astronomy *4:* 23, 48–50, 53, 56, 100, 103, 126–28, 131, 170–73, 199–202, 206–07; *5:* 82, 83, 115–18; *7:* 1, 4

Astrophysical Journal 1: 154

Astrophysics *5:* 101

Atanasoff-Berry Computer *2:* 367

Atanasoff, John Vincent *2:* 367

Atmosphere *4:* 16, 17, 19; *5:* 163

Atmospheric motion *4:* 17, 20

ATOC (Acoustic Thermometry of Ocean Climate) *5:* 130

Atomic bomb *1:* 10, 127 (ill.), 268; *2:* 402, 680, 683, 687–88, 689 (ill.); *6:* 177, 178, 182; *7:* 133, 139, 157–59

Atomic number *2:* 657–58

Atomic structure *1:* 98–100; *3:* 805–06, 811; *4:* 222, 224

Atomic theory *1:* 197, 199–201; *4:* 7, 11; *7:* 133, 134–38

Atomic weight *1:* 197, 199, 202; *2:* 656–57; *4:* 7, 9, 11

Atoms *4:* 11

Audiometer *1:* 62, 67

Audion *1:* 217, 219–21

Aurora borealis *1:* 199; *3:* 919

Australopithecus 2: 582–83

Australopithecus afarensis 2: 516, 520, 522, 584

Australopithecus africanus 2: 518; *4:* 66, 68, 70–72

The Autobiography of Bertrand Russell 3: 795, 804

Automatic Computing Engine (ACE) *4:* 233

Automatic Implantable Defibrillator *3:* 929–30

Automation *5:* 110, 111

Automobile *4:* 80, 82, 83, 85–87

Avery, Oswald *3:* 934; *6:* 93

Awakenings 3: 827–28, 830

AZT (azidothymidine) *1:* 281, 282 (ill.); *2:* 379, 471; *7:* 150

B

Baade, Walter *5:* 69

Babbage, Charles *1:* **37–43,** 37 (ill.); *4:* 233; *5:* 62; *6:* 3; *7:* 46–50, 47 (ill.)

Baby and Child Care 1: 128

Bacon, Francis *3:* 953

Bacteriology *4:* 111; *5:* 191, 192–93

Bacteriophage *1:* 77

Baez, Albert *1:* **44–47**

Bakker, Robert T. *1:* 12

Bali *2:* 636

Balinese Character: A Photographic Analysis 2: 636

Ballard, Robert D. *1:* **48–52,** 48 (ill.), 51 (ill.); *3:* 754

Ballistic missles *5:* 151, 152

Ballistite *2:* 672

Balmer, Johann *1:* 100

Bang, Bernhard L. F. *4:* 78

Banneker, Benjamin *7:* **1–8,** 1 (ill.), 5 (ill.), 8 (ill.)

Bardeen, John *3:* 864–68, 867 (ill.)

Barnard, Christiaan *2:* 506, 506 (ill.); *7:* **17–25,** 17 (ill.)

Barnett, Miles *3:* 942

Barrier Treaty *3:* 913

Banting, Frederick *7:* **9–15,** 9 (ill.)

Barton, Otis *3:* 754

Basov, Nikolai *2:* 602–03

Bass, George *1:* **53–57,** 56 (ill.)

Bathyscaphe *3:* 754, 756

Bayesian statistical analysis *5:* 21

Bayliss, William *3:* 749

Beagle, H.M.S. *1:* 204–05

Becker, Hans *2:* 642; *4:* 121

Becquerel, Henri *1:* 186–88, 188 (ill.); *3:* 789, 807–08

Bednorz, Johannes Georg *6:* 31, 32

Beebe, William *3:* 754

Bees *1:* 322–24

Begay, Fred *1:* **58–61**

Behavioral psychology *3:* 876–77, 879–80

Belchamber & Parker *5:* 149

Bell, Alexander Graham *1:* **62–67,** 62 (ill.), 65 (ill.), 248; *2:* 557; *3:* 982–83

Bell, Alexander Melville *1:* 62
Bell Burnell, Jocelyn *1:* **69–74**
Bell Telephone Laboratories
3: 863–64, 868
Benedict, Ruth Fulton *7:* **27–34,**
27 (ill.)
Benjamin Banneker's
Pennsylvania, Delaware,
Maryland and Virginia
Almanac and Ephemeris for
the Year of Our Lord, 1972
7: 6
Benjamin Franklin's
Autobiography 6: 60
Bergen cyclone model *4:* 20
Bergen Geophysical Institute
4: 15, 20, 21
Bergen school of meteorology
4: 15, 21
Bergen Weather Service *4:* 15,
19, 20
Berg, Otto *4:* 185, 186, 188
Berg, Paul *1:* **75–81,** 75 (ill.),
80 (ill.); *2:* 387, 389;
3: 871, 874
Berliner, Emile *1:* 66
Berners-Lee, Tim *5:* 18
Berson, Solomon A.
3: 1006–07, 1011
Berthe, Hans *5:* 66
Berylliosis *6:* 74–76
Beryllium *6:* 75
Berzelius, Jöns Jacob *4:* **7–14,**
7 (ill.)
Bessemer, Henry *1:* **82–87,**
82 (ill.)
Best, Charles Herbert *7:* 12–15,
13 (ill.)
Bethe, Hans *5:* 66
A Better World for Our Children
1: 128
Beyond Freedom and Dignity
3: 879–80
Bifocals *6:* 56
Big bang theory *1:* 117, 121, 270,
273; *2:* 382, 436, 438, 488,
494; *5:* 68, 101, 104; *6:* 108,
112, 113, 141, 144; *7:* 171
Bikini Atoll, Marshall Islands
1: 127 (ill.)

Biltmore Forest *6:* 149, 150
BINAC (binary automatic
computer) *2:* 367
Binary number system *6:* 102–03
Binomial nomenclature *4:* 158, 162
Biodiversity *1:* 192–94, 257;
3: 969–70, 977
Biogen *2:* 384, 388
Biological Diversity Program
1: 193
A Biologist Remembers 1: 321
The Biology of the Cell Surface
2: 546
Biotechnology *1:* 78; *2:* 387
Bipolar disorder *6:* 62, 64
Bird-flight as the Basis of Aviation
3: 990
Birds, banding of *6:* 138
Birds, territorial behavior of *6:* 138
Birth control pill *5:* 28–31
Bismarck 1: 50
Bjerknes, Jacob *4:* 17–21
Bjerknes, Vilhelm *1:* 330;
4: **15–21**
Black body radiation *1:* 100;
3: 760, 762–63
Black body radiation law *6:* 17, 19
Black Chronology 1: 230–31
Black Folk Then and Now 1: 230
Black holes *1:* 153, 156; *2:* 432,
434–36, 437 (ill.); *6:* 141,
142, 144
Black Holes and Baby Universes
and Other Essays 2: 439
Black, James *2:* 472
Blackburn, Elizabeth H.
1: **88–91**
Blackwell, David *5:* **21–27,**
21 (ill.)
Blackwell, Elizabeth *7:* **35–43,**
35 (ill.), 38 (ill.)
Blaiberg, Philip *7:* 22
Blake, Francis *1:* 66
Blalock, Alfred *3:* 897–903;
4: 208, 212, 213
Blalock-Taussig shunt *3:* 901;
4: 208, 212, 213
Bloch, Felix *1:* 9
Blodgett, Katharine Burr
1: **92–97,** 92 (ill.), 95 (ill.)

Blood banks *1:* 233, 235

Blue baby syndrome *3:* 897–98, 901–02; *4:* 208, 210, 213

Boas, Franz *2:* 634

Bohr, Niels *1:* **98–104,** 98 (ill.), 153, 289; *2:* 400, 646; *3:* 739, 809, 811, 813; *5:* 102

Bolin, Bert *1:* 34, 34 (ill.)

Bolshevik Revolution *3:* 751

Boltzmann, Ludwig *2:* 640

Bombes *4:* 231

Boolean algebra *6:* 102–04

Borlaug, Norman *1:* **105–11,** 105 (ill.)

Born Free: A Lioness of Two Worlds 4: 1, 3

Born, Max *2:* 400, 681

Born-Oppenheimer method *2:* 682

Bose, Amar *1:* 221

Bose, Satyendranath *6:* **17–21**

Bothe, Walther *2:* 642; *4:* 121

Boulton, Matthew *3:* 949–50

Boyer, Herbert W. *1:* 78

Boyle, Robert *2:* 573, 573 (ill.); *4:* 178, 181

Brahe, Tycho *1:* 135, 135 (ill.), 156; *4:* 128, 129, 131, 132; *6:* **22–29,** 22 (ill.); *7:* 62

Brattain, Walter *3:* 864–65, 867–68, 867 (ill.)

Braun, Carl Ferdinand *2:* 613; *3:* 1021

Braun, Wernher von *2:* 395, 395 (ill.); *4:* **22–32,** 22 (ill.), 27 (ill.)

Brave New World 3: 872–73, 885

Brenner, Sydney *1:* 179

Breuer, Josef *1:* 308, 310, 312

A Brief History of Time (film) *2:* 437

A Brief History of Time: From the Big Bang to Black Holes 2: 436

Bringing down the Wall: Writing on Science, Culture, and Democracy in China 5: 107

Broom, Robert *2:* 518; *4:* 70, 71

Brown, Joy Louise *3:* 885

Brown, Lester R. *1:* 258, 258 (ill.)

Brown, Robert *1:* 262, 264

Brown, William L. *3:* 970

Brownian motion *1:* 260, 262–64

Browser *5:* 14, 17

Bruce, David *4:* 78

Brucellosis *4:* 74, 76–78

Bruce, Mary Elizabeth Steele *4:* 78

Bubble chambers *1:* 7, 9, 11–12

Buckminsterfullerene *1:* 336

Bueker, Elmer *4:* 153

Bunsen, Robert *2:* 655

Burbank, Luther *1:* **112–16,** 112 (ill.), 115 (ill.)

Burbidge, E. Margaret *1:* **117–23,** 117 (ill.)

Burbidge, Geoffrey *1:* **117–23**

Bureau of Animal Population *6:* 41, 44, 45

Byron, Ada, Countess of Lovelace *7:* **45–50,** 45 (ill.)

Byron, George Gordon *7:* 45–46

C

Cairns, John, Jr. *3:* 735, 735 (ill.)

Calculating machine *6:* 102, 104

Calculus *4:* 176–77, 180, 229; *5:* 3–4; *6:* 102, 105

Caldicott, Helen *1:* **124–30,** 124 (ill.)

California Academy of Sciences *6:* 35, 38

Calypso 1: 170; *7:* 89–90

Campbell-Swinton, A. A. *3:* 1021

Camp Leakey *4:* 97

Cancer research *1:* 20; *3:* 776, 778; *7:* 105, 107–11, 125, 129–30

Cannon, Annie Jump *1:* **131–36,** 131 (ill.), 134 (ill.)

Cantor, Georg *3:* 799, 803, 803 (ill.)

Carbohydrate metabolism *1:* 163–64, 166

Carcinogens *1:* 20–22

Carnot, Nicholas *1:* 225

Carothers, Wallace *7:* **51–56,** 51 (ill.)

Carson, Benjamin *4:* **33–38,** 33 (ill.), 36 (ill.)

Cousteau Society *1:* 172; *7:* 87

Covalent bond *5:* 98

Cowings, Patricia S. *4:* 55–58, 55 (ill.)

Cow milk *4:* 76, 77

CRAY 1 *4:* 62, 63

CRAY 2 *4:* 63

CRAY 3 *4:* 63

CRAY 4 *4:* 64

Cray Computers Corporation *4:* 63, 64

Cray Research Corporation *4:* 62

Cray, Seymour *2:* 512, 512 (ill.); *4:* **59–65,** 59 (ill.)

Creation science *2:* 419

Cretaceous catastrophe *1:* 9

Crick, Francis *1:* **174–80,** 174 (ill.), 302, 304–06; *2:* 385, 469; *3:* 933, 935–37, 936 (ill.); *7:* 84 (ill.), 85

Critical Exposition of the Philosophy of Leibniz 3: 799

Crookes, William *3:* 790, 1020; *4:* 223, 225

Crop rotation *3:* 911–12, 915–16

Crossbreeding *2:* 623, 649–50

Crumpler, Rebecca Lee *7:* 42

Crutzen, Paul *6:* 123, 124, 128

Cry of the Kalahari 2: 410

Cryptology *4:* 230, 231

Curie, Jacques *1:* 181–83

Curie, Marie *1:* **181–91,** 181 (ill.), 184 (ill.); *4:* 117–19, 121, 122

Curie, Pierre *1:* **181–91,** 181 (ill.), 185 (ill.); *4:* 117–19, 121

Cuvier, Georges *1:* 206, 206 (ill.); *4:* 161

Cyanotic heart disease *3:* 897–98, 901–02; *4:* 208, 210–13

Cybernetics *3:* 959–61; *6:* 179

Cybernetics 3: 961

Cyclones *4:* 19

Cyclotrons *6:* 179; *7:* 153, 154–57, 168

Cytology *2:* 623

D

Daimler, Gottlieb *1:* 227; *4:* 83, 87 (ill.)

Daimler Motor Company *4:* 87

Dallmeier, Francisco *1:* **192–96,** 192 (ill.)

Dalton, John *1:* 98, **197–202,** 197 (ill.); *4:* 7, 9, 11

Darden, Christine *5:* **33–36,** 33 (ill.)

Dark matter *1:* 270, 272, 274; *2:* 382

Dart, Raymond A. *2:* 518, 518 (ill.); *4:* **66–73,** 66 (ill.)

Darvall, Denise *7:* 21–22

Darwin, Charles *1:* **203–10,** 203 (ill.), 322; *2:* 518; *4:* 66, 68, 70, 161, 162, 184; *5:* 81, 120, 121–22; *6:* 16, 130, 133

Davies-Hinton test *2:* 463, 465

Davies, J. A. V. *2:* 465

Davis, Noel *3:* 914

Davy, Humphry *1:* **211–16,** 211 (ill.), 276–78; *3:* 773; *4:* 9; *5:* 184

Dawson, Charles *2:* 521

DDT (Dichlorodiphenyl-trichloroethane) *1:* 106, 137–38, 140, 142

Dearborn Independent 4: 89

De arte combinatorica 6: 104

Decimal system *4:* 106

Deep Rover 1: 240–41

Deep-sea exploration *3:* 754, 756

Deforestation *4:* 166, 167

De Forest, Lee *1:* **217–23,** 217 (ill.)

Degenerative diseases *4:* 155

Delbrück, Max *3:* 934, 936

Democritus *1:* 200, 200 (ill.)

The Demon-Haunted World: Science as a Candle in the Dark 4: 205

De Niro, Robert *3:* 828

De Nova Stella 6: 26

Deoxyribonucleic acid. *See* DNA

De revolutionibus orbium coelestium 4: 50, 53

The Descent of Man 1: 209

E=mc² *1:* 260, 265, 269
Ego *1:* 314
The Ego and the Id 1: 314
Ehrlich, Anne H. *1:* 254 (ill.), 255
Ehrlich, Paul *1:* 296, 296 (ill.)
Ehrlich, Paul R. *1:* **254–59,**
    254 (ill.)
Eight Minutes to Midnight 1: 129
Einstein, Albert *1:* **260–69,**
    260 (ill.), 289; *2:* 434;
    3: 764–65, 813; *4:* 184, 221;
    5: 69, 95; *6:* 17, 109–11, 113,
    142, 178, 179, 181
Eisenhower, Dwight D. *2:* 690
Elasticity *5:* 43, 47–48
Eldredge, Niles *2:* 417
Electra complex *1:* 312
Electrical condenser *6:* 55
Electrical discharges in gases
    4: 222, 223
Electricity *6:* 53, 54, 57, 60
Electricity, alternating-current
    1: 251; *3:* 889, 891–93;
    7: 202–03
Electricity, animal *5:* 182–83
Electricity, direct-current *1:* 251;
    3: 890–92; *7:* 202
Electrocardiograph *4:* 210
Electrochemical theory *4:* 10
Electrochemistry *1:* 211–13;
    3: 775
Electrodynanics *4:* 16
Electrogasdynamics (EGD)
    2: 422, 424
Electrolytes *1:* 30–34
Electromagnetic radiation *1:* 263;
    2: 610
Electromagnetic spectrum *2:* 619
Electromagnetic theory *2:* 618;
    3: 789; *4:* 221
Electromagnetism *1:* 275–76, 278;
    2: 374; *2:* 610, 619; *3:* 806;
    4: 221
Electrons *4:* 121, 220, 222, 224,
    226; *5:* 97, 98; *6:* 168
Electrophorous *5:* 181
Electroweak force *3:* 832, 834–35
Elementary Seismology 3: 785
*Elementary Theory of Nuclear
    Shell Structure 2:* 403

Elementary Treatise on Chemistry
    2: 572
The Elements 2: 374
Elion, Gertrude Belle *2:* **468–73,**
    468 (ill.); *7:* **147–51,** 147 (ill.)
ELIZA *2:* 566
Elliot Smith, Grafton *4:* 67–70
Ellis, G. F. R. *2:* 435
El Niño *4:* 19
Elton, Charles *6:* 40–46
*The Emperor's New Mind:
    Concerning Computers, Minds,
    and the Laws of Physics*
    2: 436; *6:* 146
Encephalitis lethargica (sleeping
    sickness) *3:* 829
Endangered species *4:* 5
Endangered Species Act *5:* 91
Enders, John F. *3:* 818, 840, 843
Endocrine system *3:* 847–48, 1009
Endocrinology *5:* 9
Endostatin *7:* 110
Engineering Research Associates
    4: 60
ENIAC (electronic numerical
    integrator and computer)
    2: 367, 676; *4:* 232
Enigma machine *4:* 230; *5:* 157
Entropy *6:* 178
Environmental activism *4:* 2, 6,
    164–69, 190–93
Environmental Protection Agency
    1: 138
Eötvös force *3:* 955–56
Epidermal growth factor (EGF)
    4: 154
Epps, Maeve *2:* 584
Erbium *4:* 12
Erosion *4:* 167
Estés, Clarissa Pinkola *2:* 540
Ethanol *5:* 176–78
Ethology *1:* 320–21; *2:* 405–06,
    588, 590
Euclid *2:* 373–74, 374 (ill.), 456;
    6: 83, 84
Euclidean geometry *2:* 374;
    3: 795
Euler, Leonhard *5:* 45, 46
European Center for Nuclear
    Research (CERN) *3:* 835

German Society for Space Travel
4: 23

Germ theory *3:* 726

Gifted Hands: The Ben Carson Story 4: 38

Gilbert, Walter *1:* 81; *2:* **384–91,** 384 (ill.)

Gilbreth, Frank *5:* 51–53, 54

Gilbreth, Lillian *5:* **50–56,** 50 (ill.)

Glaser, Donald *1:* 11

Glashow, Sheldon L. *3:* 832, 835, 836 (ill.)

Glass, nonreflecting *1:* 92, 94

Glaucoma *2:* 531

Gliders *3:* 989–93

Global warming *2:* 597; *5:* 130

Goddard, Robert H. *2:* **392–98,** 392 (ill.), 397 (ill.)

Gödel, Kurt *2:* 372, 461

Goeppert-Mayer, Maria *2:* **399–404,** 399 (ill.)

Gold, Lois Swirsky *1:* 21–22

Gold, Thomas *1:* 71

Golka, Robert *3:* 891

Gombe Stream Reserve, Tanzania *2:* 405, 407, 409

Gondwanaland *3:* 956

Goodall, Jane *2:* **405–14,** 405 (ill.), 412 (ill.); *4:* 93, 94, 97

Gopher search engine *5:* 16

Gorillas in the Mist 2: 408; *4:* 93, 94, 96

Gosling, Raymond *1:* 304–06

Gough, John *1:* 198

Gould, Gordon *2:* 601, 604, 604 (ill.)

Gould, Stephen Jay *2:* **415–21,** 415 (ill.); *3:* 976

Gourdine, Meredith *2:* **422–26,** 422 (ill.), 425 (ill.)

Grand unification theory *2:* 435; *5:* 135–36

Graphophone *1:* 62, 67

Gray, Elisha *1:* 64, 66, 66 (ill.)

Gray, Laman, Jr. *7:* 21 (ill.), 23

The Great Train Robbery 1: 250

Green Belt Movement *4:* 164, 166–68

Greenhouse effect *1:* 30, 33–35

The Greenhouse Effect, Climate Change, and Ecosystems 1: 34

Green Revolution *1:* 105, 107–09

Green Was the Earth on the Seventh Day 7: 145

Gregorian calendar *6:* 26

Greylag geese *2:* 589

Grissom, Virgil I. "Gus" *4:* 26

Growing Up in New Guinea 2: 636

Growth factors *4:* 154

Guillemin, Roger *3:* 1009, 1010 (ill.)

Gutenberg, Beno *3:* 781, 784

Guyots *3:* 954

Gypsum *2:* 569

Gyroscope *4:* 52

H

Hadar, Ethiopia *2:* 519–20, 523

Hadrons *2:* 500

Hahn, Otto *1:* 289; *2:* 401, 641–42, 644–45, 647; *6:* 181

Hale, George E. *2:* 489

Half-life, radioactive *3:* 807, 809

Hall, Charles Martin *7:* **117–23,** 117 (ill.)

Hall, Lloyd A. *2:* **427–31,** 427 (ill.)

Halley, Edmond *4:* 180

Hall-Héroult process *7:* 120, 122

Hamburger, Viktor *4:* 152, 153

Hamilton, Alice *4:* **110–16;** *6:* 75

Hardy, G. H. *3:* 960

Hardy, Harriet *6:* **74–77**

Hardy-Weinberg law *2:* 552

Hargreaves, James *1:* 24–25

Harrar, George *1:* 107

Harris, Geoffrey W. *3:* 1009

Hartwell, Leland *7:* **125–31,** 125 (ill.)

Harvard University *4:* 110, 115

Hawker Hurricane fighter planes *6:* 119–22

Hawkes, Graham *1:* 239–41

Hawking, Stephen *2:* **432–40,** 432 (ill.); *6:* 141–43

Hazardous waste *4:* 190–92

Internet *5:* 14, 16–19
The Interpretation of Dreams
  1: 313–14
In the Shadow of Man 2: 405, 410
Introduction to Mathematical
  Philosophy 3: 802
An Introduction to the Study of
  Stellar Structure 1: 153
Invariant theory *2:* 454, 456
Inverse square law *4:* 177
Invertebrates *5:* 78, 79; *6:* 78, 79
The Invertebrates 6: 78
In vitro fertilization *3:* 882, 884,
  887; *5:* 31–32
Ionosphere *3:* 941–42
Iron lungs *3:* 819 (ill.)
Iroquois Confederacy *3:* 718
Islets of Langerhans *7:* 11
Isomers *4:* 7, 11
Isotopes *4:* 226
Is Peace Possible? 2: 478

J

Jackson, Robert *1:* 272
Jackson, Shirley Ann
  2: **498–501,** 498 (ill.)
Jacob, Francois *2:* 386
Janzen, Daniel H. *3:* 769, 769 (ill.)
Jarvik-7 *2:* 502, 504–05
Jarvik, Robert K. *2:* **503–07,**
  502 (ill.)
Java Man *5:* 189
Jefferson, Thomas *3:* 775
Jensen, J. Hans D. *2:* 399, 403
Jobs, Steven *2:* **508–14,** 508 (ill.)
Johanson, Donald *2:* **515–23,**
  515 (ill.), 584; *4:* 68
Johns Hopkins University *3:* 823,
  898, 900, 903
Joliot-Curie, Frédéric *1:* 288;
  2: 642; *4:* **117–25,** 117 (ill.);
  6: 179
Joliot-Curie, Irène *1:* 166, 185,
  288; *2:* 642, 644–45;
  4: **117–25,** 117 (ill.), 120 (ill.);
  6: 179
Joule, James Prescott *2:* **524–28,**
  524 (ill.); *3:* 907

Joule-Thomson effect *2:* 528;
  3: 907
Julian, Percy L. *2:* **529–35,**
  529 (ill.), 533 (ill.)
Jung, C. G. *1:* 314; *2:* **536–42,**
  536 (ill.)
Juno I *4:* 28
Juno II *4:* 28
Juno launch vehicle *4:* 22, 28
Jupiter *4:* 173
Jupiter C launch vehicle *4:* 22, 28
Jupiter missile *4:* 22, 26
Jupiter, moons of *4:* 105
Just, Ernest Everett *2:* **543–48,**
  543 (ill.)

H

Kahn, Reuben Leon *2:* 465
Kapitsa, Pyotr *3:* 891
Kaposi's sarcoma *6:* 72
Karisoke Research Center *2:* 408;
  4: 94, 96, 98
Karl Menninger School of
  Psychiatry *2:* 662
Karroo deposits *4:* 71
Keith, Arthur *2:* 521; *4:* 70
Keith, Louis *2:* **549–55,**
  549 (ill.)
Kekulé, Friedrich *3:* 741
K-electron capture *1:* 9
Kelley, William *1:* 84
Kelsey, Frances Oldham *4:* 214
Kelvin, Lord. *See* **Thomson,
  William, Lord Kelvin**
Kelvin scale *3:* 905–06, 909
Kenya Department of Wildlife
  Services *2:* 584
Kenyapithecus 2: 580
Kepler, Johannes *1:* 156, 267;
  2: 490, 490 (ill.); *4:* 51, 53,
  105, **126–32,** 126 (ill.),
  130 (ill.), 178, 183; *6:* 22, 23,
  29, 144, 157, 159; *7:* 62
Khorana, Har Gobind
  4: **133–40,** 133 (ill.), 136 (ill.)
Khush, Gurdev S. *1:* 108
Kieselguhr *2:* 671–72
Kimeu, Kamoya *2:* 585 (ill.)

Mach 1 *5:* 34
MacKay, Alan *6:* 146
Macrophage *1:* 284
Magic numbers *2:* 403
Magnetic core memory
   3: 923, 925
Magnetohydrodynamics *2:* 424
Maiman, Theodore *2:* **601–06,**
   601 (ill.)
Malaria *6:* 161–63
Mall, Franklin P. *3:* 823
Malnutrition *4:* 166, 167
Malta fever *4:* 77, 78
Mammals, origin of *4:* 71
Mammary artery implant *6:* 49
Manhattan Project *1:* 7, 10, 103,
   268–69, 285, 289–91; *2:* 399,
   402; *2:* 680, 683–85; *3:* 779,
   1002; *6:* 178, 182
Manus (people) *2:* 635, 635 (ill.)
*The Man Who Mistook His Wife
   for a Hat 3:* 827, 830
Maple Leaf Trainer II *6:* 120
Marconi, Guglielmo *1:* 218–19;
   2: **607–15,** 607 (ill.), 609 (ill.);
   3: 806, 896
Mariner 9 4: 200, 201
Mark I *3:* 924, 926; *5:* 62–63; *6:* 1
Mark II *5:* 63
Mark III *6:* 2, 5
Marriage and Morals 3: 802
Mars *4:* 129, 132, 200, 201, 204;
   7: 60, 61, 62–63
Marsden, Ernest *3:* 809, 811
Martin, Pierre-Emile *1:* 86
Marx, Karl *3:* 797
Maser *2:* 602
Mass-energy equivalence *4:* 221
Mass production *4:* 80, 82, 86, 90
Mass spectrometer *4:* 226
A Matter of Consequences 3: 880
Matthias, Bernd T. *6:* 31
Matzeliger, Jan Ernst
   5: **108–14,** 108 (ill.)
Mauchly, John William *2:* 367,
   367 (ill.)
Maunder, Annie Russell
   5: **115–18**
Maury, Antonia *1:* 133
Maxam, Allan *2:* 387

Max Planck Society *3:* 765
Maxwell, James Clerk *2:* 610,
   616–21, 616 (ill.); *3:* 789, 906,
   908; *4:* 221, 225
Maybach, Wilhelm *1:* 227; *4:* 87
Mayer, Joseph E. *2:* 400–01
Mayer, Julius *2:* 527
Mayr, Ernst *5:* **119–25,** 119 (ill.)
McCarthy, Senator Joseph *2:* 690
McClintock, Barbara *2:* **622–27,**
   622 (ill.)
McCormick, Cyrus *4:* 82
McCoy, Elijah *2:* **628–32,**
   628 (ill.)
Mead, Margaret *2:* **633–38,**
   633 (ill.), 635 (ill.); *7:* 30,
   31 (ill.)
Meaning of Evolution 2: 4160
*The Mechanism of Mendelian
   Heredity 2:* 626
*The Mechanism of the Heavens
   5:* 168
Medicine, general *5:* 57–59
Meiosis *2:* 624–25
Meitner, Lise *1:* 288; *2:* 401,
   639–47, 639 (ill.); *4:* 187;
   6: 181
Meltdown, nuclear *1:* 127
Memorial Institute for Infectious
   Diseases *4:* 112
Mendel, Gregor *1:* 209; *2:* 626,
   648–53, 648 (ill.); *6:* 132,
   172, 174
Mendel, Lafayette B. *3:* 857
Mendeleev, Dmitry *2:* **654–59,**
   654 (ill.); *4:* 185, 186; *6:* 89
Meningitis *4:* 76; *6:* 96
Menlo Park, New Jersey *1:* 248
Menninger, Charles *2:* 660
Menninger Clinic *2:* 660–61
Menninger, Karl *2:* **660–64,**
   660 (ill.)
Menninger, William *2:* 661
Mental illness *2:* 660–62;
   3: 827, 830
Mercalli scale *1:* 3; *3:* 781–82
Mercedes (automobile) *4:* 87
Mercedes-Benz automobile
   company *4:* 87
Mercury *4:* 112, 114

187–88, 260, 263, 285, 288;
2: 399, 403, 607, 613; *3:* 759,
764, 787, 792, 832, 834–35,
862, 865–66, 868, 1003, 1012,
1016; *7:* 133, 138, 153, 157,
167, 169
Nobel Prize for physiology or
medicine *1:* 161, 166, 178,
297, 302, 304, 306, 320, 325;
2: 468, 472, 483, 486, 588,
594, 622, 627; *3:* 746, 749,
841, 843, 933, 1004, 1006,
1009, 1011; *7:* 9, 14, 65, 68,
130, 147, 150, 175, 180
Nobel's Extra Dynamite *2:* 672
No-Conscription Fellowship
3: 800–01
Noddack, Ida Tacke *4:* **185–89**
Noddack, Walter *4:* 185–88
Noether, Emmy *2:* 459;
5: **138–44,** 138 (ill.)
No More War! *3:* 744
Non-Euclidean geometry
2: 371, 373
Norrish, Ronald G. W. *1:* 303
North polar sequence *5:* 83–84
Noyce, Robert *2:* **674–79,**
674 (ill.)
Nuclear chain reaction
1: 289 (ill.), 289–90; *6:* 177,
178, 181, 182
Nuclear disarmament *2:* 684;
3: 742, 744, 803
Nuclear energy *6:* 177, 182
Nuclear fission *1:* 288; *2:* 402,
639–40, 646, 683–84; *4:* 117,
119, 124, 185, 187; *6:* 181
Nuclear fusion *1:* 59–60
*Nuclear Madness: What You Can
Do!* *1:* 128
Nuclear medicine *3:* 778
Nuclear weapons testing
5: 128–29
Nuclear winter *4:* 198, 204, 205
Nucleic acids *4:* 134, 137
Nucleotides *4:* 135, 137, 138
Nurse, Paul *7:* 128–29, 129 (ill.)
Nutrition *4:* 141
Nylon *7:* 51, 55

O

O., Anna (Bertha Pappenheim)
1: 310
Oberth, Hermann *4:* 23
Occluded front *4:* 19
Occupational safety laws *4:* 113,
114
Ocean *4:* 17
Ocean Everest *1:* 240, 243
O'Connor, Daniel Basil *3:* 840
Oedipus complex *1:* 312
Oersted, Hans Christian *1:* 278
Olduvai Gorge, Tanzania *2:* 406,
516, 575–76, 579–80; *7:* 161,
162–63
Olitsky, Peter K. *3:* 816
Oliver, Thomas *4:* 113
On Aggression *2:* 592, 594
"On Computable Numbers, with
an Application to the
Entscheidungs Problem"
4: 228, 229
On Human Nature *3:* 977
*On the Economy of Manufactures
and Machinery* *1:* 40
Oort cloud *4:* 174
Oort, Jan *4:* 174
Oppenheimer, J. Robert
2: **680–91,** 680 (ill.)
Opticks *4:* 183
Oral contraceptive *5:* 28–31
Oral history *3:* 718, 720
Orangutans *4:* 97
Orgel, Leslie *1:* 177
*The Origin and Development of
the Lymphatic System* *3:* 824
*The Origin of Continents and
Oceans* *3:* 953, 956
*The Origin of Species by Means
of Natural Selection*
1: 203–04, 207
Ornithology *5:* 119, 120–21;
6: 136, 138
Ortiz, Fernando *1:* 230
Osiander, Andreas *4:* 53
Osteodontokeratic culture *4:* 72
Osteology *5:* 173
Ostwald, Friedrich Wilhelm *1:* 33
Otto, Nikolaus August *1:* 227

Progesterone *2:* 530, 532;
5: 29–31
Project Paperclip *4:* 26
Project Phoenix *1:* 72
Prokhorov, Aleksandr *2:* 602–03
Promethean Fire 3: 977
Propositiones philosophicae
5: 2–3
Proteins *4:* 138
Protons *4:* 121; *5:* 103
Protoplasm *2:* 546–47
Prusiner, Stanley *7:* **175–80,**
175 (ill.)
Psychoanalysis *1:* 308, 310,
312–14; *2:* 536, 538
Psychological Types 2: 541
Psychology *5:* 50, 52–54
Psychology of Management 5: 53
The Psychology of the
Unconscious 2: 540
Psycho-neuroimmunology *3:* 853
Pterodactyl *4:* 161
Ptolemaic system *2:* 443–44, 446;
4: 108; *6:* 157–58
Ptolemy *2:* 443; *4:* 50, 51, 54,
102, 107; *6:* **156–60,** 156 (ill.)
Public health *4:* 112, 114
Pugwash Conferences on Science
and World Affairs *2:* 684
Pulsars *1:* 69, 71, 73
Punctuated equilibrium *2:* 417
Putnam, Frederick Ward *3:* 719
Pyramids *1:* 13
Pyroelectricity *1:* 183
Pythagoras *2:* 458, 458 (ill.), 460
Pythagorean theorem *2:* 460

Q

Quantum mechanics *1:* 101, 262;
2: 680–82; *3:* 739–40; *4:* 222;
6: 142; *7:* 133, 135–38
Quantum statistics *6:* 18
Quantum theory *1:* 99–100;
3: 759–60, 763–64; *6:* 17;
7: 135–38
Quarks *3:* 835; *5:* 136; *6:* 170;
7: 170
Quarterman, Lloyd Albert *1:* 290

Quasars *1:* 70, 117, 119–22,
121 (ill.); *5:* 70, 105
Quasi-crystals *6:* 141, 142, 146
Quasi-Stellar Objects 1: 120
Queen of Shaba 4: 5
Quimby, Edith H. *3:* **776–79,**
776 (ill.)
Quinine *7:* 205, 208

R

Ra 2: 452; *7:* 144
Ra II 2: 452; *7:* 144
Rabies *3:* 731; *5:* 193
Race: Science and Politics 7: 33
Radar *1:* 7, 9; *3:* 939–41, 943
Radiata 4: 161
Radiation *1:* 125–26; *3:* 776–79,
790, 807–09
Radiation poisoning *6:* 76
Radiation sickness *1:* 187; *2:* 688
Radio *1:* 217, 222; *2:* 614
Radioactive elements *4:* 121
Radioactive fallout *2:* 688
Radioactive isotopes *3:* 776;
4: 121
Radioactive tracer analysis
4: 122, 123
Radioactivity *1:* 181, 186–88;
3: 789, 805, 807–09; *4:* 119,
121; *6:* 179
Radioimmunoassay (RIA)
3: 1004, 1006–09, 1011
Radiological Research Laboratory
3: 778
Radiometer *4:* 225
Radio waves *2:* 607–08, 610–12;
3: 893–94
Radium *1:* 181, 186, 189; *4:* 112,
114, 118, 119
Radium-D *4:* 123
Radium Institute *4:* 118, 120, 124
Rain forests *1:* 257; *3:* 766,
768–70
Raman, Chandrasekhar V. *1:* 151
Ramart-Lucas, Pauline *2:* 643
Ramsay, William *7:* **181–85,**
181 (ill.)
Randall, John T. *1:* 303

RAND Corporation *5:* 24–25
Rare earth elements *4:* 10, 12
Rational drug design *7:* 147, 149–50
Rayleigh, John *3:* 763
RCA (Radio Corporation of America) *5:* 38, 40
The Realm of the Nebulae 2: 496
Recycling *4:* 192
Redshifting *1:* 120–21, 266, 268; *2:* 381, 492
Redstone missile *4:* 22, 26, 28
Reed, Walter *6:* **161–66,** 161 (ill.); *7:* 101–03, 101 (ill.)
Reflecting telescope *4:* 176, 179
Reflections on the Decline of Science in England and on Some of Its Causes 1: 43
Reflex, conditioned *3:* 746, 749–50, 752
Reflex, unconditioned *3:* 749
Reifenstein, Edward *1:* 73
Relativity, theory of *1:* 260, 263–67, 269; *3:* 764; *5:* 140
Renewable resources *6:* 43
Repression *1:* 310, 312
Retroviruses *6:* 68, 69
Reuleaux, Franz *1:* 227
Revelle, Roger *1:* 17
Revolution of the Heavenly Spheres 2: 444
Rhenium *4:* 185–87
Rheticus, Georg *4:* 51
Rheumatic fever *4:* 210, 212; *6:* 93, 94, 96
Rheumatoid arthritis *2:* 530
Ribet, Kenneth *2:* 460
Ribosomes *4:* 137
Rice *1:* 108–10
Richer, Jean *4:* 132
Richter, Charles F. *1:* 1, 4, 328; *3:* **780–86,** 780 (ill.), 783 (ill.)
Richter scale *1:* 1, 4, 328; *3:* 780, 782
Ride, Sally *4:* 218; *7:* **187–95,** 187 (ill.)
RNA (ribonucleic acid) *1:* 76, 90–91, 304, 306
The Road Ahead 2: 370

Roads to Freedom: Socialism, Anarchism and Syndicalism 3: 802
Road to Survival 1: 255
Robbins, Frederick *3:* 818, 841, 843
Roberts, Ed *2:* 365–66
Robinson, Julia *4:* **194–97**
Rockets *2:* 393–94, 396; *4:* 24
Rockoon *3:* 920
Röntgen, Wilhelm *1:* 132; *3:* **787–93,** 787 (ill.)
Roosevelt, Franklin D. *1:* 268
Rosenwald, Julius *2:* 546
Rosing, Boris *3:* 1018
Ross, Mary *5:* **151–53**
Rotation of Earth *4:* 52
Rotblat, Joseph *2:* 684
Rothschild, Miriam *5:* **154–59**
Royal Danish Geodetic Institute *6:* 99
Royal Society *1:* 39–40
Rudolphine Tables 4: 129, 131
Russell, Bertrand *3:* **794–804,** 794 (ill.), 801 (ill.), 960
Russell, Frederick Stratten *1:* 17
Rutherford, Ernest *1:* 99, 102; *2:* 400, 641; *3:* **805–13,** 805 (ill.), 810 (ill.); *4:* 226

S

Sabin, Albert *3:* **814–21,** 814 (ill.), 841, 843, 845
Sabin Committee *3:* 826
Sabin, Florence R. *3:* **822–25,** 822 (ill.), 825 (ill.)
Sacks, Oliver Wolf *3:* **827–31,** 827 (ill.)
Sagan, Carl *2:* 418, 418 (ill.); *4:* **198–207,** 198 (ill.), 203 (ill.)
Sakharov, Andrei *2:* 686, 686 (ill.); *6:* **167–71,** 167 (ill.)
Salam, Abdus *2:* 385; *3:* **832–37,** 832 (ill.), 836 (ill.)
Salam-Weinberg theory *3:* 835
Salk Institute for Biological Research *1:* 177, 179; *3:* 846
Salk, Jonas *3:* 818, **838–46,** 838 (ill.), 845 (ill.)

Salts, decomposition of *4:* 9

Salvarsan *1:* 296

Samoa *2:* 634–35, 638

A Sand County Almanac 5: 87

Sanders, Thomas *1:* 63, 65

Sandström, Johann Wilhelm *4:* 18

Sanger, Frederick *2:* 387, 389, 389 (ill.)

Santa Rosa National Park, Costa Rica *3:* 769

Sarnoff, David *3:* 1021

Saturn *4:* 132, 173, 174; *7:* 57, 60–62

Saturn rockets *4:* 22, 24, 28, 29, 30

Savitch, Pavle *2:* 644

Sayer, Malcolm *3:* 828

The Sceptical Chymist 2: 573

Schaller, George *4:* 93, 94

Schally, Andrew V. *3:* 1009, 1010 (ill.)

Scharrer, Berta *3:* **847–54**

Scharrer, Ernst *3:* 847, 849–50, 852

Schawlow, A. L. *2:* 602–04

Scheele, Carl Wilhelm *3:* 774

Scheutz, Georg *1:* 42

Schizophrenia *6:* 62–64

Schrieffer, J. Robert *3:* 866

Schrödinger, Erwin *3:* 739

Science and the Modern World 3: 797

Scientific method *3:* 789; *4:* 183

Scientific Revolution *4:* 178, 183

Scripps Institute of Oceanography *1:* 17

Scuba (self-contained underwater breathing apparatus) *1:* 239, 241; *7:* 88

The Sea Around Us 1: 139

Sea Cliff 1: 243

Seafloor spreading *3:* 954, 958

Seaman, Gary *2:* 411

Second law of thermodynamics *6:* 178

Seeing Voices: A Journey Into the World of the Deaf 3: 831

Segrè, Emilio *3:* 1001; *4:* 188 (ill.)

Segregation, hereditary law of *2:* 650, 652

Seibert, Florence *3:* **855–61,** 855 (ill.)

Seismicity of the Earth 3: 782

Seismic tomography *1:* 5

Seismograph *1:* 4; *3:* 780, 782; *6:* 99

Seizures *4:* 37

Selenium *4:* 10

Selfridge, Thomas *3:* 995

Semiconductors *2:* 675; *3:* 862, 864–65; *4:* 59

Sequential analysis *5:* 24

Serengeti National Park *4:* 5

Serengeti Plain, Tanzania *2:* 584

Set theory *3:* 803

Seven Samurai project *1:* 272

Sex and Temperament 2: 636

Sextant *6:* 25 (ill.)

The Shaping of a Behaviorist 3: 880

Sharks *7:* 71, 74–77

Shepard, Alan *4:* 26, 29 (ill.)

Shockley, William *2:* 675; *3:* **862–69,** 862 (ill.), 867 (ill.)

Shoemaker-Levy 9 *2:* 493

Shoemaking *5:* 108, 109–13

Shute, Nevil *1:* 125

Siamese twins *4:* 33, 36, 37

Sibling rivalry *1:* 313

Sickle-cell anemia *3:* 742

Sidereus nuncius 4: 105

Siderostat *4:* 52

Siemens, Friedrich *1:* 86

Siemens, Wilhelm *1:* 86

Silent Spring 1: 137–38, 140–41; *2:* 597; *3:* 970

The Silent World 1: 168, 171; *7:* 89

Silicon *2:* 675–77; *3:* 864

Silicon Valley *2:* 676, 678; *3:* 868; *5:* 18

Silicosis *4:* 116

Simberloff, Daniel *3:* 972

Simpson, George Gaylord *2:* 416

Singer, Maxine *3:* **870–75,** 870 (ill.)

Sirius B *1:* 268

6-mercaptopurine (6MP) *2:* 471–72

Skinner, B. F. *2:* 666; *3:* **876–81,** 876 (ill.)

Subatomic particles *5:* 132, 135–37; *7:* 167–72
Sun, rotation of *4:* 105
Sunspots *4:* 105, 173; *5:* 115, 117
Supercomputer *2:* 512; *4:* 59, 61, 62, 64
Superconducting Super Collider (SSC) *7:* 171–72
Superconductivity *3:* 866
Superconductors *6:* 31–34
Superego *1:* 314
Supernova *1:* 69, 71, 73, 119, 156; *6:* 25
Surgery, heart bypass *6:* 47, 48–49, 50 (ill.); *7:* 93–95
Svedberg, Theodor *3:* 860
Sverdrup, Harald Ulrik *4:* 18, 21
Swaminathan, M. S. *1:* 110
Swan, Joseph Wilson *1:* 248–49, 251, 251 (ill.)
Swedish Academy of Science *4:* 9, 10
Synthesizer, electronic *2:* 668
Synthetic materials *7:* 51, 53–55
Syphilis *1:* 296; *2:* 463–65, 466 (ill.); *6:* 62, 64
Syphilis and Its Treatment 2: 465
Systema Naturae 4: 159
Systema Saturnium 7: 61
Szilard, Leo *1:* 268; *6:* **177–83,** 177 (ill.)

T

Taieb, Maurice *2:* 517, 519
The Tale of John Sickle 2: 591
Tales of a Shaman's Apprentice: An Ethnobotanist Searches for New Medicines in the Amazon Rain Forest 3: 768, 770
Tamm, Igor *6:* 168, 169
Taniyama, Yutaka *2:* 460
Tanjung Puting reserve, Indonesia *4:* 97
Taphonomy *4:* 72
Taussig, Helen Brooke *3:* 900–01, 901 (ill.); *4:* **208–14,** 208 (ill.), 211 (ill.)
T-cell growth factor *6:* 69

T cells *6:* 68, 69
Technetium *4:* 186, 188
Tektite II project *1:* 241
Telegraph *1:* 246, 248; *3:* 980, 983–85
Telephone *1:* 62, 64, 66; *3:* 982
Telepresence *1:* 49–50
Telescope *4:* 103
Telescope, reflector *2:* 442, 489; *4:* 176, 179
Television *3:* 1017, 1019, 1021; *5:* 37, 38–41
Telkes, Maria *3:* 967
Teller, Edward *2:* 399, 401–02
Telomerase *1:* 90
Template theory *5:* 73, 74–75
Tensegrity dome *1:* 336
Terbium *4:* 12
Tereshkova, Valentina *4:* **215–19,** 215 (ill.)
Tesla coil *3:* 894
Tesla, Nikola *1:* 251; *3:* **889–96,** 889 (ill.), 893 (ill.); *7:* 203, 203 (ill.)
Testosterone *2:* 530, 532
Test tube babies *3:* 882, 884–85
Tevatron *7:* 171
Thalidomide *4:* 208, 210, 214
Thallium *4:* 225
Thenard, Louis *1:* 215
The Theory of Games and Economic Behavior 3: 962
The Theory of Games and Statistical Decisions 5: 25–26
Theory of the Earth 2: 599
Thermodynamics *4:* 15; *5:* 97; *6:* 178
Thermodynamics and the Free Energy of Chemical Substances 5: 96
Thermometer *4:* 102
This Is Biology: The Science of the Living World 5: 124
Thomas, Vivien *3:* **897–904,** 897 (ill.); *4:* 212
Thomson, J. J. *1:* 99, 102, 102 (ill.); *3:* 806, 1021; *4:* **220–27,** 220 (ill.)
Thomson, William, Lord Kelvin *2:* 526, 611; *3:* **905–10,** 905 (ill.)

Viscose rayon industry *4:* 116

The Vitalizer 2: 431

Vitamin B12 *2:* 474, 477; *7:* 210

Vitamin C *3:* 745

Vitamin C and the Common Cold
3: 745

Vivamos Mejor/USA *1:* 47

Volta, Alessandro *1:* 213–14,
214 (ill.); *5:* **179–84,** 179 (ill.);
6: 56

Voltaic pile *1:* 214; *4:* 9; *5:* 179,
180, 183–84

Von Braun, Wernher *2:* 395,
395 (ill.); *4:* 22–32, 22 (ill.),
27 (ill.)

Von Neumann, John *3:* 962–63,
962 (ill.); *5:* 23

Vorlesungen über Thermodynamik
3: 761

Vortex rings *4:* 222

Vostok I 4: 216

Vostok 5 4: 217

Vostok 6 4: 217

Voyager: An Adventure to the
Edge of the Solar System 7: 194

Voyager space missions *4:* 202

Vries, Hugo de *2:* 626, 653

V-2 rocket *2:* 395; *3:* 919; *4:* 22,
24–26, 28

W

Walden Two 3: 878–79

Wang, An *3:* **923–28,** 923 (ill.)

Wang Laboratories
3: 923–25, 927

War Crimes Tribunal *3:* 804

Warm front *4:* 19, 20

War of the Worlds 2: 393

Washkansky, Louis *2:* 506;
7: 20–22

Wassermann, August von *2:* 465

The Watcher at the Nest 6: 139

Water frame *1:* 25, 27 (ill.)

Water pollution *3:* 734–36

Watkins, Levi, Jr. *3:* **929–32,**
929 (ill.)

Watson, James D. *1:* 174, 176,
178, 180, 302, 304–06;
2: 384–85, 469; *3:* **933–38,**

933 (ill.), 936 (ill.);
7: 84 (ill.), 85

Watson, Thomas A. *1:* 63–65

Watson-Watt, Robert *3:* **939–44**

Watt, James *3:* **945–50,** 945 (ill.)

Weak force *1:* 287; *3:* 833

Weather forecasting *4:* 15–17,
19, 20

Weber, Wilhelm *2:* 373

Webster, Arthur Gordon *2:* 393

Wegener, Alfred *3:* **951–58,**
951 (ill.)

Wegener's granulomatosis *1:* 281

Weidenreich, Franz *5:* **185–90,**
187 (ill.)

Weinberg, Steven *3:* 832, 834–35,
836 (ill.)

Weinberg, Wilhelm *2:* 552

Weizenbaum, Joseph *2:* 566

Weller, Thomas *3:* 818, 841, 843

Wells, H. Gideon *3:* 857

Westinghouse Electric Company
7: 199 (ill.), 202–03

Westinghouse, George *3:* 892;
3: 1020; *7:* **197–204,** 197 (ill.)

Wetterhahn, Karen *6:* **184–88,**
184 (ill.)

Wexler, Nancy *6:* **189–93,**
189 (ill.)

What Mad Pursuit: A Personal
View of Scientific Discovery
1: 179–80

Wheat *1:* 107–09

Wheatstone, Charles *2:* 375

Wheelwright, George *2:* 558

White dwarf star *5:* 67; *7:* 65–67

Whitehead, Alfred North
3: 796–97, 797 (ill.), 799

Whitehouse, E. O. W. *3:* 909

Whiting, Sarah Frances *1:* 132

Whitney, Eli *4:* 82

Why Men Fight: A Method of
Abolishing the International
Duel 3: 800

Wien, Wilhelm *3:* 762–63

Wiener, Norbert *3:* **959–63,**
959 (ill.)

Wigner, Eugene Paul *2:* 403

Wildlife conservation *4:* 5

Wildlife management *5:* 92

Wiles, Andrew J. *2:* 460
Wilkins, A. F. *3:* 941
Wilkins, Maurice *1:* 176–77, 302, 304, 306; *3:* 933–36
Williams, Anna W. *5:* **191–94**
Williams, Robin *3:* 828
Williamson, James S. *3:* **964–68**
Wilson cloud chamber *4:* 120
Wilson, Edmund Beecher *6:* 175
Wilson, Edward O. *3:* **969–79,** 969 (ill.)
Wilson, Woodrow *3:* 801
Wind shear *1:* 326, 330–31; *7:* 115
Winton, Alexander *4:* 83
Wireless receiver *2:* 609, 609 (ill.)
"Witch of Agnesi" *5:* 5
Wöhler, Friedrich *7:* 118
Wollaston, William Hyde *4:* 179
Woman's Medical School of Northwestern University *4:* 112
Women Who Run with the Wolves *2:* 540
Wonderful Life: The Burgess Shale and the Nature of History *2:* 420
Wong-Staal, Flossie *1:* 283, 283 (ill.)
Woods, Granville T. *3:* **980–86,** 980 (ill.)
Woods Hole Oceanographic Institute *1:* 49; *2:* 544, 547
Woodward-Hoffmann rules *7:* 210
Woodward, Robert B. *7:* **205–11,** 205 (ill.)
Woodwell, George M. *1:* 142, 142 (ill.)
Worlds in the Making *1:* 35
Worldwatch Institute *1:* 258
World Wide Web *5:* 14, 16–19
Wozniak, Stephen *2:* 508–11, 513
Wright, Almroth *1:* 293
Wright Flyer I *3:* 993
Wright Flyer III *3:* 994
Wright, Orville *3:* **987–98,** 987 (ill.), 992 (ill.)
Wright, Wilbur *3:* **987–98,** 987 (ill.), 995 (ill.)
Wu, Chien-Shiung *3:* **999–1003,** 999 (ill.), 1012, 1015
Wytham Biological Survey *6:* 43, 45

X

X chromosome *6:* 133
X-ray crystallography *1:* 177; *2:* 474–76, 478; *6:* 179
X-ray diffraction *1:* 175–76, 303–04, 306
X-ray imaging *1:* 44–45, 47
X-ray photograph *3:* 791 (ill.)
X rays *2:* 483; *3:* 776–77, 779, 787, 789–93, 807
X-ray spectroscopy *2:* 657
X-ray telescope *1:* 45

Y

Yale School of Forestry *6:* 154
Yalow, Rosalyn Sussman *3:* **1004–11,** 1010 (ill.), 1004 (ill.)
Yang, Chen Ning *3:* 999, 1002, **1012–16,** 1012 (ill.)
Y chromosome *6:* 172, 175
The Year of the Greylag Goose *2:* 592
Yellow fever *6:* 161, 162; *7:* 97, 99–103
Yerkes Observatory (University of Chicago) *2:* 489
Young, Thomas *2:* 617
Ytterite *4:* 12
Yttria *4:* 12
Yukuna (people) *3:* 768

Z

Zero Population Growth *1:* 257
Zero-sum game *5:* 24–25
Zinjanthropus *2:* 579–80
Zinn, Walter *6:* 181
Zion, Élie de *3:* 747
Zionist movement *1:* 269
Zoological Institute, University of Munich *1:* 321, 324
Zoological Philosophy *1:* 208
Zooplankton *1:* 15, 17–18
Zwicky, Fritz *1:* 156
Zworykin, Vladimir *3:* **1017–22,** 1017 (ill.); *5:* 38